INFLUENTIAL PAPERS
FROM THE 1950s

INFLUENTIAL PAPERS
FROM THE 1950s

PAPERS FROM THE DECADES IN
INTERNATIONAL JOURNAL OF PSYCHOANALYSIS
KEY PAPERS SERIES

Edited by

Andrew C. Furman and *Steven T. Levy*

International Journal of Psychoanalysis Key Papers Series
Series Editors: Paul Williams and Glen O. Gabbard

KARNAC
LONDON   NEW YORK

First published in 2003 by
H. Karnac (Books) Ltd.
6 Pembroke Buildings, London NW10 6RE

British Library Cataloguing in Publication Data

A C.I.P. for this book is available from the British Library

   ISBN 1 85575 929 2

Edited, designed, and produced by The Studio Publishing Services Ltd,
Exeter EX4 8JN

Printed in Great Britain

10 9 8 7 6 5 4 3 2 1

www.karnacbooks.com

CONTENTS

The International Journal of Psychoanalysis Key Papers Series

The IJP 'Key Papers' series brings together the most important psychoanalytic papers in the Journal's eighty-year history, in a series of accessible monographs. The idea behind the series is to approach the IJP's intellectual resource from a variety of perspectives in order to highlight important domains of psychoanalytic enquiry. It is hoped that these volumes will be of interest to psychoanalysts, students of the discipline and, in particular, to those who work and write from an interdisciplinary standpoint. The ways in which the papers in the monographs are grouped will vary: for example, a number of 'themed' monographs will take as their subject important psychoanalytic topics, while others will stress interdisciplinary links (between neuroscience, anthropology, philosophy etc. and psychoanalysis). Still others will contain review essays on, for example, film and psychoanalysis, art and psychoanalysis and the worldwide IJP Internet Discussion Group, which debates important papers before they appear in the printed journal (cf. www.ijpa.org). The aim of all the monographs is to provide the reader with a substantive contribution of the highest quality that reflects the principal concerns of contemporary psychoanalysts and those with whom they are in dialogue. This volume marks the appearance of the first in a grouping of books within the 'Key Papers' series that identifies, reproduces and discusses the most influential psychoanalytic papers produced in each decade since IJP began. By 'influential' we mean papers that not only made an important individual contribution to psychoanalytic knowledge at the time, but also went on to influence the development of psychoanalytic thinking and concepts. The objective of this and future volumes in the 'decades' collection will be to provide an overview of the development of psychoanalysis, as articulated through its principal scholarly journal.

We hope you will find this and all the 'Key Papers' monographs rewarding and pleasurable to read.

Paul Williams and Glen O. Gabbard
Joint Editors-in-Chief,
International Journal of Psychoanalysis
London, 2003

ABOUT THE EDITORS

Andrew C. Furman, M.D. is Associate Professor of Psychiatry and Behavioral Sciences, Emory University School of Medicine and Director of Clinical Services, Department of Psychiatry, Grady Memorial Hospital. He is a faculty member of the Emory University Psychoanalytic Institute.

Steven T. Levy, M.D. is Bernard Holland Professor and Vice Chair of Psychiatry and Behavioral Sciences, Emory University School of Medicine. He is Editor-Elect of the *Journal of the American Psychoanalytic Association*.

Introduction

Andrew C. Furman and Steven T. Levy

This volume presents a series of papers that appeared in the *International Journal of Psycho-Analysis* (*IJP*) during the 1950s. Chosen because of their lasting influence on psychoanalytic theory and practice, they are important contributions to our literature that have become integral to our field and are regularly referenced in subsequent published work. They express the leading themes the editors consider characteristic of psychoanalytic discourse in the pages of the *IJP* during the decade of the 1950s. Because in large measure psychoanalytic training is regularly grounded in the teaching of our literature, these papers have played a particularly important role subsequent to their appearance in *IJP* in the transmission of psychoanalytic knowledge to analysts in training.

We recognize in the pages of *IJP* in the 1950s a turning of psychoanalytic attention from the exploration of the analysand's intra-psychic experience to mapping out equally relevant psycho-analytic concerns that exist outside the analysand's mind although in connection with it. The analyst's inner world (counter-transference) and theories of early development, especially from a relational perspective (attachment and pre-Oedipal object relations), are the two leading perspectives represented among the papers chosen for this volume. They reflect increasing recognition of the centrality of the relational in understanding mental experience as well as the manner in which psychoanalytic treatment attempts to influence the latter.

If the 1940s were characterized by the great A. Freud–Klein debate, the next decade saw the increasing influence of object relational ideas on psychoanalytic understanding of a variety of issues. Introjective and projective mechanisms, crucial to unravelling pre-Oedipal development as well as integral to an exploration of counter-transference, had become by this time familiar aspects of psychoanalytic discourse across theoretical lines. While ego psychology maintained its hegemony in North American analytic circles, in the 1950s we begin to see Kleinian ideas taken seriously by North American authors. The contributions of A. Reich, and especially, Zetzel contained in this volume are examples.

Counter-transference is a concept that, after introduction by Freud in connection with the Dora Case, was viewed by classical analysts largely as an impediment to successful analysis and, with the notable exception of the work of Ferenczi, lay relatively fallow until the 1950s. What triggered a renewed interest in the topic remains unclear. It is probably due, in part, to the experience of analysts during the Second World War working with patients who had experienced significant trauma. Additionally, as the scope of analysis increasingly began to include the treatment of borderline and psychotic states, exploring the powerful and disruptive feelings working with these patients typically elicits within analysts became inevitable.

Winnicott's treatise on "Hate in the counter-transference", which appeared in the *IJP* in 1949, is included in this volume as signalling a new and more penetrating inquiry into the reciprocal quality of the therapeutic relationship. While Winnicott was speaking of work with psychotic patients, his emphasis on the continuum of the analyst's fear and hate, from approximately normal to neurotic, in response to the severely ill patient's pathology, opened the way for exploring the analyst's unconscious sensitivity to immersion in the analysand's transference in a radically new way. No longer was counter-transference an unwanted and surprising intruder into the therapeutic dialogue. It was to be expected, searched out, and utilized. While Winnicott does not spell out in any detail how, he includes in his discussion the necessity of interpreting the counter-transference, of letting the patient become aware of his impact on the analyst, which Winnicott proposes as a developmental need on the patient's part.

We have included in this volume five subsequent papers on counter-transference that carry forward the exploration of counter-transference in the direction of establishing its centrality within the psychoanalytic process. Together with the aforementioned Winnicott paper, they can be read as a dialogue among influential clinicians on three continents, opening up in increments the psychology of the analyst and his or her more personal role in the analysand's treatment. Heimann places her ideas about counter-transference, by which she means "all the feelings which the analyst experiences towards his patient", between the detached, objective Freudian analyst, and the more expressive, self-disclosing Ferenczian tradition. She emphasizes the importance of the analyst's "freely roused emotional sensibility" and links this to Freud's ideas about unconscious communication between the analytic dyad. Her position is conservative in relation to the other contributors, underlining the analyst's obligation to compare the feelings the analysand arouses with the meanings the analyst understands, to sort out what belongs to the analyst and what is generated by the patient, and to avoid burdening the patient with confessional self disclosure regarding the counter-transference. In her view, such disclosure leads away from the analysis.

Little goes considerably beyond Heimann, although like her, she emphasizes the interactive, relational elements of the analytic process. In Little's view, counter-transference must be acknowledged by the analyst, recognized by both parties and used on the patient's behalf. Little links counter-transference to empathy, both involving identification with the patient's unconscious wishes and worries. She introduces the idea of the analyst's counter-resistance, which if unrecognized, strengthens the patient's resistance. Little places counter-transference in a developmental context. The analyst's failures are linked to the parents' "irrational" behaviours which were not intended specifically for the patient but were integral to the parents' own problems. Likewise, the analyst's defensiveness about evidence of his subjective feelings in the counter-transference may be experienced by the analysand as a repetition of the parent's forbidding children from seeing. Little challenges analysts to overcome their phobic and paranoid attitudes regarding their subjective feelings aroused by patients, attitudes supported by a negative view of counter-transference and analogous to the reluctance to recognize transference by nonanalysts and, early on, by Freud. Little's work, which is built upon Klein's views of projection and introjection, places great demands on the analyst to overcome inhibitions to recognizing and using the intense feelings analysis engenders in the analyst. Unlike Heimann, and in accord with Winnicott's lead, she strongly supports the analyst's interpreting the counter-transference, particularly in the later stages of the analysis. Like Heimann, she advocates lessening the authoritarian and didactic attitudes that had come to characterize analytic work, attitudes that ignored the analyst's emotional contribution to the exchange. Little, along with Winnicott, notes the idea that with severely ill patients, the counter-transference may carry a larger portion of the work, not only in understanding, but in providing ego functions for the patient. Analysts may have to make contact at more primitive levels with such patients, foreshadowing ideas that will be more fully elaborated in the subsequent literature on projective identification, holding and containing functions in the work of Bion, Modell, Winnicott, Searles and others.

Racker spells out in greater detail than Heimann and Little the forms counter-transference may take. He describes a counter-transference neurosis analogous to the transference neurosis. Interestingly, he outlines both traditional Oedipal conflicts as they unfold in counter-transference problems with male and female patients as well as manifestations of unresolved depressive and paranoid issues, in more typically Kleinian projective and introjective terms. Racker posits counter-transference as ubiquitous and integral to the analytic process at all times.

Money-Kyrle contrasts more attitudinally neutral analytic motives such as Freud's benevolent neutrality and the notion of scientific curiosity, a necessary sublimation, with less impersonal concerns for the patient's welfare, referred to as the analyst's reparative and parental drives. The former counteracts latent destructiveness, the latter involves partial identification with the analysand as the analyst's early self. This identification can take two forms, introjective and projective, as emphasized by Melanie Klein.

According to Money-Kyrle, periods of non-understanding interfere with desired parental and reparative functions in the analyst, eliciting anxiety, particularly in analysts who make severe superego demands on themselves. Such analysts, sensing failure at such times of non-understanding, experience persecutory or depressive guilt, or as an alternative, blame the analysand. Money-Kyrle describes these alternatives in terms of prolonged introjection and projection and outlines the counter-transference difficulties that may ensue. These may include excess positive or negative attitudes towards patients. It is through continuous self-analytic reflection that the analyst can trace the patient's contributions to these difficulties and use them on behalf of the analysis.

This manuscript, familiar in Kleinian circles, but relatively less well known to analysts of other theoretical persuasions, extends the ideas of Little and Heimann, outlining the way Klein's concept of projective identification explicates the vicissitudes of normal and more problematic counter-transference. Furthermore, it provides a more searching exploration of the analyst's complex motives in doing analytic work without necessarily pathologizing them, foreshadowing recent interest in the analyst's inevitable subjectivity.

Annie Reich's work, representing the North American ego psychological school, is important for several reasons. First, it takes seriously Kleinian contributions to counter-transference and discusses them in a non-dismissive way. Reich emphasizes the importance of distinguishing different kinds of responses on the part of analysts to patients and to analytic work in general. She underlines the differences between patient-specific and more chronic counter-transference responses, the latter viewed by Reich as the analyst's transference to the patient. She gives as examples analysts who need to satisfy their narcissism, those with marked pedagogic trends and analysts who repeatedly unearth the same conflicts in all their analysands. She notes that counter-transference is necessary for the talent and interest in analysing to develop in the analyst and she takes up the question of what constitutes a well functioning sublimation. She cautions that counter-transference can easily become an overinclusive concept that conflates unconscious responsiveness with unresolved and problematic neurotic problems in the analyst that interfere with understanding and analysing.

The 1950s saw many subsequent contributions on the subject of counter-transference, papers by these same and other authors, from varying schools of psychoanalytic thought. What is clear is that object relational ideas, conceptualized around pre-Oedipal development, were viewed as central to the psychology of the analytic dyad, now considered far more interactive and subjective than the older view of the objective, removed analyst allowed. Regardless of whether this older view, pictured in a series of oft-criticized Freudian metaphors, was ever actualized, the 1950s saw a legitimization and intensification of interest in the psychology of the analysing analyst that continues unabated to this day. A particularly important integrative contribution was Zetzel's exploration of transference, which appeared after the series of papers on counter-transference discussed above. Zetzel carried forward a respectful conceptual exploration of similarities and differences between Kleinian and ego psychological perspectives on transference. The latter perspective supposes a therapeutic alliance, a term Zetzel attributes to E. Bibring, which is anchored in the ego psychological emphasis on attention to defences and anxiety in formulating interpretations. Zetzel contrasts Kleinian interpretation of primitive, pre-Oedipal material which, in the Kleinian view, decreases anxiety, with an ego psychological view which would presuppose the opposite. Furthermore, she outlines two views of the repetition compulsion, one aimed at the mastery of conflict, the other at the return to more primitive forms of gratification. Since transference is a form of repetition, this leads to two distinct views of transference. The first regards transference as a necessary regression to earlier forms of conflict preliminary to its analysis by interpretation. The second, in Zetzel's view, limits the potential of traditional analytic work for resolving conflict and leads to modifications of technique such as those advocated by Alexander. Zetzel positions Kleinian analysis, with its emphasis on pre-Oedipal material, and an ego psychological approach with its attention to alliance issues and defence analysis on a continuum, both characterized as maintaining the centrality of transference analysis, recognizing the significance and potential dangers of counter-transference manifestations, and both leading to impressive analytic achievements.

We have chosen Bion's paper, "Attacks on linking", and Segal's "Notes on symbol formation" from among a series of papers on psychosis by Rosenfeld, Klein and others appearing in *IJP* in the

1950s. Bion addresses primitive modes of thinking and their impact on more developed rational thought typical of psychoanalytic work. His work illustrates the importance of psychoanalytic treatment of very ill patients for understanding unconscious processes in more mature, analysable patients. In the 1950s, psychoanalytic treatment of psychosis remained active in many psychoanalytic circles. Bion's paper on linking focused interest on the nature of concrete mental operations and their dynamic underpinning as attempts to destroy linking to objects. Furthermore, the paper posits the importance of the availability of the analyst, as opposed to the unavailable primary object, for the temporary containment of unmanageable mental content as crucial to the analysand's gradual ability to manage intensely affective material as an analysis proceeds. This phenomenon became central to technical suggestions for dealing with disturbed patients who can eventually be treated analytically. The author brings together notions of the role of objects in fostering or inhibiting the capacity for creative thought.

Segal explores the process of symbolization and its disturbances which, following Klein, she links to disturbances in the ego's relations to its objects. In particular, problems in differentiation between ego and objects results in similarly inadequate differentiation between symbols and their referents, resulting in concrete thinking. Segal traces symbolization through the paranoid–schizoid and depressive positions, beginning with the earliest projections and identifications which constitute the origins of symbol formation. She views these earliest symbols as "symbolic equations" and sees them as central to the concrete thinking of psychotics, in whom paranoid–schizoid anxieties have not been overcome. The move to the depressive position, with its whole object relations and better differentiation between the ego and its objects, allows for symbolization proper. Here symbols, rather than being equated with the object, allow for displacement of drives away from the object. The symbol becomes a vehicle for the ego to protect its objects, modify its aggression towards objects, and allows for important subliminatory and communicative functions. Segal describes, in a manner analogous to Bion, how regressions in less disturbed patients lead to projective identifications in which symbols revert to concrete symbolic equations, interfering with analytic communication and undermining the transference attachment that carries the analytic work.

Several of the other papers selected also address the subject of psychosis and open up new treatment strategies for working analytically with patients with borderline pathology. As there was a turning outward during the 1950s, there was increasing concentration on early pre-Oedipal experiences between child and mother, and a growing recognition of the critical importance that this relationship has on subsequent development. Mahler's paper, describing her well-known developmental schema, focuses on understanding childhood psychosis, positing a fixation at either the autistic or symbiotic phases, leading to significant identity disturbances and either autism or childhood schizophrenia respectively. However, of the lasting legacies of this work, two stand out as particularly significant: it was among the first empirically derived conceptualizations of the development of serious psychopathology (or of development in general) and it laid the groundwork for exploration of the separation–individuation phase which became crucial for the understanding and treatment of infantile pre-Oedipal syndromes.

The 1950s ushered in a burgeoning interest in serious personality disturbances, the so-called widening scope of psychoanalytic patients. Psychoanalysts applied insights gained by exploring early life experiences to both theoretical and technical innovations, particularly to borderline states. Balint's paper on New Beginnings highlights this trend. Working from both the Ferenczian and Kleinian traditions, Balint disagrees with the Kleinian notion of the primacy of innate aggression and resulting unconscious phantasy. Rather, he places emphasis on the actual mother–child interaction with the supposition that, barring significant untoward trauma, paranoid, persecutory ideation arises secondarily, if at all. For Balint, this profoundly influenced his view of psychoanalytic technique. Deviations in standard interpretive technique, principally gratifications of primitive transferential desires, were warranted in patients "whose ego development was distorted by early trauma", in order to facilitate a New Beginning, "to regress to an—as yet— undefended, naïve, i.e. pretraumatic state and to begin anew to love and hate in a primitive way". Balint's technical recommendations were cautiously stated; he was well aware of the inherent risks of what, in other circles (Kleinian or Freudian), would have been considered breaches of analytic abstinence. Nonetheless, for a select group of patients, non-interpretive gratifications were a necessity. In Balint's understanding, these "parameters" allowed for the successful analysis of a broader group of patients than previously thought analysable. The impact was far-reaching, originally in the treatment of borderline conditions, but also more recently in the critical re-examination of the traditional analytic stance of anonymity, neutrality and abstinence taken up by the intersubjectivists.

Like Mahler and Balint, Winnicott had an abiding interest in early developmental phenomena. His work had enormous impact both on the treatment of "widening scope" patients as well as in elucidating the course of normal childhood development. Similar to Balint, Winnicott's rich little paper "On transference" argues for a change in technique when working with patients with pre-Oedipal pathology, with a prioritization of the setting, "the summation of all the details of management" over interpretation. The analyst, as opposed to the patient's early care-givers, as well as the more traditionally abstinent analyst working with neurotic patients, strives to be "good enough in the matter of adaptation to need", allowing for the opportunity for ego development where none had previously existed. Winnicott acknowledges that this adaptation to need on the part of the analyst is necessarily never complete, importantly so, for these limitations allow for the first time experience of anger and the beginnings of reality testing. Indeed, analytic mistakes are unavoidable, and it is the correct handling of these mistakes that lead to an analytic success. For Winnicott, resistance in these patients "indicates that the analyst has made a mistake, or in some detail has behaved badly; in fact the resistance remains until the analyst has found out the mistakes and has tried to account for it, and has used it". This is of utmost importance for, in contrast to the transferences of neurotic patients, there is a necessity for the patient to experience "objective anger about the analyst's failures", and for the "patient to become angry for the first time about the details of failure of adaptation" on the part of the original caregivers. Winnicott states that for these patients, it is not that "the past comes into the consulting room, in this work it is more true to say that the present goes back into the past, and is the past." Winnicott's rethinking of the nature of the transference and its handling in borderline and psychotic pathology, similar to Balint's New Beginning, had a profound effect on later revisions of analytic technique and our understandings of pre-Oedipal pathology.

Winnicott is perhaps best known for one of the papers we have included here, his work on transitional objects and phenomena. Winnicott, perhaps more than any other thinker of his time, appreciated the subtle, nuanced and critical dynamic that occurs between infant and mother as the infant develops into a separate being. Less concerned with the inner world of the infant than his Freudian and Kleinian predecessors, Winnicott focused attention on the relationship between mother and child, particularly that space that is between infant and mother and between internal and external worlds. This crucial area "is an intermediate area of experiencing, to which inner reality and external life both contribute. It is an area which is not challenged, because no claim is made on its behalf except that it shall exist as a resting-place for the individual engaged in the perpetual human task of keeping inner and outer reality separate yet interrelated". Transitional objects and phenomena are illusory, neither simply phantasy nor reality, a "not me" possession but not the object either. The object is used by the infant, loved and hated by the infant, as if it were the mother. However, its not being the mother, of which the infant is constantly reminded, is of crucial importance. Nor is the object merely a symbolic representation of mother (or part of mother), which, for Winnicott, implies an acknowledged distinction between internal and external. Rather it is that which allows for the development of symbolism and "gives room for the process of becoming able to accept difference and similarity".

The infant's use of transitional objects and phenomena is part of normal development and is made possible by "good enough mothering", the "mother's special capacity for making adaptation to the needs of her infant, thus allowing the infant the illusion that what the infant creates really exists", and allowing for, as the infant develops, gradual and increasingly necessary maternal failures. For Winnicott, the implications of this transitional space are enormous. It is the essence of the experience of play in the child and "throughout life is retained in the intense experiencing that belongs to the arts and to religion and to imaginative living". Winnicott's ideas have had a deep influence on analytic understanding of aesthetic experience and creativity. Like Mahler's and Balint's work, Winnicott's pre-Oedipal focus allowed for a broader understanding of borderline phenomena, and like Balint's, led to an alteration in conventional psychoanalytic technique aimed at adaptation to the special demands presented by infantile psychopathology. These ideas influenced and informed, from technical and theoretical perspectives, a dizzyingly diverse group of analysts ranging from Kohut and other Self Psychologists to Lacan and, later, Andre Green.

Similar to the work of Mahler, Balint, and Winnicott, with their focus on early mother–child interaction, Bowlby's paper on the child's tie to the mother also places emphasis on the relational rather than the intrapsychic. Bowlby re-examined this early relation in terms of a conception of attachment separate from dependency and physiologic need gratification. Drawing equally from analytic sources as from ethnography and cognitive and developmental psychology, Bowlby proposed that the infant's tie to the mother, as expressed in terms of a psychological attachment, is primary and is not mediated or necessitated by the mother's gratification of needs, e.g. hunger or warmth. With evolutionary theory as a necessary background, Bowlby described particular attachment behaviours, specific to the human species, that because of the forces of natural selection and their resulting survival value, tie the infant to the mother. These include crying, sucking, smiling, clinging, and following, and it is this constellation of attachment behaviours or instinctual responses, that are of utmost importance in the infant–mother bond. Bowlby attempted to place a psychoanalytic theory of development squarely within an evolutionary biologic structure. Bowlby's work was among the first to incorporate data from other disciplines and has had a profound impact on the work of attachment theorists and child researchers. Equally, his appeal to non-analytic investigators for help in informing and shaping analytic theory has served as a model for recognizing the importance of current explorations in cognitive neuroscience for our conceptions of mind. In this light, the influence of this paper was less technical than theoretical, influencing both our under-standing of the early relationship between mother and child and, in a broader way, the relationship of psychoanalytic theorizing to the larger field of scientific inquiry.

In Loewenstein's paper, "Some remarks on the role of speech in psychoanalytic technique", the author takes up the subject of bringing unconscious mental content into consciousness and its relationship to gaining insight. Loewenstein focuses on the role of speech and verbalization in this process, particularly as it pertains to psychoanalytic technique. The central point of reference is the barrier between something being conscious and its then being verbalized. Loewenstein emphasizes the typical analysand's resistance to verbalizing that which has already become conscious. He identifies the analyst's role as witness and as an additional memory for the patient. In this way, the analyst functions as an autonomous part of the patient's ego, lending his help to the patient's compromised ego.

Loewenstein notes that speech objectifies and makes more real; it connects affects with specific mental contents and by doing so allows for the reintegration of affects with defences, drives and other aspects of the mind. Affects once expressed in words become external as well as internal realities that can be perceived as factual in the social sense. Additionally, verbalization of transference and acting out transforms repeating into thinking, particularly about intentions and motivations. It is expected that doing so will lead to further memory of etiologic conflicts and traumatic events from the past.

In Loewenstein's view, resistance to verbalization is the last struggle of the ego's defences against making the unconscious conscious. The author draws an important distinction between the languages of the unconscious (primary process) and consciousness (secondary process). Verbalization plays a role in transforming the primary to the secondary process. The auditory perception of speech forces reality testing and distinguishes stimulation arising from the inside from that on the outside. Verbalization subjects psychic phenomena to reality testing, unravels the effect of "pathological intertwinement between past and present" and places the contents of the mind in a context that makes such content more resistant to further repression and regression. The author takes up the subject of self-analysis and points out that self-analysis usually involves "a dialogue" with a former analyst.

This paper follows a series of papers on ego psychology and interpretation that appeared in *Psychoanalytic Quarterly* in 1951 (Volume 20). It serves as an important link to subsequent efforts to define psychoanalytic technique from the perspective of the structural hypothesis. It places emphasis on the dynamics of reality and of the analyst, a central theme of the 1950s, while falling short of emphasizing the relational aspects of technique favoured by the Kleinians. In its focus on aspects of consciousness, it presages subsequent interest in conscious phenomena that continues to the present time.

We have included Lacan's 1953 "Some reflections on the ego" which, for many analysts, was their first introduction to his work. While not a source work among Lacan's output, it introduces many of his important ideas to English speaking analysts, and was the only Lacan work available in English until the mid 1970s. We find here Lacan's thoughts on the ego's opposition to reality, the importance of the negative, the centrality of language in defining reality, emphasis on subjectivity, and especially the profound organizing influence of the body image or imago and its origins in the mirror phase. Lacan's work can be seen as leading away from ego psychological perspectives that emphasize the ego's reliance on the reality principle, the ego's adaptational purposes, the ego's mastery of drives, and the diminishing importance of the body. While Lacan was most important to French analysis, we find in this manuscript ideas that resonate with Kleinian, intersubjectivist, self-psychological and other perspectives and that have gradually influenced the ego-psychological, structural approaches they were, in part, a reaction against.

In choosing these "most influential" papers appearing in the *IJP* during the 1950s, the editors were struck by their modernity. The contemporary psychoanalytic literature remains preoccupied with the same themes, the subjectivity of the analyst (our contemporary term for counter-transference), preverbal and pre-Oedipal maturational failures, the reparative potential of the therapeutic relationship seen from a developmental perspective, empirical studies of attachment behaviour, the analyst as witness, the analytic playspace, the limits of neutrality. One might ask whether psychoanalysis has made much progress in the fifty years subsequent to the appearance of these papers. We would answer that the nature of psychoanalytic inquiry predicts a return to the same issues. Unlike most other fields of scholarly investigation, the discoveries of psychoanalysis are often unwelcome, meet with powerful resistance, are easily abandoned and thus require repeated rediscovery.

The very search for what is new and innovative in our field may represent avoidance and repression as much as it does creativity and progress. To be sure, each rediscovery or return to crucial psychoanalytic concerns must account for the changes wrought by the influence of altered cultural and philosophical perspectives as well as progressive discoveries in adjacent fields. But progress in our field needs to be measured in relation to how we preserve what we know as much as by what is newly discovered. We hope that our readers will appreciate this as they return to these modern papers of half a century ago.

CHAPTER ONE

Hate in the counter-transference[1]

D. W. Winnicott

In this paper I wish to examine one aspect of the whole subject of ambivalency, namely, hate in the counter-transference. I believe that the task of the analyst (call him a research analyst) who undertakes the analysis of a psychotic is seriously weighted by this phenomenon, and that analysis of psychotics becomes impossible unless the analyst's own hate is extremely well sorted-out and conscious. This is tantamount to saying that an analyst needs to be himself analysed, but it also asserts that the analysis of a psychotic is irksome as compared with that of a neurotic, and inherently so.

Apart from psychoanalytic treatment, the management of a psychotic is bound to be irksome. From time to time I have made acutely critical remarks about the modern trends in psychiatry, with the too easy electric shocks and the too drastic leucotomies. Because of these criticisms that I have expressed I would like to be foremost in recognition of the extreme difficulty inherent in the task of the psychiatrist, and of the mental nurse in particular. Insane patients must always be a heavy emotional burden on those who care for them. One can forgive those who do this work if they do awful things. This does not mean, however, that we have to accept whatever is done by psychiatrists and neurosurgeons as sound according to principles of science.

Therefore although what follows is about psychoanalysis, it really has value to the psychiatrist, even to one whose work does not in any way take him into the analytic type of relationship to patients.

To help the general psychiatrist the psychoanalyst must not only study for him the primitive stages of the emotional development of the ill individual, but also must study the nature of the emotional burden which the psychiatrist bears in doing his work. What we as analysts call the counter-transference needs to be understood by the psychiatrist too. However much he loves his patients he cannot avoid hating them, and fearing them, and the better he knows this the less will hate and fear be the motive determining what he does to his patients.

Statement of theme

One could classify counter-transference phenomena thus:

1. Abnormality in counter-transference feelings, and set relationships and identifications that are under repression in the analyst. The comment on this is that the analyst needs more analysis, and we believe this is less of an issue among psychoanalysts than among psychotherapists in general.
2. The identifications and tendencies belonging to an analyst's personal experiences and personal development which provide the positive setting for his analytic work and make his work different in quality from that of any other analyst.
3. From these two I distinguish the truly objective counter-transference, or if this is difficult, the analyst's love and hate in reaction to the actual personality and behaviour of the patient, based on objective observation.

I suggest that if an analyst is to analyse psychotics or anti-socials he must be able to be so thoroughly aware of the counter-transference that he can sort out and study his objective reactions to the patient. These will include hate. Counter-transference phenomena will at times be the important things in the analysis.

The motive imputed to the analyst by the patient

I wish to suggest that the patient can only appreciate in the analyst what he himself is capable of feeling. In the matter of motive; the obsessional will tend to be thinking of the analyst as doing his work in a futile obsessional way. A hypo-manic patient who is incapable of being depressed, except in a severe mood swing, and in whose emotional development the depressive position has not been securely won, who cannot feel guilt in a deep way, or a sense of concern or responsibility, is unable to see the analyst's work as an attempt on the part of the analyst to make reparation in respect of his own (the analyst's) guilt feelings. A neurotic patient tends to see the analyst as ambivalent towards the patient, and to expect the analyst to show a splitting of love and hate; this patient, when in luck, gets the love, because someone else is getting the analyst's hate. Would it not follow that if a psychotic is in a "coincident love–hate" state of feeling he experiences a deep conviction that the analyst is also only capable of the same crude and dangerous state of coincident love–hate relationship? Should the analyst show love he will surely at the same moment kill the patient.

This coincidence of love and hate is something that characteristically recurs in the analysis of psychotics, giving rise to problems of management which can easily take the analyst beyond his resources. This coincidence of love and hate to which I am referring is something which is distinct from the aggressive component complicating the primitive love impulse and implies that in the history of the patient there was an environmental failure at the time of the first object-finding instinctual impulses.

If the analyst is going to have crude feelings imputed to him he is best forewarned and so forearmed, for he must tolerate being placed in that position. Above all he must not deny hate that really exists in himself. Hate that is justified in the present setting has to be sorted out and kept in storage and available for eventual interpretation.

If we are to become able to be the analysts of psychotic patients we must have reached down to very primitive things in ourselves, and this is but another example of the fact that the answer to many obscure problems of psychoanalytic practice lies in further analysis of the analyst. (Psychoanalytic research is perhaps always to some extent an attempt on the part of an analyst to carry the work of his own analysis further than the point to which his own analyst could get him.)

A main task of the analyst of any patient is to maintain objectivity in regard to all that the patient brings, and a special case of this is the analyst's need to be able to hate the patient objectively. Are there not many situations in our ordinary analytic work in which the analyst's hate is justified? A patient of mine, a very bad obsessional, was almost loathsome to me for some years. I felt bad about this until the analysis turned a corner and the patient became lovable, and then I realized that his unlikeableness had been an active symptom, unconsciously determined. It was indeed a wonderful day for me (much later on) when I could actually tell the patient that I and his friends had felt repelled by him, but that he had been too ill for us to let him know. This was also an important day for him, a tremendous advance in his adjustment to reality.

In the ordinary analysis the analyst has no difficulty with the management of his own hate. This hate remains latent. The main thing, of course, is that through his own analysis he has become free from vast reservoirs of unconscious hate belonging to the past and to inner conflicts. There are other reasons why hate remains unexpressed and even unfelt as such:

1. Analysis is my chosen job, the way I feel I will best deal with my own guilt, the way I can express myself in a constructive way.
2. I get paid, or I am in training to gain a place in society by psychoanalytic work.
3. I am discovering things.
4. I get immediate rewards through identification with the patient, who is making progress, and I can see still greater rewards some way ahead, after the end of the treatment.
5. Moreover, as an analyst I have ways of expressing hate. Hate is expressed by the existence of the end of the "hour".

I think this is true even when there is no difficulty whatever, and when the patient is pleased to go. In many analyses these things can be taken for granted, so that they are scarcely mentioned, and the analytic work is done through verbal interpretations of the patient's emerging unconscious transference. The analyst takes over the role of one or other of the helpful figures of the patient's childhood. He cashes in on the success of those who did the dirty work when the patient was an infant. These things are part of the description of ordinary psychoanalytic work, which is mostly concerned with patients whose symptoms have a neurotic quality.

In the analysis of psychotics, however, quite a different type and degree of strain is take by the analyst, and it is precisely this different strain that I am trying to describe.

Illustration of counter-transference anxiety

Recently for a period of a few days I found I was doing bad work. I made mistakes in respect of each one of my patients. The difficulty was in myself and it was partly personal but chiefly associated with a climax that I had reached in my relation to one particular psychotic (research) patient. The difficulty cleared up when I had what is sometimes called a "healing" dream. (Incidentally I would add that during my analysis and in the years since the end of my analysis I have had a long series of these healing dreams which, although in many cases unpleasant, have each one of them marked my arrival at a new stage in emotional development.)

On this particular occasion I was aware of the meaning of the dream as I woke or even before I woke. The dream had two phases. In the first I was in the gods in a theatre and looking down on the people a long way below in the stalls. I felt severe anxiety as if I might lose a limb. This was associated with the feeling I have had at the top of the Eiffel Tower that if I put my hand over the edge it would fall off on to the ground below. This would be ordinary castration anxiety.

In the next phase of the dream I was aware that the people in the stalls were watching a play and I was now related to what was going on on the stage through them. A new kind of anxiety now developed. What I knew was that I had no right side of my body at all. This was not a castration dream. It was a sense of not having that part of the body.

As I woke I was aware of having understood at a very deep level what was my difficulty at that particular time. The first part of the dream represented the ordinary anxieties that might develop in respect of unconscious fantasies of my neurotic patients. I would be in danger of losing my hand or my fingers if these patients should become interested in them. With this kind of anxiety I was familiar, and it was comparatively tolerable.

The second part of the dream, however, referred to my relation to the psychotic patient. This patient was requiring of me that I should have no relation to her body at all, not even an imaginative one; there was no body that she recognized as hers and if she existed at all she could only feel herself to be a mind. Any reference to her body produced paranoid anxieties because to claim that she had a body was to persecute her. What she needed of me was that I should have only a mind speaking to her mind. At the culmination of my difficulties on the evening before the dream I had become irritated and had said that what she was needing of me was little better than hair-splitting. This had had a disastrous effect and it took many weeks for the analysis to recover from my lapse. The essential thing, however, was that I should understand my own anxiety and this was represented in the dream by the absence of the right side of my body when I tried to get into relation to the play that the people in the stalls were watching. This right side of my body was the side related to this particular patient and was therefore affected by her need to deny absolutely even an imaginative relationship of our bodies. This denial was producing in me this psychotic type of anxiety, much less tolerable than ordinary castration anxiety. Whatever other interpretations might be made in respect of this dream the result of my having dreamed it and remembered it was that I was able to take up this analysis again and even to heal the harm done to it by my irritability which had its origin in a reactive anxiety of a quality that was appropriate to my contact with a patient with no body.

Postponement of interpretation

The analyst must be prepared to bear strain without expecting the patient to know anything about what he is doing, perhaps over a long period of time. To do this he must be easily aware of his own fear and hate. He is in the position of the mother of an infant unborn or newly born. Eventually, he ought to be able to tell his patient what he has been through on the patient's behalf, but an analysis may never get as far as this. There may be too little good experience in the patient's past to work on. What if there be no satisfactory relationship of early infancy for the analyst to exploit in the transference?

There is a vast difference between those patients who have had satisfactory early experiences which can be discovered in the transference, and those whose very early experiences have been so deficient or distorted that the analyst has to be the first in the patient's life to supply certain environmental essentials. In the treatment of the patient of the latter kind all sorts of things in analytic technique become vitally important that can be taken for granted in the treatment of patients of the former type.

I asked an analyst who confines his attention to neurotics whether he does analysis in the dark, and he said, "Why, no! Surely our job is to provide an ordinary environment, and the dark would be extraordinary". He was surprised at my question. He was orientated towards analysis of neurotics. But this provision and maintenance of an ordinary environment can be in itself a vitally important thing in the analysis of a psychotic, in fact it can be, at times, even more important than the verbal interpretations which also have to be given. For the neurotic the couch and warmth and comfort can be symbolical of the mother's love; for the psychotic it would be more true to say that these things are the analyst's physical expression of love. The couch is the analyst's lap or womb, and the warmth is the live warmth of the analyst's body. And so on.

Objective hate under test

There is, I hope, a progression in my statement of my subject. The analyst's hate is ordinarily latent and is easily kept latent. In analysis of psychotics the analyst is under greater strain to keep his hate latent, and he can only do this by being thoroughly aware of it. Now I want to add that in certain stages of certain analyses the analyst's hate is actually sought by the patient, and what is then needed is hate that is objective. If the patient seeks objective or justified hate he must be able to reach it, else he cannot feel he can reach objective love.

It is perhaps relevant here to cite the case of the child of the broken home, or the child without parents. Such a child spends his time unconsciously looking for his parents. It is notoriously inadequate to take such a child into one's home and to love him.

What happens is that after a while a child so adopted gains hope, and then he starts to test out the environment he has found, and to seek proof of his guardians' ability to hate objectively. It seems that he can believe in being loved only after reaching being hated.

During the second world war a boy of nine came to a hostel for evacuated children, sent from London not because of bombs but because of truancy. I hoped to give him some treatment during his stay in the hostel, but his symptom won and he ran away as he had always done from everywhere since the age of six when he first ran away from home. However, I had established contact with him in one interview in which I could see and interpret through a drawing of his that in running away he was unconsciously saving the inside of his home and preserving his mother from assault, as well as trying to get away from his own inner world which was full of persecutors.

I was not very surprised when he turned up in the police station very near my home. This was one of the few police stations that did not know him intimately. My wife very generously took him in and kept him for three months, three months of hell. He was the most lovable and most maddening of children, often stark staring mad. But fortunately we knew what to expect. We dealt with the first phase by giving him complete freedom and a shilling whenever he went out. He had only to ring up and we fetched him from whatever police station had taken charge of him.

Soon the expected change-over occurred, the truancy symptom turned round, and the boy started dramatizing the assault on the inside. It was really a whole-time job for the two of us together, and when I was out the worst episodes took place.

Interpretation had to be made at any minute of day or night, and often the only solution in a crisis was to make the correct interpretation, as if the boy were in analysis. It was the correct interpretation that he valued above everything. The important thing for the purpose of this paper is the way in which the evolution of the boy's personality engendered hate in me, and what I did about it.

Did I hit him? The answer is no, I never hit. But I should have had to have done so if I had not known all about my hate and if I had not let him know about it too. At crises I would take him by bodily strength, and without anger or blame, and put him outside the front door, whatever the weather or the time of day or night.

There was a special bell he could ring, and he knew that if he rang it he would be readmitted and no word said about the past. He used this bell as soon as he had recovered from his maniacal attack.

The important thing is that each time, just as I put him outside the door, I told him something; I said that what had happened had made me hate him. This was easy because it was so true.

I think these words were important from the point of view of his progress, but they were mainly important in enabling me to tolerate the situation without letting out, without losing my temper and every now and again murdering him.

This boy's full story cannot be told here. He went to an Approved School. His deeply rooted relation to us has remained one of the few stable things in his life. This episode from ordinary life can be used to illustrate the general topic of hate justified in the present; this is to be distinguished from hate that is only justified in another setting but which is tapped by some action of a patient (child).

A mother's love and hate

Out of all the complexity of the problem of hate and its roots I want to rescue one thing, because I believe it has an importance for the analyst of psychotic patients. I suggest that the mother hates the baby before the baby hates the mother, and before the baby can know his mother hates him.

Before developing this theme I want to refer to Freud's remarks. In "Instincts and their vicissitudes" (1915) (where he says so much that is original and illuminating about hate), Freud says: "we might at a pinch say of an instinct that it 'loves' the objects after which it strives for purposes of satisfaction, but to say that it 'hates' an object strikes us as odd, so we become aware that the attitudes of love and hate cannot be said to characterize the relation of instincts to their objects, but are reserved for the relations of the ego as a whole to objects. ..." This I feel is true and important. Does this not mean that the personality must be integrated before an infant can be said to hate? However early integration may be achieved—perhaps integration occurs earliest at the height of excitement or rage—there is a theoretical earlier stage in which whatever the infant does that hurts is not done in hate. I have used the word "ruthless love" in describing this stage. Is this acceptable? As the infant becomes able to feel a whole person, so does the word hate develop meaning as a description of a certain group of his feelings.

The mother, however, hates her infant from the word go. I believe Freud thought it possible that a mother may under certain circumstances have only love for her boy baby; but we may doubt this. We know about a mother's love and we appreciate its reality and power. Let me give some of the reasons why a mother hates her baby, even a boy.

(a) The baby is not her own (mental) conception.
(b) The baby is not the one of childhood play, father's child, brother's child, etc.
(c) The baby is not magically produced.
(d) The baby is a danger to her body in pregnancy and at birth.
(e) The baby is an interference with her private life, a challenge to preoccupation.
(f) To a greater or lesser extent a mother feels that her own mother demands a baby, so that her baby is produced to placate her mother.
(g) The baby hurts her nipples even by suckling, which is at first a chewing activity.
(h) He is ruthless, treats her as scum, an unpaid servant, a slave.
(i) She has to love him, excretions and all, at any rate at the beginning, till he has doubts about himself.
(j) He tries to hurt her, periodically bites her, all in love.
(k) He shows disillusionment about her.
(l) His excited love is cupboard love, so that having got what he wants he throws her away like orange peel.
(m) The baby at first must dominate, he must be protected from coincidences, life must unfold at the baby's rate and all this needs his mother's continuous and detailed study. For instance, she must not be anxious when holding him, etc.
(n) At first he does not know at all what she does or what she sacrifices for him. Especially he cannot allow for her hate.
(o) He is suspicious, refuses her good food, and makes her doubt herself, but eats well with his aunt.
(p) After an awful morning with him she goes out, and he smiles at a stranger, who says: "Isn't he sweet!"

(q) If she fails him at the start she knows he will pay her out for ever.

(r) He excites her but frustrates—she mustn't eat him or trade in sex with him.

I think that in the analysis of psychotics, and in the ultimate stages of the analysis, even of a normal person, the analyst must find himself in a position comparable to that of the mother of a newborn baby. When deeply regressed the patient cannot identify with the analyst or appreciate his point of view any more than the foetus or newly born infant can sympathize with the mother.

A mother has to be able to tolerate hating her baby without doing anything about it. She cannot express it to him. If, for fear of what she may do, she cannot hate appropriately when hurt by her child she must fall back on masochism, and I think it is this that gives rise to the false theory of a natural masochism in women. The most remarkable thing about a mother is her ability to be hurt so much by her baby and to hate so much without paying the child out, and her ability to wait for rewards that may or may not come at a later date. Perhaps she is helped by some of the nursery rhymes she sings, which her baby enjoys but fortunately does not understand?

> "Rockabye Baby, on the tree top,
> When the wind blows the cradle will rock,
> When the bough breaks the cradle will fall,
> Down will come baby, cradle and all."

I think of a mother (or father) playing with a small infant; the infant enjoying the play and not knowing that the parent is expressing hate in the words, perhaps in birth symbolism. This is not a sentimental rhyme. Sentimentality is useless for parents, as it contains a denial of hate, and sentimentality in a mother is no good at all from the infant's point of view.

It seems to me doubtful whether a human child as he develops is capable of tolerating the full extent of his own hate in a sentimental environment. He needs hate to hate.

If this is true, a psychotic patient in analysis cannot be expected to tolerate his hate of the analyst unless the analyst can hate him.

Practical problem of interpretation

If all this is accepted there remains for discussion the question of the interpretation of the analyst's hate to the patient. This is obviously a matter fraught with danger, and it needs the most careful timing. But I believe an analysis is incomplete if even towards the end it has not been possible for the analyst to tell the patient what he, the analyst, did unbeknown for the patient whilst he was ill, in the early stages. Until the interpretation is made the patient is kept to some extent in the position of infant, one who cannot understand what he owes to his mother.

Summary

An analyst has to display all the patience and tolerance and reliability of a mother devoted to her infant, has to recognize the patient's wishes as needs, has to put aside other interests in order to be available and to be punctual, and objective, and has to seem to want to give what is really only given because of the patient's needs.

There may be a long initial period in which the analyst's point of view cannot be (even unconsciously) appreciated by the patient. Acknowledgment cannot be expected because at the primitive root of the patient that is being looked for there is no capacity for identification with the analyst, and certainly the patient cannot see that the analyst's hate is often engendered by the very things the patient does in his crude way of loving.

In the analysis (research analysis) or in ordinary management of the more psychotic type of patient, a great strain is put on the analyst (psychiatrist, mental nurse) and it is important to study the ways in which anxiety of psychotic quality and also hate are produced in those who work with severely ill psychiatric patients. Only in this way can there be any hope of the avoidance of therapy that is adapted to the needs of the therapist rather than to the needs of the patient.

Article citation

1. Winnicott, D. (1949). Hate in the counter-transference. *International Journal of Psycho-Analysis, 30*: 69–74.

CHAPTER TWO

On counter-transference[1]

Paula Heimann

This short note on counter-transference has been stimulated by certain observations I made in seminars and control analyses. I have been struck by the widespread belief amongst candidates that the counter-transference is nothing but a source of trouble. Many candidates are afraid and feel guilty when they become aware of feelings towards their patients and consequently aim at avoiding any emotional response and at becoming completely unfeeling and "detached".

When I tried to trace the origin of this ideal of the "detached" analyst, I found that our literature does indeed contain descriptions of the analytic work which can give rise to the notion that a good analyst does not feel anything beyond a uniform and mild benevolence towards his patients, and that any ripple of emotional waves on this smooth surface represents a disturbance to be overcome. This may possibly derive from a misreading of some of Freud's statements, such as his comparison with the surgeon's state of mind during an operation, or his simile of the mirror. At least these have been quoted to me in this connection in discussions on the nature of the counter-transference.

On the other hand, there is an opposite school of thought, like that of Ferenczi, which not only acknowledges that the analyst has a wide variety of feelings towards his patient, but recommends that he should at times express them openly. In her warm-hearted paper "Handhabung der bertragung auf Grund der Ferenczischen Versuche" (*Int. Zeitschr. f. Psychoanal.*, Bd. XXII, 1936) Alice Balint suggested that such honesty on the part of the analyst is helpful and in keeping with the respect for truth inherent in psychoanalysis. While I admire her attitude, I cannot agree with her conclusions. Other analysts again have claimed that it makes the analyst more "human" when he expresses his feelings to his patient and that it helps him to build up a "human" relationship with him.

For the purpose of this paper I am using the term "counter-transference" to cover all the feelings which the analyst experiences towards his patient.

It may be argued that this use of the term is not correct, and that counter-transference simply means transference on the part of the analyst. However, I would suggest that the prefix "counter" implies additional factors.

In passing it is worth while remembering that transference feelings cannot be sharply divided from those which refer to another person in his own right and not as a parent substitute. It is often pointed out that not everything a patient feels about his analyst is due to transference, and that, as the analysis progresses, he becomes increasingly more capable of "realistic" feelings. This warning itself shows that the differentiation between the two kinds of feelings is not always easy.

My thesis is that the analyst's emotional response to his patient within the analytic situation represents one of the most important tools for his work. The analyst's counter-transference is an instrument of research into the patient's unconscious.

The analytic situation has been investigated and described from many angles, and there is general agreement about its unique character. But my impression is that it has not been sufficiently stressed that it is a relationship between two persons. What distinguishes this relationship from others, is not the presence of feelings in one partner, the patient, and their absence in the other, the analyst, but above all the degree of the feelings experienced and the use made of them, these factors being interdependent. The aim of the analyst's own analysis, from this point of view, is not to turn him into a mechanical brain which can produce interpretations on the basis of a purely intellectual procedure, but to enable him, to sustain the feelings which are stirred in him, as opposed to discharging them (as does the patient), in order to subordinate them to the analytic task in which he functions as the patient's mirror reflection.

If an analyst tries to work without consulting his feelings, his interpretations are poor. I have often seen this in the work of beginners, who, out of fear, ignored or stifled their feelings.

We know that the analyst needs an evenly hovering attention in order to follow the patient's free associations, and that this enables him to listen simultaneously on many levels. He has to perceive the manifest and the latent meaning of his patient's words, the allusions and implications, the hints to former sessions, the references to childhood situations behind the description of current relationships, etc. By listening in this manner the analyst avoids the danger of becoming preoccupied with any one theme and remains receptive for the significance of changes in themes and of the sequences and gaps in the patient's associations.

I would suggest that the analyst along with this freely working attention needs a freely roused emotional sensibility so as to follow the patient's emotional movements and unconscious phantasies. Our basic assumption is that the analyst's unconscious understands that of his patient. This rapport on the deep level comes to the surface in the form of feelings which the analyst notices in response to his patient, in his "counter-transference". This is the most dynamic way in which his patient's voice reaches him. In the comparison of feelings roused in himself with his patient's associations and behaviour, the analyst possesses a most valuable means of checking whether he has understood or failed to understand his patient.

Since, however, violent emotions of any kind, of love or hate, helpfulness or anger, impel towards action rather than towards contemplation and blur a person's capacity to observe and weigh the evidence correctly, it follows that, if the analyst's emotional response is intense, it will defeat its object.

Therefore the analyst's emotional sensitivity needs to be extensive rather than intensive, differentiating and mobile.

There will be stretches in the analytic work when the analyst who combines free attention with free emotional responses does not register his feelings as a problem, because they are in accord with the meaning he understands. But often the emotions roused in him are much nearer to the heart of the matter than his reasoning, or, to put it in other words, his unconscious perception of the patient's unconscious is more acute and in advance of his conscious conception of the situation.

A recent experience comes to mind. It concerns a patient whom I had taken over from a colleague. The patient was a man in the forties who had originally sought treatment when his marriage broke down. Among his symptoms promiscuity figured prominently. In the third week of his analysis with me he told me, at the beginning of the session, that he was going to marry a woman whom he had met only a short time before.

It was obvious that his wish to get married at this juncture was determined by his resistance against the analysis and his need to act out his transference conflicts. Within a strongly ambivalent attitude the desire for an intimate relation with me had already clearly appeared. I had thus many reasons for doubting the wisdom of his intention and for suspecting his choice. But such an attempt to short-circuit analysis is not infrequent at the beginning of, or at a critical point in, the treatment and usually does not represent too great an obstacle to the work, so that catastrophic conditions need not arise. I was therefore somewhat puzzled to find that I reacted with a sense of apprehension and worry to the patient's remark. I felt that something more was involved in his situation, something beyond the ordinary acting out, which, however, eluded me.

In his further associations which centred round his friend, the patient, describing her, said she had had a "rough passage". This phrase again registered particularly and increased my misgivings. It dawned on me that it was precisely because she had had a rough passage that he was drawn to her. But still I felt that I did not see things clearly enough. Presently he came to tell me his dream: he had acquired from abroad a very good second-hand car which was damaged. He wished to repair it, but another person in the dream objected for reasons of caution. The patient had, as he put it, "to make him confused" in order that he might go ahead with the repair of the car.

With the help of this dream I came to understand what before I had merely felt as a sense of apprehension and worry. There was indeed more at stake than the mere acting-out of transference conflicts.

When he gave me the particulars of the car—very good, second-hand, from abroad—the patient spontaneously recognized that it represented myself. The other person in the dream who tried to stop him and whom he confused, stood for that part of the patient's ego which aimed at security and happiness and for the analysis as a protective object.

The dream showed that the patient wished me to be damaged (he insisted on my being the refugee to whom applies the expression "rough passage" which he had used for his new friend). Out of guilt for his sadistic impulses he was compelled to make reparation, but this reparation was of a masochistic nature, since it necessitated blotting out the voice of reason and caution. This element of confusing the protective figure was in itself double-barrelled, expressing both his sadistic and his masochistic impulses: in so far as it aimed at annihilating the analysis, it represented the patient's sadistic tendencies in the pattern of his infantile anal attacks on his mother; in so far as it stood for his ruling out his desire for security and happiness, it expressed his self-destructive trends. Reparation turned into a masochistic act again engenders hatred, and, far from solving the conflict between destructiveness and guilt, leads to a vicious circle.

The patient's intention of marrying his new friend, the injured woman, was fed from both sources, and the acting-out of his transference conflicts proved to be determined by this specific and powerful sadomasochistic system.

Unconsciously I had grasped immediately the seriousness of the situation, hence the sense of worry which I experienced. But my conscious understanding lagged behind, so that I could decipher the patient's message and appeal for help only later in the hour, when more material came up.

In giving the gist of an analytic session I hope to illustrate my contention that the analyst's immediate emotional response to his patient is a significant pointer to the patient's unconscious processes and guides him towards fuller understanding. It helps the analyst to focus his attention on the most urgent elements in the patient's associations and serves as a useful criterion for the selection of interpretations from material which, as we know, is always overdetermined.

From the point of view I am stressing, the analyst's counter-transference is not only part and parcel of the analytic relationship, but it is the patient's creation, it is a part of the patient's personality. (I am possibly touching here on a point which Dr Clifford Scott would express in terms of his concept of the body-scheme, but to pursue this line would lead me away from my theme.)

The approach to the counter-transference which I have presented is not without danger. It does not represent a screen for the analyst's shortcomings. When the analyst in his own analysis has worked through his infantile conflicts and anxieties (paranoid and depressive), so that he can easily establish contact with his own unconscious, he will not impute to his patient what belongs to himself. He will have achieved a dependable equilibrium which enables him to carry the roles of the patient's id, ego, superego, and external objects which the patient allots to him or—in other words—projects on him, when he dramatizes his conflicts in the analytic relationship. In the instance I have given the analyst was predominantly in the roles of the patient's good mother to be destroyed and rescued, and of the patient's reality-ego which tried to oppose his sadomasochistic impulses. In my view Freud's demand that the analyst must "recognize and master" his counter-transference does not lead to the conclusion that the counter-transference is a disturbing factor and that the analyst should become unfeeling and detached, but that he must use his emotional response as a key to the patient's unconscious. This will protect him from entering as a co-actor on the scene which the patient re-enacts in the analytic relationship and from exploiting it for his own needs. At the same time he will find ample stimulus for taking himself to task again and again and for continuing the analysis of his own problems. This, however, is his private affair, and I do not consider it right for the analyst to communicate his feelings to his patient. In my view such honesty is more in the nature of a confession and a burden to the patient. In any case it leads away from the analysis. The emotions roused in the analyst will be of value to his patient, if used as one more source of insight into the patient's unconscious conflicts and defences; and when these are interpreted and worked through, the ensuing changes in the patient's ego include the strengthening of his reality sense so that he sees his analyst as a human being, not a god or demon, and the "human" relationship in the analytic situation follows without the analyst's having recourse to extra-analytical means.

Psychoanalytic technique came into being when Freud, abandoning hypnosis, discovered resistance and repression. In my view the use of counter-transference as an instrument of research can be recognized in his descriptions of the way by which he arrived at his fundamental discoveries. When he tried to elucidate the hysterical patient's forgotten memories, he felt that a force from the patient opposed his attempts and that he had to overcome this resistance by his own psychic work. He concluded that it was the same force which was responsible for the repression of the crucial memories and for the formation of the hysterical symptom.

The unconscious process in hysterical amnesia can thus be defined by its twin facets, of which one is turned outward and felt by the analyst as resistance, whilst the other works intrapsychically as repression.

Whereas in the case of repression counter-transference is characterized by the sensation of a quantity of energy, an opposing force, other defence mechanisms will rouse other qualities in the analyst's response.

I believe that with more thorough investigation of counter-transference from the angle I have attempted here, we may come to work out more fully the way in which the character of the counter-transference corresponds to the nature of the patient's unconscious impulses and defences operative at the actual time.

Note

1. Paper read at the 16th International Psycho-Analytical Congress, Zürich, 1949. After presenting this paper at the Congress my attention was drawn to a paper by Leo Berman: "Counter-transferences and attitudes of the analyst in the therapeutic process", *Psychiatry*, XII(2), May, 1949. The fact that the problem of the counter-transference has been put forward for discussion practically simultaneously by different workers indicates that the time is ripe for a more thorough research into the nature and function of the counter-transference. I agree with

Berman's basic rejection of emotional coldness on the part of the analyst, but I differ in my conclusions concerning the use to be made of the analyst's feelings towards his patient.

Article citation

Heimann, P. (1950). On counter-transference. *International Journal of Psycho-Analysis, 31*: 81–84.

CHAPTER THREE

Counter-transference and the patient's response to it[1]

Margaret Little

I

I will begin with a story.

A patient whose mother had recently died was to give a wireless talk on a subject in which he knew his analyst was interested; he gave him the script to read beforehand, and the analyst had the opportunity of hearing the broadcast. The patient felt very unwilling to give it just then, in view of his mother's death, but could not alter the arrangement. The day after the broadcast he arrived for his analysis in a state of anxiety and confusion.

The analyst (who was a very experienced man) interpreted the patient's distress as being due to a fear lest he, the analyst, should be jealous of what had clearly been a success and be wanting to deprive him of it and of its results. The interpretation was accepted, the distress cleared up quite quickly, and the analysis went on.

Two years later (the analysis having ended in the meanwhile) the patient was at a party which he found he could not enjoy, and he realized that it was a week after the anniversary of his mother's death. Suddenly it came to him that what had troubled him at the time of his broadcast had been a very simple and obvious thing, sadness that his mother was not there to enjoy his success (or even to know about it), and guilt that he had enjoyed it while she was dead had spoilt it for him. Instead of being able to mourn for her (by cancelling the broadcast) he had had to behave as if he denied her death, almost in a manic way. He recognized that the interpretation given, which could be substantially correct, had in fact been the correct one at the time for the analyst, who had actually been jealous of him, and that it was the analyst's unconscious guilt that had led to the giving of an inappropriate interpretation. Its acceptance had come about through the patient's unconscious recognition of its correctness for his analyst and his identification with him. Now he could accept it as true for himself in a totally different way, on another level—i.e. that of his jealousy of his father's success with his mother, and guilt about himself having a success which represented success with his mother, of which his father would be jealous and want to deprive him. The analyst's behaviour in giving such an interpretation must be attributed to counter-transference.

II

Surprisingly little has been written on counter-transference apart from books and papers on technique chiefly meant for students in training. The writers of these all emphasize the same two points— the importance and potential danger of counter-transference and the need for thorough analysis of analysts. Much more has been written about transference, and a lot of that would apply equally well to counter-transference. I found myself wondering why, and also why different people use the term counter-transference to mean different things.

The term is used to mean any or all of the following:

(a) the analyst's unconscious attitude to the patient;
(b) repressed elements, hitherto unanalysed, in the analyst himself which attach to the patient in the same way as the patient "transfers" to the analyst affects, etc. belonging to his parents or to the objects of his childhood: i.e. the analyst regards the

patient (temporarily and varyingly) as he regarded his own parents;
(c) some specific attitude or mechanism with which the analyst meets the patient's transference;
(d) The whole of the analyst's attitudes and behaviour towards his patient. This includes all the others, and any conscious attitudes as well.

The question is why it is so undefined or undefinable. Is it that true isolation of counter-transference is impossible while the comprehensive idea of it is clumsy and unmanageable? I found four reasons.

1. I would say that unconscious counter-transference is something which cannot be observed directly as such, but only in its effects; we might compare the difficulty with that of the physicists who try to define or observe a force which is manifested as light waves, gravity, etc. but cannot be detected or observed directly.
2. I think part of the difficulty arises from the fact that (considering it metapsychologically) the analyst's total attitude involves his whole psyche, id and any superego remnants as well as ego (he is also concerned with all these in the patient), and there are no clear boundaries differentiating them.
3. Any analysis (even self-analysis) postulates both an analysand and an analyst; in a sense they are inseparable. And similarly transference and counter-transference are inseparable; something which is suggested in the fact that what is written about the one can so largely be applied to the other.
4. More important than any of these, I think there is an attitude towards counter-transference, i.e. towards one's own feelings and ideas, that is really paranoid or phobic, especially where the feelings are or may be subjective.

In one of his papers on technique Freud pointed out that the progress of psychoanalysis had been held up for more than ten years through fear of interpreting the transference, and the attitude of psychotherapists of other schools to this day is to regard it as highly dangerous and to avoid it. The attitude of most analysts towards counter-transference is precisely the same, that it is a known and recognized phenomenon but that it is unnecessary and even dangerous ever to interpret it. In any case, what is unconscious one cannot easily be aware of (if at all), and to try to observe and interpret something unconscious in oneself is rather like trying to see the back of one's own head—it is a lot easier to see the back of someone else's. The fact of the patient's transference lends itself readily to avoidance by projection and rationalization, both mechanisms being characteristic for paranoia, and the myth of the impersonal, almost inhuman analyst who shows no feelings is consistent with this attitude. I wonder whether failure to make use of counter-transference may not be having a precisely similar effect as far as the progress of psychoanalysis is concerned to that of ignoring or neglecting the transference; and if we can make the right use of counter-transference may we not find that we have yet another extremely valuable, if not indispensable, tool?

In writing this paper I found it very difficult to know which of the meanings of the term counter-transference I was using, and I found that I tended to slip from one to another, although at the start I meant to limit it to the repressed, infantile, subjective, irrational feelings, some pleasurable, some painful, which belong to the second of my attempted definitions. This is usually the counter-transference which is regarded as the source of difficulties and dangers.

But unconscious elements can be both normal and pathological, and not all repression is pathological any more than all conscious elements are "normal". The whole patient–analyst relationship includes both "normal" and pathological, conscious and unconscious, transference and counter-transference, in varying proportions; it will always include something which is specific to both the individual patient and the individual analyst. That is, every counter-transference is different from every other, as every transference is different, and it varies within itself from day to day, according to variations in both patient and analyst and the outside world.

Repressed counter-transference is a product of the unconscious part of the analyst's ego, that part which is nearest and most closely belonging to the id and least in contact with reality. It follows from this that the repetition compulsion is readily brought to bear on it; but other ego activities besides repression play a part in its development, of which the synthetic or integrative activity is most important. As I see it, counter-transference is one of those compromise formations in the making of which the ego shows such surprising skill; it is in this respect essentially of the same order as a neurotic symptom, a perversion, or a sublimation. In it libidinal gratification is partly forbidden and partly accepted; an element of aggression is woven in with both the gratification and the prohibition, and the distribution of the aggression determines the relative proportions of each. Since counter-transference, like transference, is concerned with another person, the mechanisms of projection and introjection are of special importance.

By the time we have paranoia linked with counter-transference we have a mammoth subject to discuss, and to talk about the patient's response may be just nonsense unless we can find some simple way of approach. Many of our difficulties, unfortunately, seem to me to come from trying to over-simplify, and from an almost compulsive attempt to separate out conscious from unconscious, and repressed unconscious from what is unconscious but not repressed, often with an ignoring of the dynamic aspects of the thing. So once again I would like to say here that although I am talking mainly about the repressed elements in counter-transference I am not limiting myself strictly to this, but am letting it flow over into the other elements in the total relationship; and at the risk of being disjointed my "simple approach" is chiefly a matter of talking about a few things and then trying to relate them to the main theme.

Speaking of the dynamic aspects brings us to the question: what is the driving force in any analysis? What is it that urges the patient on to get well? The answer surely is that it is the combined id urges of both patient and analyst, urges which in the case of the analyst have been modified and integrated as a result of his own analysis so that they have become more directed and effective. Successful combination of these urges seems to me to depend on a special kind of identification of the analyst with the patient.

III

Consciously, and surely to a great extent unconsciously too, we all want our patients to get well, and we can identify readily with them in their desire to get well, that is with their ego. But unconsciously we tend to identify also with the patient's superego and id, and thereby with him, in any prohibition on getting well, and in his wish to stay ill and dependent, and by so doing we may slow down his recovery. Unconsciously we may exploit a patient's illness for our own purposes, both libidinal and aggressive, and he will quickly respond to this.

A patient who has been in analysis for some considerable time has usually become his analyst's love object; he is the person to whom the analyst wishes to make reparation, and the reparative impulses, even when conscious, may through a partial repression come under the sway of the repetition compulsion, so that it becomes necessary to make that same patient well over and over again, which in effect means making him ill over and over again in order to have him to make well.

Rightly used, this repetitive process may be progressive, and the "making ill" then takes the necessary and effective form of opening up anxieties which can be interpreted and worked through. But this implies a degree of unconscious willingness on the part of the analyst to allow his patient to get well, to become independent and to leave him. In general we can agree that these are all acceptable to any analyst, but failures of timing of interpretation such as that which I have described, failure in understanding, or any interference with working-through, will play into the patient's own fear of getting well, with all that it involves in the way of losing his analyst, and they cannot be put right until the patient himself is ready to let the opportunity occur. The repetition compulsion in the patient is here the ally of the analyst, if the analyst is ready not to repeat his former mistake and so once more strengthen the patient's resistances.

This unconscious unwillingness on the analyst's part to let his patient leave him can sometimes take very subtle forms, in which the analysis itself can be used as a rationalization. The demand that a patient should not "act out" in situations outside the analysis may hinder the formation of those very extra-analytic relationships which belong with his recovery and are evidence of his growth and ego development. Transferences to people outside the analysis need not be an actual hindrance to the analytic work, if the analyst is willing to use them, but unconsciously he may behave exactly like the parents who, "for the child's own good", interfere with his development by not allowing him to love someone else. The patient of course needs them just as a child needs to form identifications with people outside his home and parents.

These things are so insidious that our perception of them comes slowly, and in our resistance to them we are allying with the patient's superego, through our own superego. At the same time, we are showing our own inability to tolerate a splitting either of something in the patient, or of the therapeutic process itself; we are demanding to be the only cause of the patient's getting well.

A patient whose analysis is "interminable" then may perhaps be the victim of his analyst's (primary) narcissism as much as of his own, and an apparent negative therapeutic reaction may be the outcome of a counter-resistance of the kind I have indicated in my story.

We all know that only a few of several possible interpretations are the important and dynamic ones at any given point in the analysis, but as in my story, the interpretation which is the appropriate one for the patient may be the very one which, for reasons of counter-transference and counter-resistance, is least available to the analyst at that moment, and if the interpretation given is the one that is appropriate for the analyst himself the patient may, through fear, submissiveness, etc., accept it in precisely the same way as he would accept the "correct" one, with immediate good effect. Only later does it come out that the effect obtained was not the one required, and that the patient's resistance has been thereby strengthened and the analysis prolonged.

IV

It has been said that it is fatal for an analyst to become identified with his patient, and that empathy (as distinct from sympathy) and detachment are essential to success in analysis. But the basis of empathy, as of sympathy, is identification, and it is the detachment which makes the difference between them. This detachment comes about partly at least by the use of the ego function of reality testing with the introduction of the factors of time and distance. The analyst necessarily identifies with the patient, but there is for him an interval of time between himself and the experience which for the patient has the quality of immediacy—he knows it for past experience, while to the patient it is a present one. That makes it at that moment the patient's experience, not his, and if the analyst is experiencing it as a present thing he is interfering with the patient's growth and development. When an experience is the patient's own and not the analyst's an interval of distance is introduced automatically as well, and it is on the preservation of these intervals of time and distance that successful use of the counter-transference may depend. The analyst's identification with the patient needs of course to be an introjective, not a projective, one.

When such an interval of time is introduced the patient can feel his experience in its immediacy, free from interference, and let it become past for him too, so that a fresh identification can be made with his analyst. When the interval of distance is introduced the experience becomes the patient's alone, and he can separate himself off psychically from the analyst. Growth depends on an alternating rhythm of identification and separation brought about in this way by having experiences and knowing them for one's own, in a suitable setting.

To come back to the story with which I began, what happened was that the analyst felt the patient's unconscious repressed jealousy as his own immediate experience, instead of as a past, remembered, one. The patient was immediately concerned with his mother's death, feeling the necessity to broadcast just then as an interference with his process of mourning, and the pleasure proper to it was transformed into a manic one, as if he denied his mother's death. Only later, after the interpretation, when his mourning had been transferred to the analyst and so become past, could he experience the jealousy situation as an immediate one, and then recognize (as something past and remembered) his analyst's counter-transference reaction. His immediate reaction to the analyst's jealousy was a phobic one—displacement by (introjective) identification, and re-repression.

Failures in timing such as this, or failures to recognize transference references, are failures of the ego function of recognizing time and distance. Unconscious mind is timeless and irrational, "What's yours is mine, what's mine's my own"; "What's yours is half mine, and half the other half's mine, so it's all mine" are infantile ways of thinking which are used in relation to feelings and experiences as much as to things, and counter-transference becomes a hindrance to the patient's growth when the analyst uses them. The analyst becomes the blind man leading the blind, for neither has the use of the necessary two dimensions to know where he is at any given moment. But when the analyst can keep these intervals in his identification with his patient it becomes possible for the patient to take the step forward of eliminating them again and to go on to the next experience, when the process of establishing the interval has to be repeated.

This is one of the major difficulties of the student in training or the analyst who is undergoing further analysis—he is having to deal with things in his patients' analysis which have still the quality of present-ness, or immediacy, for him himself, instead of that past-ness which is so important. In these circumstances it may be impossible for him always to keep this time interval, and he has then to defer as full an analysis as the patient might otherwise achieve until he has carried his own analysis further, and wait until a repetition of the material comes.

V

The recent discussions here of Dr Rosen's work brought the subject of counter-transference to the surface with a fresh challenge to us to know and understand much more clearly what we are doing. We heard how in the space of a few days or weeks patients who for years had been completely inaccessible had shown remarkable changes which, from some points of view at least, must be regarded as improvement. But, what was not originally meant to be in the bargain, they seem to have remained permanently dependent on and attached to the therapist concerned. The description of the way in which the patients were treated, and of the results, stirred and disturbed most of us profoundly, and apparently aroused a good deal of guilt among us, for several members in their contributions to the discussion beat their breasts and cried *mea culpa*.

I have tried to understand where so much guilt came from, and it seemed to me that a possible explanation of it might lie in the unconscious unwillingness to let patients go. Many seriously ill patients, especially psychotic cases, are not able, either for internal (psychological) reasons, or for external (e.g. financial) ones, to go through with a full analysis and bring it to what we regard as a satisfactory conclusion, that is with sufficient ego development for them to be able to live successfully in real independence of the analyst. In such cases a superficial relationship of dependence is continued (and rightly continued) indefinitely, by means of occasional "maintenance" sessions, the contact being preserved deliberately by the analyst. Such patients we can keep in this way without guilt, and the high proportion of successes in the treatment of these patients, it seems to me, may well depend on that very freedom from guilt.

But over and above this there is perhaps a tendency to identify particularly with the patient's id in psychotic cases generally; in fact it would sometimes be difficult to find the ego to identify with! This will be a narcissistic identification on the level of the primary love–hate, which nevertheless lends itself readily to a transformation into object-love. The powerful stimulus of the extensively disintegrated personality touches on the most deeply repressed and carefully defended danger spots in the analyst and, correspondingly, the most primitive (and incidentally least effective) of his defence mechanisms are called into play. But at the same time a small fragment of the patient's shattered ego may identify with the ego of the therapist (where the therapist's understanding of the patient's fears filters through to him, and he can introject the therapist's ego as a good object); he is then enabled to make a contact with reality via the therapist's contact with it. Such contact is tenuous and easily broken at first, but is capable of being strengthened and extended by a process of increasing introjection of the external world and re-projection of it, with a gradually increasing investment of it with libido derived originally from the therapist.

This contact may never become sufficient for the patient to be able to maintain it entirely alone, and in such a case continued contact with the therapist is essential, and will need to vary in frequency according to the patient's changing condition and situation. I would compare the patient's position to that of a drowning man who has been brought to a boat, and while still in the water his hand is placed on the gunwale and held there by his rescuer until he can establish his own hold.

It follows from this perhaps, a truth already recognized, that the more disintegrated the patient the greater is the need for the analyst to be well integrated.

It may be that in those psychotic patients who do not respond to the usual analytic situation in the ordinary way, by developing a transference which can be interpreted and resolved, the counter-transference has to do the whole of the work, and in order to find something in the patient with which to make contact the therapist has to allow his ideas and the libidinal gratifications derived from his work to regress to a quite extraordinary degree. (We may wonder, for instance, about the pleasure an analyst derives from his patients sleeping during their analytic sessions with him!) It has been said that greater therapeutic results are found when a patient is so disturbed that the therapist experiences intense feelings and profound disturbance, and the underlying mechanism for this may be identification with the patient's id.

But these outstanding results are found in the work of two classes of analyst. One consists of beginners who are not afraid to allow their unconscious impulses a considerable degree of freedom because, through lack of experience, like children, they do not know or understand the dangers, and do not recognize them. It works out well in quite a high proportion of cases, because the positive feelings preponderate. Where it does not the results are mostly not seen or not disclosed—they may even be repressed. We all have our private graveyards, and not every grave has a headstone.

The other class consists of those experienced analysts who have gone through a stage of over-cautiousness, and have reached the point at which they can trust not only directly to their unconscious impulses as such (because of the modifications resulting from their own analyses) but also to being able at any given moment to bring the counter-transference as it stands then into consciousness enough to see at least whether they are advancing or retarding the patient's recovery—in other words to overcome counter-transference resistance.

At times the patient himself will help this, for transference and counter-transference are not only syntheses by the patient and analyst acting separately, but, like the analytic work as a whole, are the result of a joint effort. We often hear of the mirror which the analyst holds up to the patient, but the patient holds one up to the analyst too, and there is a whole series of reflections in each, repetitive in kind, and subject to continual modification. The mirror in each case should become progressively clearer as the analysis goes on, for patient and analyst respond to each other in a reverberative kind of way, and increasing clearness in one mirror will bring the need for a corresponding clearing in the other.

The patient's ambivalence leads him both to try to break down the analyst's counter-resistances (which can be a frightening thing to do) and also to identify with him in them and so to use them as his own. The question of giving him a "correct" interpretation is then of considerable importance from this point of view.

VI

When such a thing happens as I have quoted in this story, to neutralize the obstructive effect of a mistimed or wrongly emphasized interpretation giving the "correct" interpretation when the occasion arises may not be enough. Not only should the mistake be admitted (and the patient is entitled not only to express his own anger but also to some expression of regret from the analyst for its occurrence, quite as much as for the occurrence of a mistake in the amount of his account or the time of his appointment), but its origin in unconscious counter-transference may be explained, unless there is some definite contraindication for so doing, in which case it should be postponed until a suitable time comes, as it surely will. Such explanation may be essential for the further progress of the analysis, and it will have only beneficial results, increasing the patient's confidence in the honesty and good-will of the analyst, showing him to be human enough to make mistakes, and making clear the universality of the phenomenon of transference and the way in which it can arise in any relation-ship. Only harm can come from the withholding of such an interpretation.

Let me make it clear that I do not mean that I think counter-transference interpretations should be unloaded injudiciously or without consideration on the heads of hapless patients, any more than transference interpretations are given without thought today. I mean that they should neither be positively avoided nor perhaps restricted to feelings which are justified or objective, such as those to which Dr Winnicott refers in his paper on "Hate in the counter-transference" (*International Journal of Psycho-Analysis, 30, 1949*). (And of course they cannot be given unless something of the counter-transference has become conscious.) The subjectivity of the feelings needs to be shown to the patient, though their actual origin need not be gone into (there should not be "confessions"); it should be enough to point out one's own need to analyse them; but above all the important thing is that they should be recognized by both analyst and patient.

In my view a time comes in the course of every analysis when it is essential for the patient to recognize the existence not only of the analyst's objective or justified feelings, but also of the analyst's subjective feelings; that is, that the analyst must and does develop an unconscious counter-transference which he is nevertheless able to deal with in such a way that it does not interfere to any serious extent with the patient's interests, specially the progress of cure. The point at which such recognition comes will of course vary in individual analyses, but it belongs rather to the later stages of analysis than to the earlier ones. Occasionally, mistakes in technique or mistakes such as errors in accounts, etc., make it necessary to refer to unconscious mental processes in the analyst (i.e. to counter-transference) at an earlier time than one would choose, but the reference can be a slight one, sufficient only for the purpose of relieving the immediate anxiety. Too much stress on it at an early time would increase anxiety to what might be a really dangerous degree.

So much emphasis is laid on the unconscious phantasies of patients about their analysts that it is often ignored that they really come to know a great deal of truth about them—both actual and psychic. Such knowledge could not be prevented in any case, even if it were desirable, but patients do not know they have it, and part of the analyst's task is to bring it into consciousness, which may be the very thing to which he has himself the greatest resistance. Analysts often behave unconsciously exactly like the parents who put up a smoke-screen, and tantalize their children, tempting them to see the very things they forbid their seeing; and not to refer to counter-transference is tantamount to denying its existence, or forbidding the patient to know or speak about it.

The ever-quoted remedy for counter-transference difficulties—deeper and more thorough analysis of the analyst—can at best only be an incomplete one, for some tendency to develop unconscious infantile counter-transferences is bound to remain. Analysis cannot reach the whole of the unconscious id, and we have only to remember that even the most thoroughly analysed person still dreams to be reminded of this. Freud's saying "Where id was ego shall be" is an ideal, and like most other ideals is not fully realizable. All that we can really aim at is reaching the point at which the analyst's attitude to his own id impulses is no longer a paranoid one and so is safe from his patients' point of view, and to remember besides that this will still vary in him from day to day, according to the stresses and strains to which he is exposed.

To my mind it is this question of a paranoid or phobic attitude towards the analyst's own feelings which constitutes the greatest danger and difficulty in counter-transference. The very real fear of being flooded with feeling of any kind, rage, anxiety, love, etc., in relation to one's patient and of being passive to it and at its mercy, leads to an unconscious avoidance or denial. Honest recognition of such feeling is essential to the analytic process, and the analysand is naturally sensitive to any insincerity in his analyst, and will inevitably respond to it with hostility. He will identify with the analyst in it (by introjection) as a means of denying his own feelings, and will exploit it generally in every way possible, to the detriment of his analysis.

I have shown above that unconscious (and uninterpreted) counter-transference may be responsible for the prolonging of analysis. It can equally well be responsible for the premature ending, and I feel that it is again in the final stages that most care is needed to avoid these things. Analysts writing about the final stages of analysis and its termination speak over and over again of the way in which patients reach a certain point, and then either slip away and break off the analysis just at the moment when to continue is vital for its ultimate success, or else slip again into another of their interminable repetitions, instead of analysing the anxiety situations. Counter-transference may perhaps be the deciding factor at this point, and the analyst's willingness to deal with it may be the all-important thing.

I should perhaps add that I am sure that valuable unconscious counter-transferences may also very often be responsible for the carrying through to a successful conclusion of analyses which have appeared earlier to be moving towards inevitable failure, and also for quite a lot of the post-analytic work carried on by patients when analyses have been terminated prematurely.

In the later stages of analysis then, when the patient's capacity for objectivity is already increased, the analyst needs especially to be on the look-out for counter-transference manifestations, and for opportunities to interpret it, whether directly or indirectly, as and when the patient reveals it to him. Without it patients may fail to recognize objectively much of the irrational parental behaviour which has been so powerful a factor in the development of the neurosis, for wherever the analyst does behave like the parents, and conceals the fact, there is the point at which continued repression of what might otherwise be recognized is inevitable. It brings great relief to a patient to find that irrational behaviour on the part of his parents was not intended for him personally, but was already transferred to him from their parents, and to find his analyst doing the same kind of thing in minor ways can give conviction to his understanding and make the whole process more tolerable to him than anything else can do. There will of course be phantasies in every analysis about the analyst's feelings towards his patient—we know that from the start—and they have to be interpreted like any other phantasies, but beyond these a patient may quite well become aware of real feelings in his analyst even before the analyst himself is fully aware of them. There may be a great struggle against accepting the idea that the analyst can have unconscious counter-transference feelings, but when once the patient's ego has accepted it certain ideas and memories which have been inaccessible till then may be brought into consciousness, things which would otherwise have stayed repressed.

I have spoken of the patient revealing the counter-transference to the analyst, and I mean this quite literally, though it may sound like the dangerous blood-sport of "analysing the analyst". The "analytic rule" as it is usually worded nowadays is more helpful to us than in its original form. We no longer "require" our patients to tell us everything that is in their minds. On the contrary, we give them permission to do so, and what comes may on occasion be a piece of real counter-transference interpretation for the analyst. Should he not be willing to accept it, re-repression with strengthened resistance follows, and consequently interruption or prolonging of the analysis. Together with the different formulation of the analytic rule goes a different way of giving interpretations or comments; in the old days analysts, like parents, said what they liked when they liked, as by right, and patients had to take it. Now, in return for the permission to speak or withhold freely, we ask our patients to allow us to say some things, and allow them too to refuse to accept them. This makes for a greater freedom all round to choose the time for giving interpretations and the form in which they are given, by a lessening of the didactic or authoritarian attitude.

Incidentally, a good many of the transference interpretations which are ordinarily given are capable of extension to demonstrate the possibility of counter-transference, for instance: "You feel that I am angry, as your mother was when . . ." can include "I'm not angry as far as I know, but I'll have to find out about it and, if I am, to know why, for there's no real reason for me to be". Such things of course are often said, but they are not always thought of as counter-transference interpretations. In my view that is what they are, and their use might well be developed consciously as a means of freeing counter-transferences and making them more directly available for use.

In her paper read at the Zürich Congress (*International Journal of Psycho-Analysis*, *31*, 1950) Dr Heimann has referred to the appearance of some counter-transference feelings as a kind of signal comparable to the development of anxiety as a warning of the approach of a traumatic situation. If I have understood her correctly the disturbance which she describes is surely in fact anxiety, but a secondary anxiety which is justified and objective and brings a greater alertness and awareness of what is happening. She specifically states that in her opinion counter-transference interpretations are best avoided. But anxiety serves first of all another purpose; it is primarily a method of dealing with an actual trauma, however ineffective it may be in this capacity. It can happen that this secondary anxiety with its awareness and watchfulness can mask very effectively anxiety of a more primitive kind. Below the level of consciousness analyst and patient can be sensitive to each other's paranoid fears and persecutory feelings, and become so to speak synchronized (or "in phase") in them, so that the analysis itself can be used by both as defence and the analyst may swing over from an introjective identification with the patient to a projective one, with a loss of those intervals of time and distance of which I spoke earlier, while the patient may defend himself by an introjective identification with the analyst, instead of being able to project on to him the persecuting objects.

Resolution of this situation can come about through conscious recognition of the counter-transference either by the analyst or by the patient. Failure to recognize it may lead to either premature interruption of the analysis, or to prolonging it; in each case there will be re-repression of what might otherwise have become conscious, and strengthening of the resistances. Premature interruption is not necessarily fatal to the ultimate success of the analysis, any more than its prolongation is, for the presence of sufficient understanding, and some valuable counter-transference may make further progress possible even after termination, by virtue of other introjections already made.

The ideal analyst of course exists only in imagination (whether the patient's or the analyst's), and can only be made actual and living in rare moments. But if the analyst can trust to his own modified id impulses, his own repressions of a valuable kind, and to something positive in his patient as well (presumably something which helped to decide him to undertake the analysis in the first place) then he can provide enough of that thing which was missing from the patient's early environment and so badly needed—a person who can allow the patient to grow without either interference or over-stimulation. Then a benign circle forms in the analytic situation which the patient can use to develop his own basic rhythmic patterns, and on those patterns to build up the more complex rhythms which are needed to deal with the world of external reality and his own continuously growing inner world.

VII

I have tried to show how patients respond to the unconscious counter-transferences of their analysts, and in particular the importance of any paranoid attitude in the analyst to the counter-transference itself. Counter-transference is a defence mechanism of a synthetic kind, brought about by the analyst's unconscious ego, and is easily brought under the control of the repetition compulsion; but transference and counter-transference are still further syntheses in that they are products of the combined unconscious work of patient and analyst. They depend on conditions which are partly internal and partly external to the analytic relationship, and vary from week to week, day to day, and even moment to moment with the rapid intra- and extra-psychic changes. Both are essential to psychoanalysis, and counter-transference is no more to be feared or avoided than is transference; in fact it cannot be avoided, it can only be looked out for, controlled to some extent, and perhaps used.

But only in so far as analysis is a true sublimation for the analyst and not a perversion or addiction (as I think it sometimes may be) can we avoid counter-transference neurosis. Patches of transitory counter-transference neurosis may appear from time to time even in the most skilled, experienced and well-analysed analysts, and they can be used positively to help patients towards recovery by means of their own transferences. According to the analyst's attitude to counter-transference (which is ultimately his attitude to his own id impulses and his own feelings) paranoid anxiety, denial, condemnation, or acceptance, and the degree of his willingness to allow it to become conscious to his patient as well as to himself, the patient will be encouraged to respond either by exploiting it repetitively, or to use it progressively to good purpose.

Interpretation of counter-transference along the lines which I have tried to indicate would make much heavier demands on analysts than before; but so did interpretation of transference at the time when it began to be used. Nowadays that is something which is taken for granted, and it has been found to have its compensations in that the analyst's libidinal impulses and creative and reparative wishes find effective gratification in the greater power and success of his work. I believe that similar results might follow a greater use of counter-transference if we can find ways of using it, though I must stress the tentativeness with which I am putting forward any of these ideas.

Note

1. Paper read at a meeting of the British Psycho-Analytical Society on 7 June, 1950.

Article citation

Little, M. (1951). Counter-transference and the patient's response to it. *International Journal of Psycho-Analysis, 32*: 32–40.

CHAPTER FOUR

A contribution to the problem of counter-transference[1]

Heinrich Racker

I

The significance given to counter-transference and the importance attached to the corresponding problems depends on the significance given to the role of the analyst in the cure. This role is considered as a twofold one. First, he is the interpreter of the unconscious processes, and secondly, he is the object of these same processes. An immediate consequence of this is the twofold role of the counter-transference: it may intervene and interfere, firstly, inasmuch as the analyst is an interpreter, and secondly, inasmuch as he is the object of the impulses. As regards the former the counter-transference may help, distort, or hinder the perception of the unconscious processes. Or again, the perception may be correct but the percept may provoke neurotic reactions which impair his interpretive capacity. As regards the latter—the analyst as object—the counter-transference affects his manner and his behaviour which in turn influence the image the analysand forms of him. Through the analyst's interpretations, the form he gives them, his voice, through every attitude he adopts towards the patient, the latter perceives (consciously or unconsciously) the psychological state he happens to be in—not to speak of the debatable question of telepathic perception. Thus the counter-transference, by affecting the analyst's understanding and behaviour, influences the patient and especially his transference, that is to say, the process on which the transformation of his personality and object-relations so largely depend.

Just as the whole of the patient's personality, the healthy part and the neurotic part, his present and past, reality and phantasy, are brought into play in his relation with the analyst, so it is with the analyst, although with qualitative and quantitative differences, in his relation with the patient. These two relations differ, above all, through the different external and internal situations of patient and analyst in analytical treatment and through the fact of the latter's having already been analysed.

Nevertheless the previous statement still holds. For neither is the analyst free of neurosis. Part of his libido remains fixated in phantasy—to the introjected objects—and so apt to be transferred. Part of his psychic conflicts remain unsolved and strive after a solution by means of relations with external objects. His profession, too, and his resulting social and financial situation are subject to the transference of central inner situations. Finally the direct relation with the patient lends itself to transference, for the psychoanalyst's choice of profession, like all such choices, is itself based upon the object-relations of infancy. Just as the whole of the patient's images, feelings, and impulses towards the analyst, insofar as they are determined by the past, is called transference and its pathological expression is denominated transference neurosis, in the same way the whole of the analyst's images, feelings and impulses towards the patient, insofar as they are determined by the past, is called counter-transference and its pathological expression may be denominated counter-transference neurosis.

The transference is always present and always reveals its presence. Likewise counter-transference is always present and always reveals its presence, although, as in the case of transference, its manifestations are sometimes hard to perceive and interpret.

What interests us most is the neurotic part of counter-transference that perturbs the analyst's work. Every analyst knows quite well that he himself is not wholly free of infantile dependence, of neurotic representations of object and subject and of pathological defence-mechanisms. But certain facts—named hereunder—call to mind the two different ways of "knowing" of which Freud speaks when he refers to the significance of the resistances. For the analyst's knowledge of neurotic counter-transference is, as a rule, at first only a theoretical knowledge. Here also resistances must be overcome for him to become really "conscious of his unconscious" and here also elaboration must follow. Besides, it seems that this evolutionary process is governed by the same fundamental Haeckelian law that governs biogenetic processes: just as the counter-transference processes represent relatively late discoveries in the history—the phylogenesis—of the science of psychoanalysis, so it is—although with individual differences—in the history of each member and perhaps also in that of each group of the analytic movement.

I shall now cite some of the facts that point to the existence of this resistance.

Above all, little is written or spoken about this subject.[2] The fact that the number of officially published works is very small and that in these the subject is not dealt with very amply or very thoroughly might be accounted for on the grounds that the subject is unsuitable for publication. But even in "esoteric" analytical literature there are very few writings under this heading.[3] In case histories counter-transference is seldom mentioned, still less treated with any profundity. To my mind these facts are due, in part at least, to a resistance. It would seem that among analytic subjects counter-transference is treated somewhat like a child of whom the parents are ashamed. But this "shame", or, I should say, the danger that threatens the analyst's self-esteem and others' esteem for him in owning that he, an analysed person analysing others, continues to be neurotic, is no more than a superficial expression of the causes of his resistance to becoming aware of the counter-transference. Beneath this there lie all the fears and defences inherent in his neurosis, and his professional situation only clothes the old impulses, images and anxieties in a new language.[4]

Observation of my own counter-transference and afterwards of that of candidates (under analysis or control) and the awareness of its great importance in therapy have led me to report some of these experiences. My main intention in the present paper is to suggest a point of view from which counter-transference may be advanta-geously regarded. The pathological part of counter-transference is

an expression of neurosis like any other and should be investigated
with all the means of which psychoanalysis disposes.

II

In the same way as the original neurosis and the transference
neurosis, the "counter-transference neurosis" is also centred in the
Oedipus complex.[5] At this level every male patient fundamentally
represents the father and every female patient the mother. In a
similar fashion to the transference neurosis, the real factors such as
the age of the object (in this case, of the patient), his bodily
appearance, his general psychological state, his moods, etc., evoke
one aspect or another of what is already performed in the analyst as
his inner oedipic situation.

Here I shall consider counter-transference separately for the two
sexes.

Towards the female patient the analyst has a latent predisposition to experience all the feelings and impulses that he directed on
to his mother during the oedipic phase. In accordance with the
originally positive nature of this relation, he is predisposed to
positive feelings and genital impulses, even before meeting the
patient. Owing to the prohibition of active-phallic impulses both in
the past oedipic situation and in the present analytical situation in
which genital behaviour is forbidden to the analyst in an analogous
way, these feelings and impulses easily acquire a passive-phallic
character. The unconscious desire may now be (at this level) that the
patient should fall in love with the analyst's penis. In this desire
there may lie, in part, the origin of his wish that she should make a
good positive transference.

This counter-transference situation has most important consequences. Whenever there exists a desire for the patient to fall in love
(or for positive transference) and this desire is seriously frustrated,
rejection and hatred of the patient arise. The desire to bind the
mother erotically may also find expression in the desire that the
patient should not establish any new extratransferential erotic
relations. This danger is increased by circumstance that the rule of
abstinence (with regard to acting out) lends itself to the rationalization of this desire. On the other hand, he may find himself inhibited

from advising obedience to the rule of abstinence (or—as is customary nowadays—from interpreting in this sense), as a reaction-formation against the guilty desire to bind the patient and against using this rule in the service of this desire.

The desire to bind the patient also corresponds to the desire of parents not to "let go of" their children. As the liberation of the patient from the infantile dependence and its transferential equivalent is the core of analytical treatment, we must admit that this desire on the analyst's part acts as a tendency not to cure the patient. Thus together with the desire to cure (which likewise has deep roots in the unconscious) we find tendencies in the analyst in the opposite direction.[6] We shall meet later on with other examples, such as sexual envy, etc.

In the erotic transference the patient sooner or later feels the analyst as a rejecting object (father) and frequently tends to an acting out. This may consist in a flirtation, with greater or less direct realization, aimed at flight into freedom (to free herself from the transferential bond) and revenge on the rejecting object. This revenge may be lived by the analyst in his unconscious as hatred and unfaithfulness towards him and in turn provoke irritation and hatred in him. In this case the analyst may, through the patient's words, relive the primal scene, in a direct or symbolical form, as what it had meant to him as a child, i.e. as a grave aggression against him from the parents—here, especially the mother. Something analogous may occur in regard to the sexual act between the patient and her husband.[7] A patient who had started with a good positive transference—and the young analyst with a good counter-transference—completely eliminated him at a certain moment from the associations she communicated. This rejection on the patient's part, together with an intensification of her sexual life with her husband, was experienced by the analyst in connection with his own oedipic situation so that he was once again the child whose parents have sexual relations, satisfying themselves and excluding and rejecting him. The analyst felt disappointed and reacted inwardly with irritation against the patient—the bad mother—and with feelings of inferiority and envy towards her sexual partner, the husband. The patient's hatred of the image she had projected upon the analyst expressed itself in an intense resistance against complying with the fundamental rules of treatment. Thus to the analyst's oedipic frustration there was added a further frustration in his profession, which also has its oedipic significance.

In cases where the patient's transference was superficially very positive, where the analyst represented the intensely desired father, the patient's husband represented, at this level, the prohibiting mother. But, for the analyst's unconscious, the husband was his father, whom the mother deceives with him. This situation was on the one hand satisfactory; on the other hand, sometimes there appeared expressions of castration—anxiety and guilt feelings towards the father (the husband). But with the analyst's "victory" the husband became the rejected son, that is to say, at bottom, the analyst himself. This identification with the husband then enabled the analyst to desire even unconsciously that the patient should have good sexual relations with her husband. But he could not admit any other man who would once again represent the father who robs him sexually of his mother.

Another aspect of the oedipic trauma was relived by a young analyst in the case of a girl who, after several months of analysis, confessed that she had not been frank with him, but had withheld the fact that she was no longer a virgin and even prior to treatment had started sexual relations and had continued them for a time while under analysis. The declaration came to the analyst as a violent repetition of an old trauma; it resembled the experience of "sexual enlightenment", as if he were thinking once again, "My parents have always been doing 'that', i.e. coitus, but have hidden it from me and forbidden me it; they have deceived me". The counter-transference with this patient had been very positive—too much so; she had been the "pure" mother, but now she had become a "whore".

Besides this sexual, affective, and narcissistic frustration, the analyst also underwent a professional frustration; the patient's lack of sincerity doubtless delayed the wished for therapeutic success. The profession, it is known, also has an oedipic significance which is added to the direct oedipic counter-transference to the person under treatment.

The analyst had known that there were conscious resistances in the patient; but, apart from the girl's skill in hiding the facts, there were neurotic obstacles in himself that hindered his surmising what she was later to confess. These obstacles were, firstly, his desire for a strong positive transference on the girl's part which made him overrate it, and, secondly, his desire for a "pure" mother, both of which desires spring from the Oedipus complex.

To sum up: in counter-transference various aspects of the oedipic situation are repeated. Sometimes the analyst loves the patient genitally and desires her genital love towards him; he hates her if she then loves another man, feels rivalry of this man and jealousy and envy (heterosexual and homosexual) of their sexual pleasure. Sometimes he hates her if she hates him, and loves her if she suffers, for in this case he is revenged for the oedipic deceit. He feels satisfaction when the transference is very positive, but also castration-anxiety and guilt-feelings towards the husband, etc.

The dangers entailed in these reactions are plain. I have already mentioned the analyst's tendency to bind the patient to him and the consequent difficulties for the interpretation of the acting out. To this must be added, for instance, the fear of those persons for whom the patient is an important (erotic) object inasmuch as she tends to abandon them; fear of oedipic aggression projected on the husband may arise in the analyst if the patient turns towards another object; or fear of oedipic aggression projected on the parents, should a virgin girl begin to have sexual relations when under analysis (fear of making a prostitute of her; oedipic degradation of sexuality), etc.

Although the neurotic reactions of counter-transference may be sporadic, the predisposition to them is continuous.[8] They come about when certain circumstances in the patient's life and personality encounter certain internal and external circumstances in the analyst. The question now arises whether or no these situations are of a general character. If it is admitted that neurosis and analysis are interminable, so is the Oedipus complex. Under one aspect or another it will express itself, then, in every counter-transference. What varies is the form of its elaboration, the consciousness of it, and its degree of intensity. These not only vary from person to person but in each one they vary from hour to hour and are different at different periods of life. But even in the best of cases there are external and internal forces to make one "go back to one's first love", first hatred and fear. So I think that in spite of the individual features peculiar to the individual oedipic constellations I have reported, the above exposition rests on a general basis and hence possesses a certain general validity.

Towards the male patient, also, we find, under certain circumstances, a position corresponding to the positive Oedipus complex, i.e. rivalry and hatred. This occurs with special intensity where the patient has lived (or is living) certain tendencies of the Oedipus complex that the analyst himself has particularly wished to satisfy but had suppressed, as, for instance, the desire to steal another's wife. In consequence there may arise in the analyst not only envy and hatred of the patient, which perturb his internal analytical position, but also malicious satisfaction in finding inhibitions and fears in other aspects of the patient's life. The possible consequences and dangers of such a counter-transference situation are clear. In order not to lengthen this section unduly, I refrain from furnishing more examples or entering into any further detail. I only wish to add that I have the impression that the positive Oedipus complex appears, as a rule, more often when dealing with a woman than with a man, and, *vice versa*, the negative Oedipus complex more often with a man than with a woman. This may possibly be owing to the fact that the analyst usually has from the start a pre-eminently libidinous position towards patients of either sex.

III

Corresponding to the above-mentioned castration-anxiety, oedipic guilt-feelings, and heterosexual disappointment in the positive oedipic experience, we have the position belonging to the negative Oedipus complex. The counter-transference situation that most frequently manifests itself at this level is, perhaps, the desire to be loved by the male patient. We are dealing here, no less than in the case of the female patient, with a very complex desire which will later concern us still further. At the level we are now considering, this desire aims at being possessed by the father anally. As this desire is violently rejected it is often converted into the desire to possess the father actively. The father's anus may be replaced by his mouth, and both the anal act and the fellatio imply at the same time that the man (father, brother), submits to the subject through his libidinous desire for his penis and can be dominated because of this dependence.

Towards the male patient, then, there is, virtually or really, the desire to be loved by him, the desire for him to submit, and, more deeply, all tendencies of a homosexual nature, both passive and active. This finds expression, for instance, in the analyst's love for the patient when the latter works well in his analysis, overcomes resistances, obeys "my fundamental rule" (as a candidate said), and submits in this way to the analyst. If he does not do so, the analyst's homosexual desires are thwarted; behind the patient's resistance he may sense hatred, which, added to the frustration suffered, sometimes arouses hatred in the analyst also.

The patient's anal or oral submission and his homosexual love mean to the analyst that the father belongs to him and not to the mother. In this way the analyst is also protected against his latent envy and hatred of his father for his sexual satisfaction with the mother, protected against his envy and hatred of the woman for her sexual satisfaction with the man, and against his anger with either of them for giving what he wants to someone else and not to him.

As an example I will present the experience of a candidate in dealing with a male patient with intense reaction formations against anal and oral dependence and a very marked tendency to take revenge for the frustrations suffered at the positive oedipic level. Indeed, one of the unconscious reasons that led this patient to analysis was the desire to be better able to take revenge on his mother and father. Now this desire existed repressed in the analyst too. Thus the patient carried out perversely what the analyst rejected neurotically. (It is clear that a repressed tendency should disharmonize with the corresponding perversion carried out by somebody else. The perception of the perversion renews the neurotic conflict and provokes hatred as a defence.) The analyst thus perceived the patient's marked aggressiveness towards men in general and himself in particular, which meant the frustration of his homosexual desires towards the patient. The frustration opened his eyes to the nature of the unpleasant feelings (hatred and its consequences, envy, etc.) against which the patient's homosexual love should protect him—apart from the satisfaction entailed in attaining it.

The negative Oedipus complex once again finds expression when the patient's wife, as a rival of the analyst, seeks to perturb the positive relationship between him and her husband. In this case the image of the wife may become fused with that of the mother-rival in the analyst's negative Oedipus complex.

When the patient is female, the image the analyst forms of her may also be fused with that of the hated mother in the negative Oedipus complex. For the moment I only mention the example of the patient's undermining a positive internal relationship between her husband and the analyst, who, in his unconscious, has already established (albeit from afar) a homosexual relationship with the former. It is evident that all these counter-transference situations corresponding to the negative oedipic level, once they attain a certain intensity and remain unconscious and out of control, will occasion serious difficulties to the analyst in his understanding and interpretation of the case and in his behaviour towards the patient.

IV

To continue, allow me first to recall some well-known facts. The infantile oedipic experience (which we have been dealing with up to now) leads to the setting-up of the superego, the formation of which has already been prepared at previous levels of experience. Herewith an internal situation is brought about which can be synthesized in these words. The libido is, in part, attached to the introjected objects in the superego (the father, more deeply: the mother, etc.). The guilt-feelings exacerbate the need to be loved by these objects. Acceptance of the ego by the superego or by the reprojected parents must avert the catastrophe, i.e. especially castration and object loss.

In the counter-transference situation these introjected objects may be transferred onto the patient in either of two forms: firstly, on the patient as an individual, and secondly, on the patient as an important factor within other object-relationships of the analyst. As for the first form—the direct one—most of the counter-transference situations described hitherto belong here; the patients themselves represented the father or the mother. The second form refers to transference of the introjected objects either upon society as a whole, by which, for instance, he wishes "to be accepted" through his professional and scientific activity, or upon a social group such as the analytic group, or upon some individual (an analyst, a member of the family, a friend, etc.). In all these cases (of the second form) also, the introjected objects are at the same time transferred onto the patient, but in an indirect way; one might here speak of a sub-transference, to differentiate it from direct transference, in which the analyst wishes to be loved, etc., by the patient himself.[9] As a rule both forms of counter-transference, the direct and the indirect, will manifest themselves in a greater or lesser degree.

To arrive at a deeper understanding of these aspects of the "neurosis of counter-transference", I will set forth some concrete situations.

I shall refer in the first place to situations in which the candidate or analyst lived the position of sub-transference as regards his patients, while making a direct transference of the superego on some other real object as, for instance, an analyst of "higher rank", a "father analyst". I shall first set forth some cases in which there was danger of the treatment failing. In some of these patients there was also a possibility of their committing suicide. When faced with such dangers the analyst will experience a greater or lesser degree of anxiety. What are these dangers, considered analytically? In some cases the idea occurred to the analyst that if the treatment should fail, he would be violently criticized and persecuted by his accusers. These were represented either by another analyst (for example, a friend of the patient's), or by one of the patient's relations, or by the didactic analyst, the control-analyst, or the Executive Committee of the Institute of Psycho-analysis. The superego, as I have said, was projected upon these real objects. The danger threatening the analyst was, in the first place, castration, as to practise the profession means, on the oedipic level, to castrate the father and conquer the mother. Castration-anxiety then led to regressive processes and old defence-mechanisms, entailing a revival of what has been called the basic depressive conflict of neuroses and psychoses.[10] In defence against this situation, that is to say, where the ego is defending itself against persecution by a very severe superego, there arise paranoiac, manic and other mechanisms. The cruel superego is, on the oedipic level, the father that castrates; on anterior levels the threatening danger is that of being eaten, being destroyed, etc.

Hitherto I have been concerned with the genital and anal levels of the "counter-transference neurosis". Now I shall describe some counter-transference experiences in their oral expression, in close connection with the aspects of the matter under consideration.

(1) One of the defence mechanisms against the dangers pointed out above is that of masochistic submission to the desires of the introjected objects. A female patient had been sent to the candidate by a "father-analyst", whose esteem as regards his capacity as a future analyst was very important to him. The patient had a great deal of anxiety and a great deal of "hunger". The candidate "fed" her as much as he could and after a few months she had remarkably improved. But proportionally to the gravity of the patient's illness, the candidate felt anxiety, for so long as she was ill, he had not been fulfilling the wishes of the introjected and reprojected object, that is to say, the "father-analyst". In his efforts he was giving himself to her, and abandoning himself, "tearing himself to pieces", "ruining himself" or "killing himself" for her; all these expressions faithfully reflected the situation of the ego submitted to the archaic persecuting superego.

Finally, the candidate himself fell ill. He knew that his illness was connected with the analysis of the patient. Inside himself he blamed her and her "vampirism", and hated her until he grasped the fact that he was projecting, and that in reality it was his own "hunger" and the danger of the corresponding frustrations that caused his ailment. His own "hunger" corresponded to the voracity of his superego which he had projected, and *vice versa*. In other words, he admitted her eating from him so that he could eat too; he "castrated" himself and "killed" himself a little so as not to be castrated and killed completely.

(2) Another defence mechanism against the above-mentioned catastrophes is the identification with the projected superego and the projection of the bad and guilty object introjected in the ego. In superficial terms: "I am not incompetent, but it is the patient who is no good". In a case of a female patient, the candidate's dependence on his superego was brought markedly into play by the circumstance of its being the first case he presented in the technique seminar. The patient hardly spoke, and what little she said was not always sincere. It was a very difficult case, and the candidate was particularly anxious for her to progress: he wished to show the seminar what he knew and what he was capable of. But it was all in

vain. At the same time the candidate was conscious that he was a beginner, that is to say, that the case could certainly be handled better. Scarcely any of his interpretations were successful with the patient, and it came to the point where he had moments of hating her. To defend himself against his feeling of helplessness and inferiority, he inwardly accused the patient. Threatened by failure, he was thus exposed to persecution by the superego which he had projected in a direct way on the seminar, the director, etc., and in an indirect way upon the patient. She became a persecuting object, and he the persecuted. But in rebellion and defence against this unbearable state of affairs, and relying on the support of important objects (opinions of the director, and of advanced candidates in the seminar), he inverted the situation: he became the persecuting subject and the patient the persecuted object. But in view of the fact that the basic situation remained unaltered, the situation now created should be more precisely formulated as follows: he was the victim turned persecutor and she the persecutor turned victim.

(3) While in this situation the superego continues to act, at bottom, as a persecutor, we may find other states in which (a) the bad object (originally introjected into the ego and now projected upon the patient) is subjectively and temporarily experienced as "overcome" or "eliminated" or else (b) where the superego shows itself to be a good object that loves and accepts. In both cases manic situations arise. Here also the depressive situation still continues at bottom, but the defensive battle is—temporarily—won and the (apparent) victory frees the subject from anxiety and conflict.

For each of these situations, (a) and (b), an example.

(a) A direct "elimination" of the bad object was brought about in the following case, which I shall set forth in greater detail, because besides the manic mechanism, it shows the basic depressive situation as well as the paranoiac and masochistic defences of the "counter-transference neurosis" of the analyst in question.

The patient was a woman of 35 years of age, unmarried, who had come to analysis at her fiancé's request. His reasons for this were her great aggressiveness towards him and her complete frigidity. The case soon proved to be very serious, with a marked melancholic nucleus and manifold paranoiac ramifications (attempts at suicide, erotomania, erythrophobia, etc.); at the same time the patient displayed little awareness of her illness. The conscious and unconscious resistances were very great, and the young analyst soon began to doubt whether he would be able to help her. Nevertheless, he did not wish to drop the case, for he knew, so he said, that, however unlikely the cure, analysis was the woman's one real hope. The analyst's superego therefore demanded that he help her, but his ego was helpless. In view of the further fact that the woman was closely connected with the analytical circle, the idea of the treatment failing took on, for his unconscious, the significance of castration, or loss of the introjected objects. Against this danger and the resulting anxiety, the analyst defended himself by (inwardly) accusing the patient. He began to hate her.

This hatred aroused guilt-feelings in him. While the patient's state remained unchanged, the analyst oscillated inwardly between accusations against her and self-recriminations. But one day an external event provoked a change in the situation. The fiancé broke off all relations with the patient for good. She fell into a state of depression and thought seriously of suicide. The analyst's hatred, now satisfied, ceased, and his guilt-feelings became acute. He had hated her and in his unconscious he was—magically—responsible for her misfortune. The patient now transferred in great part upon him her hatred and accusation of the primary objects and of the fiancé. The analyst, persecuted by the accusations and threats of his superego, utterly submitted to her oral aggressiveness and "hunger". He offered her his free hours, and frequently at week-ends she stayed in his house for several hours, crying, accusing him, threatening him with suicide, etc. The analyst masochistically let himself be eaten, bitten, and partially castrated for her, to fend off total catastrophe.

Little by little the patient got better, though only superficially. A cure or far-reaching improvement was more than the analyst could hope for. So, when she found a new love-object, he agreed to her abandoning analysis, a thing he had not accepted while she was depressed. What he felt at the moment she left off analysis was a truly manic state. He was "set free" of the "bad object", and "free" of the persecuting superego, both of which had been alternately (sub-)transferred on to the patient.

(b) In the case just reported the mania was brought about by means of the pseudo-real elimination of the persecuting object. In other cases mania was experienced through the fact that the superego changed into a good object, which loves and accepts. This happened, for instance, where there was at first a hard therapeutic struggle in which the analyst—as in the case under (1) above—was persecuted by the superego (the patient and the "father–analyst" of that case), and then a genuine and noteworthy improvement in the patient was produced which was recognized, furthermore, by these very objects.

In all the cases set forth in this section the activity as analyst constituted the external field, in which the basic inner conflict was lived. More precisely, it was success or failure in therapeutic activity that was decisive for the situation between the ego and the superego. A similar part—although a lesser one in intensity and frequency—is also played by other activities in the psychoanalytic profession, such as, for example, scientific writings. In the case of one patient (female) the analyst had considered writing a report of his treatment. The patient's symptoms were very interesting and the beginning of the analysis had been quite satisfactory. In his contentment at being able to do interesting work and being accepted accordingly by the superego (and its projection on the analytical circle), there arose a strong positive counter-transference. But a few weeks later great difficulties began and the analyst had more and more the impression that he was dealing with a scientifically sterile case. He felt the hatred lying behind the patient's intense resistances, and although consciously he knew well enough that this aggressiveness was directed against the introjected childhood objects and now projected upon him, he reacted inwardly with annoyance and hatred against the "unjust hatred" of the patient. But in reality, the patient's hatred was "just", doubly "just", and this also the analyst knew, consciously very well. For the hatred not only corresponded exactly, insofar as the patient felt it, to the badness of her introjected objects, but it also corresponded exactly, insofar as it was the analyst who suffered under it, to the badness of his own introjected objects. The degree of severity of his superego, the degree of anxiety it induced in him, his feelings of guilt and inferiority, which he had tried to placate by means of the scientific report—an intention later thwarted—the intensity of all these factors determined the intensity of his own hatred.

The psychoanalytic profession, as both therapeutic and scientific work, thus held—in the cases dealt with here—the unconscious meaning of denying or avoiding the basic depressive situation, and the aim of being loved by the introjected and projected objects, of dominating them, etc.

As a consequence of the basic depressive situation, an intense exhibitionism is also often to be met with, as a tendency to deny the various guilt and inferiority feelings (incest and castration,[11] homosexuality, oral sadism, etc.). This exhibitionism (before the introjected and projected objects) not only intervenes in important aspects of the profession, as we have already seen, but also in many small details, as, for example, the analyst's satisfaction and the consequent heightening of his love for the patient when the latter affords him a chance to make an interesting observation, confirm a cherished opinion, etc.

Naturally the situation of inner and outer dependence described in this section will be met with as a rule more in the case of a beginner in the profession than in that of an experienced analyst. But since we are dealing essentially with an internal situation of a universal character, considerations regarding it are, as said above, of general validity.

V

While the previous section dealt with those manifestations of the basic depressive situation and the defences against it in which the superego was sub-transferred on to the patient, I shall now consider the situation where the basic conflict is lived in a direct form with the patient. In these cases the latter becomes, in an immediate way, a screen for the images of the introjected objects and that of the subject himself (the analyst's self-images) and becomes, at the same time, the object of the tendencies directed towards these images.

I have already mentioned multiple sources of the analyst's need of being loved by the patient (feminine or masculine): the positive and negative Oedipus complex, the corresponding guilt-feelings, the rejection of active impulses and the consequent passive desires. We may here add passive oral love on the one hand, and oral sadism on the other, the unconscious perception of which is charged with intense guilt-feelings, which in their turn increase the need of being loved; this last situation constitutes the core of the basic depressive conflict. If the analyst's need of being loved is thwarted, the danger arises that his capacity of objective perception concerning his patients may be perturbed by the interference of hatred archaic images; the image of the bad mother (breast) that will not give, that eats and robs, or the self-image of the "vampire", etc.

Instead of the former transference or the latter projection of a paranoiac character, there may also occur a depressive confrontation with this or another self-image, or manic reactions may come about, etc. Some examples may serve to illustrate this.

(1) In the case of a candidate, when faced with female patients who repressed their sexual transference, an old thought of his would come back to him: the woman could not fall in love with him because he was too ugly or because he was not instinctive enough. In this thought, in addition to the positive Oedipus complex, the homosexual conflict, and the accompanying guilt and inferiority feelings, there is also an expression of the specific depressive conflict: he is ugly and hateful because he has too much hatred (oral): he is not instinctive enough, because he does not love enough, because he only wishes to receive, take, rob (guilt-feelings over oral receptivity and passivity, and before all over his oral sadism).

(2) The oral frustration at the root of the tendencies just mentioned leads, on the one hand, to the image of the bad, voracious, and miserly mother, and on the other hand, to the oral envy and the corresponding hatred. This hated image is further strengthened by the paranoiac projection of the thieving self-image. All this creates "direct" counter-transferential dangers of a paranoiac nature, especially in cases where the patient satisfies those oral-sadistic tendencies that the analyst represses, as often happens when dealing with a "Don Juan" or a "Vamp". The counter-transference position as regards behaviour in money matters is also frequently perturbed by the same factors: hatred of avarice, of the object's "voracity", etc.

Before furnishing an example of the above, I should like to add at this point some general remarks on counter-transference reactions to the patient's resistances, for they are often connected with the analyst's paranoiac mechanisms which have just been described.

The resistances sometimes provoke annoyance and even intense hatred; this will be the greater, the more helpless the analyst feels about the problem confronting him.[12] This hatred may generally be traced to his fear of failure and all that this would mean. It is thus the expression of the same paranoiac mechanism that we saw in the previous section, in dealing with "indirect counter-transference".

The feeling often arises in the analyst that the resistance is hatred the patient feels for him. We might think that this sensation was only an expression of the childhood equation: frustration = (is equal to) hatred to the frustrator. Upon reflexion we see that that feeling reflects an objective truth. The main resistances are a manifestation of conflicts with introjected objects which, by reason of their frustrating nature, are feared, rejected, and hated. Hence resistance, in one of its aspects, is hatred, to which the analyst sometimes reacts with hatred on his part, and so falls into a trap laid for him by his own neurosis. For the analyst believes the patient when the latter unconsciously attributes badness to him; that is to say, he believes himself to be as bad as the patient's introjected objects, which have been projected upon him and which account for the patient's main resistances. And he believes him because the patient has a powerful ally within the analyst's own personality—the latter's own bad introjected objects which hate him and which he hates. And in the same measure an analyst may come to hate a patient who is in intense resistance. For this resistance sometimes leads to the analyst's being persecuted by his own superego; he defends himself against this persecution by means of projection of the bad introjected objects in the ego and simultaneous identification with the superego projected upon the patient, which, in turn, leads to his feeling hatred and "becoming angry".

I shall now mention an example in which this reaction to resistance was added to a paranoiac reaction of "direct counter-transference". One of the expressions of a (female) patient's great resistance was her way of talking; it gave the analyst the impression that she was reciting. It seemed to him that by this means she wished to appear especially refined, sensitive, and feminine, and was trying to get him to fall in love with her so as to dominate him. He felt an intense rejection of this unconscious manoeuvre on her part. Upon analysing the rejection, he discovered, among other things, that this pseudo-romantic and deceitful part of the patient represented a part of himself, a rejected self-image. It was his own desire to dominate his introjected and projected objects that sometimes induced him to adopt a seeming submissiveness, and just such a comedy of delicacy, sensitivity, and romantic goodness; it was the wolf in sheep's clothing which he hated in himself and outside himself. Two things should be shown by this example: Firstly, the mechanism of anger on meeting with resistance. The resistance was, in one aspect, the expression of her hatred of her bad internal objects which she wanted to dominate. Her hatred found an ally in the analyst's superego, for the resistances (in threatening the success of the analysis) also provoked in him fear of the superego. The analyst defended himself against this superego aggression with his hatred of the patient. Secondly, this example illustrates "direct" paranoiac counter-transference, for the hated "wolf" in the patient was really a repressed self-image (or tendency) of his own.

The patient's intense resistance represents, as a rule, a frustration for the analyst, which in itself would explain his annoyance. But the external frustration is regularly added, as shown, to internal frustrations of an infantile origin. In this sense, the analyst's feeling of annoyance with the patient is always, in part at least, neurotic. The frustration that the patient affords us springs from the resistances, but it is just because of them that he comes for treatment. If we are annoyed by his resistances, we behave (if only internally) like a doctor who is annoyed by a physical disease, and, for instance, gets angry with the patient when he feels that his medical skill is insufficient. In the case of a patient who will not take the medicine that would cure him, it is understandable for the doctor to get angry, but not for a psychologist to do so, for he should know that behind the refusal of the medicine—here: behind the rejection of the analytical rules, of interpretations, etc. —there lie psychological conflicts. The analyst's irritation is thus, partly, of an infantile nature. It cannot be completely avoided, but it is important to know its origin, so that the child within the psychologist should not disturb him more than can be helped, and so that the two children—the one inside the analyst and the one inside the patient—should not come to blows. To say this may sound like carrying coals to Newcastle, but as these struggles never come to an end, neither should the analysis of their origin ever be regarded as concluded.

(3) We have seen under (1) and (2) the basic depressive conflict and the paranoiac defence in "direct counter-transference". Just as the "bad woman", or the patient that does not love the analyst, may evoke in him paranoiac hatred or depression, the patient who loves him sometimes evokes a mild mania ; and this—as in the above-mentioned mechanisms—in spite of the fact that the analyst is conscious of the transferential character of this love. In the same sense the doubt may enter his mind whether it is really "only transference". The unconscious reasons for this doubt are clear.

(4) The guilt-feelings over his own lack of love (over his own oedipic hatred, his oral sadism, etc.) that the analyst feels with some patients, may also lead him to a masochistic submissiveness. The case referred to in Section IV, 3, is an example of this. With the indirect counter-transference (previously described) there was mixed the paranoiac hatred of the "direct" type; for the analyst's unconscious, the patient was the bad mother who frustrated him genitally, who took his father from him, withheld the breast, hated him, consumed him orally, etc. The guilt-feelings and need for punishment for the hatred that this image provoked in the analyst were one of the reasons for his submitting himself to the patient's voracity and aggression. This also expressed itself in his behaviour as regards payment. Thus for instance he did not charge her for the extra sessions he gave her during her weeks of depression and even for the regular ones he did not wish to take more than "four cents a session", as was revealed by a lapsus of his. In a similar way this analyst submitted to the oral and anal avarice of another patient, also because of guilt-feelings over his own envy and oedipic and oral hatred.

Thus similarly to the situation of indirect counter-transference, we also find in direct relationship with the patient, under certain circumstances, the same neurotic dependence, the same basic depressive conflict, and the same defence mechanisms.

VI

Many problems calling for further analysis arise in connexion with the above exposition, some of which have already been outlined. The most immediate problems are those referring to the various consequences of neurotic counter-transference. How does it affect the analyst's understanding, his interpretations and his behaviour? And what consequences has it for the patient's relationship with the analyst, especially for the re-experience of childhood that is to be rectified? Furthermore, what deductions could be made from the counter-transferential states that are provoked by the patient as regards the latter's psychological situations? What influence, more-over, has the analyst's life outside his consulting-room upon his counter-transference and *vice versa*? What practical conclusions are to be drawn?

In view of the length this paper has already reached, I will only refer briefly to some of these problems. As for the first question, namely, the influence of counter-transference upon the analyst's understanding, we must remember, above all, what processes this understanding is based on. H. Deutsch[13] differentiates two components: (a) the identification of the analyst with certain parts of the patient's ego (i.e. the impulses and defences) and (b) the "complementary position", or the identification with the patient's images (according to the phantasies of transference). Thus, if the analyst reacts, for instance, with oral resentment to the avarice of a (female) patient, this does not prevent him from identifying himself intellectually with her defence mechanisms and object images, and he is able to understand that she is avaricious because for her he is a thief (namely, her rapacious mother), but it does prevent him from doing so emotionally, because for his feelings it is she that has these meanings. Moreover, the counter-transference is instrumental in bringing to his notice a psychological fact about the patient, for his experience of frustration and his ensuing hatred made him aware of the patient's avarice.[14] Nevertheless, his inner reaction is neurotic; he is not prevented from understanding but from reacting under-standingly. The latter will only be possible for him once he has analysed and overcome his situation and is able to identify himself with the patient's ego emotionally as well. Even the most elementary rule of keeping silent in such moments of "irritation" is not always complied with. In such situations the patient often senses the analyst's aggressive feelings in the content or in the formulation of the interpretation, or in his voice, and so finds himself once again facing an archaic object. And this time with real grounds, as it is indeed the analyst's own archaic objects that awaken his hostility, this being frequently the expression of his identification with these objects, in defence against the anxiety they provoked in him. The consequence of such happenings for the patient's transference are clear.

In the same way we may say—to vary a definition of counter-transference, due to F. Hann-Kende—that transference is a function of the patient's transferences and the analyst's counter-transferences.[15] Just as the above-mentioned patient perceived—even though only unconsciously—the counter-transferential hatred, another patient detected the analyst's wish to dominate from his tone of voice and reacted with a greater repression of his positive transference. Another became aware of the analyst's anxiety, so that he lost confidence and increased his resistances. It is naturally of great importance to see and analyse the influence of these and other expressions of counter-transference upon transference.[16]

A special danger involved in neurotic counter-transference is what might be called counter-transferential induction or counter-transferential grafting. By this, I mean the well-known danger of the analyst's "inducing" or "grafting" his own neurosis upon the patient. This danger also is only to be averted in the degree to which the analyst knows his "personal equation", that is to say his proneness to certain specific errors as a consequence of his own neurosis.

The serious consequences of such mistakes which are "induced" into the patient were to be seen in the case of a patient whom a young analyst wished to bring to an independence that he did not possess himself, and just for this very reason. The analyst felt he was neurotic in this respect; he had, moreover, a neurotic ideal of independence and wanted the patient (his "son") to achieve what he (the "father") had been unable to. He did not incite him directly to "independent" living—his conscience as an analyst would not allow of that—but, on the other hand, he asked him certain questions. By persuading himself that they were only questions, the analyst satisfied the demands of his professional conscience. Yet the questions led the patient to what the analyst desired, namely, "independent" living, and in this way the analyst satisfied his desires too. These questions obeyed the same process of formation as neurotic symptoms, being a transaction between the id, ego and superego. These stimuli to action only lead, as a rule, to apparent changes; though we know it, it seems difficult for us to free ourselves from the "educator" within us, with all his neurotic impulses and the corresponding ideals. The realization of our relative unconsciousness as regards our own neurotic processes of counter-transference should constitute a reason for doubly observing the fulfilment of the rule of abstinence with respect to acting out; and I am referring to acting out not only on the part of the patient but also on the part of the analyst. A cure is to be achieved—as Freud repeatedly stressed—only by overcoming the resistances.

I should like to add a few words about the most immediate practical conclusions that follow from this exposition. There is, in the first place, an evident need of keeping watch on the resistances regarding counter-transference and the corresponding problems. Just as in controls, in the publications of case-histories, etc., the processes of transference are given due consideration, so also should the essential processes of counter-transference be regarded. The need of continuing didactic analysis until the candidate has faced up squarely to his own counter-transference neurosis has already been stressed by M. Langer ("Dificultades psicológicas del psicoanalista principiante" (read to the Argentine Psycho-Analytic Association, 1948; unpublished)) and others. The breakdown of the corresponding resistances in the candidate will then lead to a lessening of his neurotic dependence on his didactic analyst and so favour the introjection of a good object. In the programmes of technical lecture-courses, counter-transference should—in so far as this has not been carried out already—receive the attention it deserves.

One last word: Freud once said that his pupils had learnt to bear a part of the truth about themselves. The deepening of our knowledge of counter-transference accords with this principle. And I believe we should do well if we learnt to bear this truth about each one of us being also known by some other people.

Notes

1. Lecture delivered to the Argentine Psycho-Analytic Association, September, 1948. This date also explains why the references to papers on counter-transference, published in the last five years, appear only in some footnotes added subsequently.

2. This statement has, in the meantime, lost part of its validity. During the years following the presentation of this paper there have appeared a series of important studies on counter-transference. (Winnicott, 1949; Heimann, 1950; Reich, 1951; Little, 1951; Gitelson, 1952; all published in the *International Journal of Psycho-Analysis*).

3. I only know of two such papers: Fenichel, O., "Theoretical implications of the didactic analysis" (mimeographed by the Topeka Inst. of Psycho-Anal.) and Langer, M., "Dificultades psicológicas del psicoanalista principiante" (read to the Argentine Psycho-Analytic Association, 1948; unpublished).

4. M. Little stresses the frequent "paranoid or phobic attitude towards counter-transference ... especially where the feelings are, or may be, subjective". ("Counter-transference and the patient's response to it", *International Journal of Psycho-Analysis*, 32, Part I, p. 33, 1951.).

5. I shall confine myself to what concerns the male analyst.

6. M. Little ("Counter-transference and the patient's response to it", *International Journal of Psycho-Analysis*, 32, Part I, p. 34), by a somewhat different approach, arrives at the same conclusions.

7. Compare M. Langer, "Dificultades psicológicas del psicoanalista principiante" (read to the Argentine Psycho-Analytic Association, 1948; unpublished).

8. So long as the analyst knows himself to be under the influence of a neurotic impulse, he should, of course, postpone communicating any interpretation, if possible, until he has analysed his state and overcome it. A guide of a certain practical value for knowing whether it is the neurosis that is driving him, is the compulsiveness with which he feels the need to give the interpretation. Behind this compulsiveness there clearly lies the invariable sign of neurotic reaction—anxiety.

9. This differentiation accords, in essence, with differentiations made by Fenichel, O. ("Theoretical implications of the didactic analysis" (mimeographed by the Topeka Institute of Psycho-Analysis)) and by Reich, A. ("On counter-transference", *International Journal of Psycho-Analysis*, 32, Part I, 1951, p. 26). This authoress draws a distinction between "counter-transference in the proper sense" and "the expressions of the analyst's using the analysis for acting-out purposes", and she considers that in these latter cases "... the patients are frequently not real objects onto whom something is transferred ..." I think, nevertheless, that where, for instance, the patient's improvement helps the analyst "to master guilt feelings" (A. Reich), the patient represents a "real Object" which the analyst (even if only in phantasy) had damaged and is now repairing.

10. Pichon Rivière, E.: "Psicoanálisis de la Esquizofrenia", Revista de Psicoanálisis, V(2), 1947.
11. See also the passive–phallic position described above. The desire that the penis should be loved has the further significance, besides those mentioned above, of the denial of castration.
12. Fenichel, in his "Problems of analytical technique" (1939) says on this point: "Whenever one is blocked in any piece of work to which one is devoted, one always becomes angry". (Psychoanal. Quarterly, 8(2), p. 184). In the following lines an attempt is made to enter into the problem that Fenichel here indicates.
13. H. Deutsch (1934). "Okkulte Vorgänge während der Psychoanalyse" (Hidden processes during psycho-analysis), Imago, 12, 1934.
14. It is mainly with this aspect—the counter-transference as "one of the most important tools for the analyst's work"—that P. Heimann deals in her paper "On counter-transference" (International Journal of Psycho-Analysis, 30, 1950, Parts I and II, p. 81).
15. In his paper "Zur bertragung und Gegenübertragung in der Psychoanalyse" (On transference and counter-transference in psycho-analysis), Int. Zeitschr. f. Psychoanalyse, 1936, 22, p. 478). F. Hann-Kende defines counter-transference as "a function of the transferences of the patient and of the analyst".
16. D. W. Winnicott (1949). "Hate in the counter-transference", International Journal of Psycho-Analysis, 30, 1949, pp. 69–74), M. Little "Counter-transference and the patient's response to it", International Journal of Psycho-Analysis, 32, Part I, and M. Gitelson (1952). "The emotional position of the analyst in the psychoanalytic situation", International Journal of Psycho-Analysis, 33, pp. 1–10, deal with the problem of analysing with the patient the counter-transferential situations, their causes and effects.

Article citation

Racker, H. (1953). A contribution to the problem of counter-transference. International Journal of Psycho-Analysis, 34: 313–324.

CHAPTER FIVE

Normal counter-transference and some of its deviations[1]

R. E. Money-Kyrle

Introductory

Counter-transference is an old psychoanalytic concept which has recently been widened and enriched. We used to think of it mainly as a personal disturbance to be analysed away in ourselves. We now also think of it as having its causes, and effects, in the patient and, therefore, as an indication of something to be analysed in him.

I believe this more recently explored aspect of counter-transference can be used, in the way described, for example, by Paula Heimann (1950), to achieve an important technical advance.[2] But of course the discovery that counter-transference can be usefully employed does not imply that it has ceased ever to be a serious impediment. And as both aspects in fact exist, we may surmise that there may be a problem about their similarities and differences which still deserves investigation. Perhaps this problem may be put in the form of three related questions: what is "normal" counter-transference? How and under what conditions is it disturbed? And how can disturbances be corrected and in the process perhaps used to further an analysis?

Normal counter-transference

As to the analyst's correct or normal attitude to the patient, there are a number of aspects which have been mentioned both in papers and discussions. Freud spoke of a "benevolent neutrality". This I take to imply that the analyst is concerned for the welfare of his patient, without becoming emotionally involved in his conflicts. It also implies, I think, that the analyst, in virtue of his understanding of psychic determinism, has a certain kind of tolerance which is the opposite of condemnation, and yet by no means the same as indulgence or indifference.

Many analysts have stressed the element of scientific curiosity, and certainly we should not get far without this sublimation. But, by itself, it seems a little too impersonal. Concern for the patient's welfare comes, I think, from the fusion of two other basic drives: the reparative, which counteracts the latent destructiveness in all of us, and the parental. Of course, if too intense, they betray excessive guilt about inadequately sublimated aggressiveness which can be the cause of very disturbing anxieties. But, in some degree, both are surely normal. The reparative satisfactions of analysis are obvious and often referred to. So, in some degree, the patient must stand for the damaged objects of the analyst's own unconscious phantasy, which are still endangered by aggression and still in need of care and reparation. The parental aspect has been mentioned, in discussions, by Paula Heimann (1954).[3] No one would suggest that the patient stands only for a child, and not sometimes for a sibling, or even for a parent. But it is with the unconscious child in the patient that the analyst is most concerned; and because this child so often treats the analyst as parent, the analyst's unconscious can hardly fail to respond in some degree by regarding the patient as his child.

Now, to a parent, a child stands, at least in part, for an early aspect of the self. And this seems to me important. For it is just because the analyst can recognize his early self, which has already been analysed, in the patient, that he can analyse the patient.[4] His empathy and insight, as distinct from his theoretical knowledge, depend on this kind of partial identification.[5]

But identification can take two forms—introjective and projective —a distinction latent in Freud's concept, the significance of which

Melanie Klein has recently brought out.[6] We may therefore expect
to find both forms in the analyst's partial identification with his
patient.

I will try to formulate what seems to be happening when the
analysis is going well. I believe there is a fairly rapid oscillation
between introjection and projection. As the patient speaks, the
analyst will, as it were, become introjectively identified with him,
and having understood him inside, will reproject him and interpret.
But what I think the analyst is most aware of is the projective
phase—that is to say, the phase in which the patient is the
representative of a former immature or ill part of himself, including
his damaged objects, which he can now understand and therefore
treat by interpretation, in the external world.

Meanwhile the patient is receiving effective interpretations,
which help him to respond with further associations that can be
understood. As long as the analyst understands them, this
satisfactory relationship—which I will call the "normal" one—
persists. In particular, the analyst's counter-transference feelings
will be confined to that sense of empathy with the patient on which
his insight is based.

Periods of non-understanding

Everyone, the analyst no less than the patient, would be happy if the
situation I have just described, and called the "normal" one, would
persist throughout the whole course of an analysis. Unfortunately, it
is normal only in the sense of being an ideal. It depends for its
continuity on the analyst's continuous understanding. But he is not
omniscient. In particular, his understanding fails whenever the
patient corresponds too closely with some aspect of himself which
he has not yet learnt to understand. Moreover some patients are
much less co-operative than others. There are patients with whom
the best of analysts find great difficulty in maintaining contact—
with whom the "normal" relationship is the exception rather than
the rule. And even with co-operative patients, it is subject to fairly
frequent breaks.

We recognize these breaks at once by our feeling that the
material has become obscure, and that we have somehow lost the

thread. Now whatever has in fact been missed, the fact of missing it creates a new situation which may be felt as a strain by the analyst as well as by the patient. Of course some analysts—for example, those who most crave the reassurance of continuous success—feel such strains more acutely then others. But, apart from individual differences, there is a peculiarity in the very nature of the analytic technique which must impose some strain on all of us—especially at moments when we cannot help a patient who is in obvious distress. For, if my argument so far is right, we all have some need to satisfy our parental and reparative drives to counteract the Death Instinct; but we are much more restricted in the ways in which we can do so than a real parent, an educationalist or any other kind of therapist. We are restricted to the giving of interpretations;[7] and our capacity to give them depends upon our continuing to understand the patient. If this understanding fails, as fail from time to time it must, we have no alternative therapy to fall back on. Here, then, is a situation peculiar to analysis, when lack of understanding is liable to arouse conscious or unconscious anxiety, and anxiety still further to diminish understanding. It is to the onset of this kind of vicious spiral that I am inclined to attribute every deviation in normal counter-transference feeling.

If the analyst is in fact disturbed, it is also likely that the patient has unconsciously contributed to this result, and is in turn disturbed by it. So we have three factors to consider: first, the analyst's emotional disturbance, for he may have to deal with this silently in himself before he can disengage himself sufficiently to understand the other two; then the patient's part in bringing it about; and finally its effect on him. Of course, all three factors may be sorted out in a matter of seconds, and then indeed the counter-transference is functioning as a delicate receiving apparatus. But I will discuss the first stage first, as if it were a lengthy process—as it sometimes is.

The role of the analyst's superego

The extent to which an analyst is emotionally disturbed by periods of non-understanding will probably depend, in the first instance, on another factor: the severity of his own superego. For analysis is also a form of work required of us by this inner figure—which, incidentally, a demanding patient may sometimes come to represent. If our superego is predominantly friendly and helpful, we can tolerate our own limitations without undue distress, and, being undisturbed, will be the more likely soon to regain contact with the patient. But if it is severe, we may become conscious of a sense of failure as the expression of an unconscious persecutory or depressive guilt. Or, as a defence against such feelings, we may blame the patient.

The choice of one or other of these alternatives seems to me to determine something else as well. For when that interplay between introjection and projection, which characterizes the analytic process, breaks down, the analyst may tend to get stuck in one or other of these two positions; and what he does with his guilt may determine the position he gets stuck in. If he accepts the guilt, he is likely to get stuck with an introjected patient. If he projects it, the patient remains an incomprehensible figure in the external world.

Examples of prolonged introjection and projection

An example of the first, that is, the introjective, alternative may be seen when the analyst gets unduly worried, both on his own and his patient's behalf, about a session that has gone badly. He may feel as if he had regained some of his own old troubles and become almost physically burdened with his patient's as well. Only when he separates the two can he see what he has missed and get the patient out of him again.

Often, it is something towards the end of a session, or of a week, which he feels he has missed, and then he has all the patient's supposed frustration in himself. This may look like a self-punishment for having unconsciously intended to hurt the patient. But we may wonder whether the patient has not contributed to the analyst's distress—whether the leaving of his analyst with an unsolved problem about himself is not his way of projecting himself into the analyst both to punish him for, and to avoid, the threatened separation.

In other words, there may be a symbiosis between the analyst's tendency to prolong the introjection of a patient whom he cannot understand or help and the patient's tendency to project parts of himself, in the way described by Melanie Klein, into the analyst who is not helping him. (This may be particularly disturbing if what the patient is most anxious to get rid of is his own destructiveness.)

In such cases the ultimate cause of the analyst's slowness in understanding and reprojecting the patient may be that the patient has come to stand for something which he has not yet learnt to understand quickly in himself. If he still fails to do so, and cannot tolerate the sense of being burdened with the patient as an irreparable or persecuting figure inside him, he is likely to resort to a defensive kind of reprojection which shuts out the patient and creates a further bar to understanding.

If so, a new complication may arise if the analyst, in projecting the patient, projects aspects of himself as well. Then he will have the chance to explore within himself the workings of those mechanisms of projective identification which, under the influence of Melanie Klein, Rosenfeld and others have so fruitfully explored in schizophrenic patients.[8] Nor need we be surprised at this, for the discovery of pathological mechanisms in mental illness is usually followed by the recognition of their less obvious presence in normal people too. A "slow-motion" example of the kind of process I have in mind may be seen in another fairly common weekend experience. For a little time after he has finished his week's work, the analyst may be consciously preoccupied with some unsolved problem of his patients. Then he forgets them; but the period of conscious concern is followed by a period of listlessness in which he is depleted of the private interests that usually occupy his leisure. I suggest this is because, in phantasy, he has projected parts of himself together with his patients and must wait, as it were, till these return to him.

When this partial loss of self occurs within a session, it is often experienced as the loss of intellectual potency; the analyst feels stupid. The patient may well have contributed to this result. Perhaps, frustrated by not getting an immediate interpretation, he has unconsciously wished to castrate his analyst, and by treating him as if he were, has helped to make him feel castrated.[9]

A complicated example taken from my own experience would seem to illustrate the simultaneous operation of all these processes. For while the dominant theme was my introjection of a patient who wished to project his illness into me, I also experienced a sense of being robbed of my wits by him.

A neurotic patient, in whom paranoid and schizoid mechanisms were prominent, arrived for a session in considerable anxiety because he had not been able to work in his office. He had also felt vague on the way as if he might get lost or run over; and he despised himself for being useless. Remembering a similar occasion, on which he had felt depersonalized over a week-end and dreamed that he had left his "radar" set in a shop and would be unable to get it before Monday, I thought he had, in phantasy, left parts of his "good self" in me. But I was not very sure of this, or of other interpretations I began to give. And he, for his part, soon began to reject them all with a mounting degree of anger; and, at the same time, abused me for not helping. By the end of the session he was no longer depersonalized, but very angry and contemptuous instead. It was I who felt useless and bemused.

When I eventually recognized my state at the end as so similar to that he had described as his at the beginning, I could almost feel the relief of a re-projection. By then the session was over. But he was in the same mood at the beginning of the next one—still very angry and contemptuous. I then told him I thought he felt he had reduced me to the state of useless vagueness he himself had been in; and that he felt he had done this by having me "on the mat", asking questions and rejecting the answers, in the way his legal father did. His response was striking. For the first time in two days, he became quiet and thoughtful. He then said this explained why he had been so angry with me yesterday: he had felt that all my interpretations referred to my illness and not to his.

I suggest that, as in a slow motion picture, we can here see several distinct processes which, in an ideal or "normal" analytic period, should occur extremely quickly. I think I began, as it were, to take my patient in, to identify introjectively with him, as soon as he lay down and spoke about his very acute distress. But I could not at once recognize it as corresponding with anything already understood in myself; and, for this reason, I was slow to get it out of me in the process of explaining, and so relieving it in him. He, for his part, felt frustrated at not getting effective interpretations, and reacted by projecting his sense of mental impotence into me, at the same time behaving as if he had taken from me what he felt he had lost, his father's clear, but aggressive, intellect, with which he attacked his impotent self in me. By this time, of course, it was useless to try to pick up the thread where I had first dropped it. A new situation had arisen which had affected us both. And before my patient's part in bringing it about could be interpreted, I had to do a silent piece of self-analysis involving the discrimination of two things which can be felt as very similar: my own sense of incompetence at having lost the thread, and my patient's contempt for his impotent self, which he felt to be in me. Having made this interpretation to myself, I was eventually able to pass the second half of it on to my patient, and, by so doing, restored the normal analytic situation.

According to Bion (1955), the capacity to make this kind of discrimination, and much more quickly than in the example, is an important part of the capacity to use one's counter-transference in the interests of analysis.

Positive and negative counter-transference

Coming now to counter-transference in the narrow sense of an excess of positive or negative feeling, this too is often an indirect result of the frustrations arising when a distressed patient is not understood, and no effective interpretations can be given. For the analyst whose reparative impulse is thwarted of its analytically normal outlet may be unconsciously inclined either to offer some form of love instead, or to become hostile to his patient. Meanwhile, the patient may be facilitating the process by trying to provoke one or other of these affects in his analyst, who is the more likely to respond to his patient's mood just because he has lost his empathy with it.

Now however scrupulously we may suppress an excess of positive or negative feeling of this kind, the patient is likely to sense it unconsciously. Then a new situation arises in which his response to our mood may itself have to be interpreted.

If, for example, the counter-transference is too positive, the patient may respond to our increased emotional concern by complaining that we have no emotional concern. We do not contradict him as he may wish. But it may be appropriate to tell him that he believes we are attracted to him and has to deny it in order to avoid the responsibility for a seduction. For an important early pattern may be involved. As a child, he may have been unconsciously aware that his caresses embarrassed one of his parents, for example, his mother, because she was afraid of being aroused by them; and the sense of being rebuffed may have rankled all his life, because it was needed to counteract his guilt for trying to seduce her. If so, the interpretation of the repetition of this pattern in the transference may enable the patient to reassess, not only his analyst's, but his real parent's attitude to him.

But if it goes unnoticed, and its effects unobserved, the unconscious offering of love in lieu of effective interpretations may disturb the analysis in many ways. For instance, the analyst may foster the split, directly in his own mind and indirectly in his patient's, between himself as a good parent and the real parents as bad ones. Then the patient may never become aware of his guilt towards them—a guilt which, paradoxically enough, is likely to be all the greater if they were really bad; for it is in proportion to his own ambivalence. If this guilt is not recovered in analysis, the patient cannot work through that early stage described by Melanie Klein as the depressive position, in which the developing infant begins to become aware of, and miserable about, the conflict between his hatred and his love.

As to the negative attitudes to a patient which may also result from a temporary failure to understand him, these would seem especially to arise when the patient becomes a persecution because he is felt to be incurable. Then, as before, the analyst's triple task is first to become aware of this defensive mechanism in himself, then of his patient's part in bringing it about, and lastly of its effect on him. To take the last point first: The sort of paranoid patient I mentioned earlier, who hated me for years and seemed to make no noticeable progress, can easily come to stand for one's own bad and persecutory objects, which one would like to get rid of. Such feelings betray themselves in one's sigh of relief after the last session of the week, or before a holiday. One's first impulse may be to suppress such hostile feelings; but if one does not allow oneself to become aware of them, one may miss their influence on the patient's unconscious. For instance, I came to feel that the occasions on which this patient repudiated me with more than ordinary violence, followed rather than preceded, moments when I would really have been glad to see the last of him. And then my interpretation that it was he who felt rebuffed met with more success.

I also noticed more clearly that the times when I was aware of disliking him followed moments in which I had despaired of helping him. And I began to wonder whether he, on his side, was not trying to make me despair and, if so, what his motives were. Several seemed to be involved, of which perhaps the most important was that, in his phantasy, getting well was equated with the renunciation of an unacknowledged homosexual component in himself. He unconsciously wished to prove to me that this could not be done. Meanwhile, he attacked me consciously for not curing him, that is, for not removing the impulse; and unconsciously for not satisfying it for him.

Conclusion

If what I have said so far touches only the fringe of an immensely complicated subject, it at least suggests the possibility of approximate answers to the questions I began with: what is normal counter-transference? How and under what conditions is it disturbed? And how can disturbances be corrected and in the process perhaps used to further an analysis?

The analyst's motive is a blend of curiosity with parental and reparative drives. His equipment consists both of his theoretical knowledge about the unconscious, and of his personal acquaintance with its manifestations which he has gained in his own analysis. But it is with his use of the second that we are here concerned; that is, with his insight, for this consists in his ability, by means of a partial identification with his patient, to apply his acquaintance with his own unconscious to the interpretation of his patient's behaviour. When all is going well, this identification seems to oscillate between its introjective and projective forms. The analyst, as it were, absorbs the patient's state of mind through the medium of the associations he hears and the postures he observes, recognizes it as expressing some pattern in his own unconscious world of phantasy, and reprojects the patient in the act of formulating his interpretation. In this phase he may get that sense of helpfully understanding his patient from within which satisfies both his curiosity and his reparative drives. To some degree, his interest is also a parental one; for, to the parent, the child is his early self, and it is with the same child in the patient that the analyst is most concerned. His sense of being in touch with it, his empathy, comprises his "normal" counter-transference feeling.

What keeps the process going is the analyst's repeated acts of recognition, in the introjective phase, that such and such a pattern of absorbed emotion expresses such and such a phantasy in his own unconscious. And what causes a break in this relationship is a failure in this recognition.

The cause of a failure may be something still feared, because not yet fully understood, within the analyst to which the patient has come too close. But the result need be no more than a retardation in the analytic process, which enables us the better to observe its separate phases. This happens particularly when it is the first or introjective phase which is slowed down. The analyst then feels burdened with the patient and with some of his old immature self as well. He has to do more slowly, what at other times he does at once; become conscious of the phantasies within him, recognize their source, separate the patient's from his own, and so objectify him again.

But the analyst may also have to deal with two other factors, which are much less in evidence when the process is going quickly. These are the patient's contribution—in particular his use of projective identification—to the analyst's disturbed emotions, and the effect which these in turn may be having on the patient.

It may be, however, that the analyst does not succeed in sorting all this out within himself before he reprojects the patient as something not understood, or foreign, in the external world. Then, since his reparative impulses can find no outlet in effective interpretations, he may be tempted to fall back on some form of reassurance instead. Or, if he despairs of his reparative powers, he may defend himself against depression by feeling angry with his patient. In either case, his intuition has temporarily gone so that any interpretations he makes can be based only on his knowledge of theory, which by itself is likely to be a sterile substitute for a fruitful combination of the two.

If we were omniscient analysts, the only counter-transference we should experience would be that belonging to those intuitive periods when all is going well. In fact, the less satisfactory states I have tried to describe, in which our feelings are at least in some degree disturbed, probably take up a lot more analytic time than we readily remember or admit. Yet it is precisely in them, I think, that the analyst, by silently analysing his own reactions, can increase his insight, decrease his difficulties, and learn more about his patient.

Notes

1. Read at the 19th International Psychoanalytical Congress, Geneva, 24–28 July, 1955.
2. The use of counter-transference as an "instrument of research" has been especially studied by Paula Heimann (1950). That is to say, she has stressed its causes in the patient, while Margaret Little (1951). has stressed its effects on him. This, too, is clearly an important aspect. But, in interpreting the patient's response to our counter-transference, opinions differ about whether, as she thinks, we should occasionally be prepared to admit to him what our counter-transference was—instead of confining ourselves to interpreting what is in his mind, namely, his beliefs about our attitude.
3. The sublimation of curiosity and of parental impulses have been stressed respectively by Clifford Scott and Paula Heimann in scientific discussions in the British Psycho-Analytical Society. But I have not found specific references to these points in any of their published papers. In "Problems of the training analysis" (1954). However, Paula Heimann does implicitly refer to the dangers of an excess of parental sublimation.
4. Conversely, by discovering new patterns in a patient, the analyst can make "post-graduate" progress in his own analysis.
5. Annie Reich speaks of a "short-lived identification", and Paula Heimann of identification in both introjective and projective forms in her "Problems of the training analysis" quoted above.
6. I think the distinction between introjective and projective identification is implicit, though not very clearly brought out, in Freud's Group Psychology and the Analysis of the Ego.
7. The extent to which we are in fact restricted to pure interpretations depends, in some degree, upon our school. We are all agreed that our main role is to give interpretations. No one denies that we also arrange a certain framework within which to give them: we provide the physical comfort of a couch; and we preserve a certain courtesy of manner with minor variations according to the requirements of different patients, some wishing to shake hands before or after every session, others not, and so on. But opinions differ about whether the framework, once established, should be deliberately manipulated. Thus Winnicott, if I understand him rightly, has argued that some psychotic patients can only form a relation to an ideal object which they have never had, and that the analyst may have to play this role before analysis proper can be started; in other words, that it is not alone sufficient to interpret the patient's efforts to force this role on him.

8. If so, the patient is also likely to introject him in this condition and then feel in more desperate need of external help than ever. At such moments, the analyst may become disagreeably aware that the patient is still more urgently demanding that which he is still less able to give—consciously, a good interpretation, unconsciously a breast or penis which now neither feel they have.

9. How exactly a patient does succeed in imposing a phantasy and its corresponding affect upon his analyst in order to deny it in himself is a most interesting problem. I do not think we need assume some form of extrasensory communication; but the communication can be of a preverbal and archaic kind—similar perhaps to that used by gregarious animals in which the posture or call of a single member will arouse a corresponding affect in the rest. In the analytic situation, a peculiarity of communications of this kind is that, at first sight, they do not seem as if they had been made by the patient at all. The analyst experiences the affect as being his own response to something. The effort involved is in differentiating the patient's contribution from his own.

References

Bion, W. R. (1955). Language and the schizophrenic. In: M. Klein, P. Heimann & R. E. Money-Kyrle (Eds.), *New Directions in Psycho-Analysis*, Chapter 9.

Heimann, P. (1950). On counter-transference. *International Journal of Psycho-Analysis*, 31:

Klein, M. (1946). Notes on some schizoid mechanisms. *International Journal of Psycho-Analysis*, 27:

Little, M. (1951). Counter-transference and the patient's response to it. *International Journal of Psycho-Analysis*, 32:

Reich, A. (1951). On counter-transference. *International Journal of Psycho-Analysis*, 32:

Rosenfeld, H. (1952). Transference phenomena and transference analysis in an acute catatonic schizophrenic patient. *International Journal of Psycho-Analysis*, 33:

Article citation:

Money-Kyrle, R. (1956) Normal counter-transference and some of its deviations. *International Journal of Psycho-Analysis*, 37:360–366

CHAPTER SIX

On counter-transference[1,2]

Annie Reich

The act of understanding the patient's productions in analysis and the ability to respond to them skilfully is not based solely on logical conclusions. Frequently the analyst can observe that insight into the material comes suddenly as if from somewhere within his own mind. Suddenly the confusing incomprehensible presentations make sense; suddenly the disconnected elements become a Gestalt. Equally suddenly, the analyst gets inner evidence as to what his interpretation should be and how it should be given. This type of understanding impresses one as something which is experienced almost passively; "it happens". It is not the result of an active process of thinking, like the solution of a mathematical problem. It seems obvious that this kind of insight into the patient's problem is achieved via the analyst's own unconscious. If is as if a partial and short-lived identification with the patient had taken place. The evidence of what is going on in the patient's unconscious, then, is based on an awareness of what is now going on in the analyst's own mind. But this identification has to be a short-lived one. The analyst has to be able to swing back to his outside position in order to be capable of an objective evaluation of what he has just now felt from within.

Anyhow, the tool for understanding is the analyst's own unconscious. When Freud advises that the analyst should listen with free floating attention, he has exactly this in mind. The material should be absorbed by the analyst's unconscious; there should not be any aim-directed censoring or conscious elimination through the analyst's attempts at rational thinking. This method of listening will guarantee the analyst's ability to remember, in an effortless way, those parts of the patient's previous material which connect with or serve to explain the new elements which are presented.

It is obvious what hazards may arise. If the analyst has some reasons of his own for being preoccupied, for being unable to associate freely, for shrinking back from certain topics, or if he is unable to identify with the patient, or has to identify to such a degree that he cannot put himself again outside the patient—to mention only a few of the possible difficulties—he will be unable to listen in this effortless way, to remember, to understand, to respond correctly.

Furthermore, there are more tasks for the analyst. He has to be the object of the patient's transference. He has to be the screen on to which the patient can project his infantile objects, to whom he can react with infantile emotions and impulses, or with defences against these. The analyst has to remain neutral in order to make this transference possible. He must not respond to the patient's emotion in kind. He must be able to tolerate love and aggression, adulation, temptation, seduction and so on, without being moved, without partiality, prejudice or disgust. It is, indeed, not an easy task to be able, on the one side, to feel oneself so deeply into another person as the analyst has to do in order to understand, and, at the same time, to remain uninvolved. Without having faced his own unconscious, his own ways and means of solving conflicts, that is, without being analysed himself, the analyst would not be able to live up to these difficult requirements.

To be neutral in relationship to the patient, to remain the screen, does not, of course, imply that the analyst has no relationship at all to the patient. We expect him to be interested in the patient, to have a friendly willingness to help him. He may like or dislike the patient. As far as these attitudes are conscious, they have not yet anything to do with counter-transference. If these feelings increase in intensity, we can be fairly certain that the unconscious feelings of the analyst, his own transferences on to the patient, i.e. counter-transferences, are mixed in. Intense dislike is frequently a reaction to not understanding the patient; or it may be based on deeper "real counter-transference". Too great, particularly sexualized, interest in the patient can most frequently be understood also as a counter-transference. We shall come back to this point.

A situation in which the analyst really falls in love with the patient is infrequent. In such a situation the analysis becomes impossible, and the patient should be sent to somebody else.

Counter-transference thus comprises the effects of the analyst's own unconscious needs and conflicts on his understanding or technique. In such cases the patient represents for the analyst an object of the past on to whom past feelings and wishes are projected, just as it happens in the patient's transference situation with the analyst. The provoking factor for such an occurrence may be something in the patient's personality or material or something in the analytic situation as such. This is counter-transference in the proper sense.

In a discussion before the psychoanalytic study group in Prague in 1938 between Dr Otto Fenichel and myself on the topic of counter-transference, which Dr Fenichel later on used as the basis of a paper entitled "The implications of the didactic analysis" (mimeographed by the Topeka Institute of Psychoanalysis), the conception of counter-transference was understood in a much wider sense. We included under this heading all expressions of the analyst's using the analysis for acting-out purposes.

We speak of acting out whenever the activity of analysing has an unconscious meaning for the analyst. Then his response to the patient, frequently his whole handling of the analytic situation, will be motivated by hidden unconscious tendencies. Though the patients in these cases are frequently not real objects on to whom something is transferred but only the tools by means of which some needs of the analyst, such as to allay anxiety or to master guilt-feelings, are gratified, we have used the term counter-transference. This seemed to us advisable because this type of behaviour is so frequently mixed up and fused with effects of counter-transference proper that it becomes too schematic to keep the two groups apart. The simplest cases in the proper sense of counter-transference are those which occur suddenly, under specific circumstances and with specific patients. These are, so to speak, acute manifestations of counter-transference. I give you a simple example which was related to me recently:

An analyst was ill, suffering pain but being able to continue work with the help of rather large doses of analgesics. One of his patients chose this time to accuse the analyst of neglecting her, of not giving her enough time, and so on. The complaints were brought forth with the nagging persistence of a demanding oral aggressive individual. The analyst became violently annoyed with the patient and had great difficulty in restraining the expression of his anger. What had been going on is fairly obvious. The analyst resented the fact that the patient was able to make these aggressive demands for attention while he, the analyst, was in a situation which would have justified similar demands, but he had to control himself. The unexpressed demands then tie up with deeper material which is irrelevant in this connexion.

The analyst is here in a special situation in which his mental balance is shaken by illness. In this condition, he cannot tolerate the patient who, as a mirror, reflects his own repressed impulses. The counter-transference reaction is based on an identification with the patient. Identifications of this kind belong to the most frequent forms of counter-transference.

Another example: a young analyst, not yet finished with his own training, feels irked by one of his patients and feels a desire to get rid of him. Why? The patient has expressed homosexual tendencies which the analyst is not inclined to face within himself. Here again the patient is the mirror that reflects something that is intolerable.

Counter-transference phenomena are by no means always manifestations of defence against the impulse, as in these last examples, but they may be simple impulse derivatives. I remember the case of a colleague who came for a second analysis because he had a tendency to fall in love with young attractive women patients. The analysis revealed that he was not really interested in these women but in identification with them, he wanted to be made love to by the analyst and in this way to gratify the homosexual transference fantasies which in his first analysis had remained unanalysed.

The sexual interest in the patient which could be called the most simple and direct manifestation of counter-transference is here the result of an identification with the patient. This is most typical. Most of the so-called "simple" manifestations of that kind are built after that pattern. The patients are not really the objects of deeper drives but they reflect the impulses of the analyst as if they were fulfilled. But identification is certainly not the only possible danger. At other times, for instance, one is faced with counter-transference reactions which are provoked by the specific content of the patient's material. For instance: certain material of a patient was understood by an analyst as a representation of the primal scene. Whenever the material was touched upon by the patient the analyst reacted to it with the defence reaction he had developed in the critical situation in his childhood: he became sleepy and had difficulties in concentrating and remembering.

Sometimes the disturbances are of a more general nature, not dependent on any special situation of the analyst or special material. It is the analytic relationship as such and some special aspects of the relationship to patients which cause the analyst to be disturbed by manifestations of counter-transference. For instance, an inclination to accept resistances at face value, a feeling of inability to attack or analyse them, was based, in two cases which I could observe in analysis, on an unconscious identification with the patient, just because he was in the position of a patient. The analyst expressed in that identification a passive masochistic wish (in one case, a homosexual one; in the other case, of a woman analyst, a predominantly masochistic one) to change places with the patient and to be in the passive position. Both were tempted to let themselves be accused and mistreated by the patient. In both cases, to be a patient corresponded to an infantile fantasy.

Such manifestations of counter-transference, of course, do not represent isolated episodes but reflect permanent neurotic difficulties of the analyst. Sometimes the counter-transference difficulties are only one expression of a general character problem of the analyst. For instance, unconscious aggression may cause the analyst to be over-conciliatory, hesitant and unable to be firm when necessary. Unconscious guilt feelings may express themselves in boredom or therapeutic overeagerness. These attitudes naturally represent serious handicaps for the analyst.

Another example of this kind is a paranoid attitude which makes the analyst concentrate on "motes" in other people's eyes in order not to see the "beams" in his own. This can degenerate into complete projection of his own contents or may remain within the frame of usefulness and enable the analyst to develop an uncanny sense of smell, so to speak, for these particular contents. He does not invent them in his patients but is able to unearth them, even if they exist only in minimal quantities. Obviously the analytic situation is a fertile field for such behaviour. This mechanism may originally even have created the interest in analysis. Frequently, though, the analytic situation is not the only battleground for these forces, which extend also to other fields of life. This attitude cannot be considered as a pure counter-transference phenomenon in the proper sense any more. It belongs more to the "acting out" group, which I mentioned earlier, and of which I would like to bring just one example:

> An analyst had the need to prove that he was not afraid of the unconscious, not afraid of his own unconscious drives. This led to a compulsion to "understand" the unconscious intellectually, as if to say: "Oh, I know and understand all that, I am not scared". This caused a tendency to preserve a safe distance from the patient's unconscious by helping to keep up an intellectual isolation and induced the analyst to overlook the patient's defence mechanisms like isolations. The aim of this acting out was, of course, to master the analyst's anxiety. Such mechanisms are double-edged. They work only for a certain time and tend to break down when the intensity of anxiety becomes too great. The analyst, being afraid of his breakdown, was frightened by any emotional breakthrough or outburst of anxiety in his patient and avoided anything which could help the patient to reach greater emotional depth. Under such conditions it became important not to identify himself with the patient at all, or, at least, only with the resistances, which then were not recognized as such but were taken at their face value, this again seriously interfering with the analyst's tasks.

The bad relationship of the analyst with his own unconscious may lead to constant doubt of the veracity of the expressions of the unconscious. Such a doubt is sometimes overcompensated by the extraordinary stress which is placed on any bit of unconscious material that can be recognized. Deep interpretations are then given in a compensatory way to overcome the analyst's doubts before the patient is ready for them. In other cases I have seen a fear of interpretations. I shall refrain from giving any other examples for "acting out" in order not to overburden the reader with too many details. But there is one more group that should be mentioned. Here the analyst misuses the analysis to get narcissistic gratifications and assurances for himself. A specific form of this kind might be called the "Midas touch". It is as if whatever the analyst touches was transformed into gold. He is a magic healer. He restores potency and undoes castration. His interpretations are magic gifts. His patients become geniuses just because they are his patients. It is obvious what enormous gratification the analyst can get from such an attitude and how dangerous it is. It easily can lead to unrealistic evaluations of the patients, to inability to observe soberly, to therapeutic overambition and hostility against the patient who fails to give his analyst the narcissistic gratification of becoming cured by him. In general, the slow cumbersome process of analysis makes high demands on the analyst's patience and narcissistic equilibrium. It is obvious how detrimental it may become if this equilibrium is shaky, that is, if the analyst depends on his patients for narcissistic supplies.

Related to this are attitudes which one might call pedagogic ones. The analyst feels tempted to fulfil thwarted infantile desires of patients and thus to teach them that the world is not as terrible as they in their childish ways of thinking assume. Thus anxiety is smoothed over, reassurance is given instead of real analysis of the anxiety. The psychotherapeutic past with which most of our students recently come to analytic training presents us frequently with tendencies of this kind.

I remember the case of a colleague, for instance, who would constantly answer all the questions of a patient relating to the analyst's private affairs. The analyst was unable to let a frustration situation come to a peak, which would have led into the analysis of the childhood situation. Instead, he had to gratify and reassure the patient. It was as if he were saying to the patient: "I am not treating you as you were treated, that is—mistreated—by your parents". which means: "I am not treating you as I was treated by my parents or by my former analyst. I am healing what they damaged". Sometimes pedagogic attitudes like this may stand under the opposite sign: "I shall treat you as I was treated. I will do to you what was done to me". Here something that was originally passively experienced is transformed into something which is actively done to somebody else. This is one of the most effective forms of anxiety mastering.

I shall not continue to enumerate and describe here how the variety of possible disturbances in the activity of analysing is as manifold as the whole psychopathology of neuroses, character disturbances included. In all similar types of behaviour in which the activity of analysing is used in some way for extraneous unconscious purposes, mostly in order to keep up the analyst's inner equilibrium, the patient, as I mentioned before, is not a real object but is only used as a fortuitous tool to solve a conflict situation. Fenichel has coined a specific term to describe this situation: the patient is used as a witness to whom the analyst has to prove, for instance, that he can master the unconscious, or that he has no reason to feel guilty.

Let me stop here and look back. I have given many more examples of the permanent kind than of the acute one. This may be due to the material available to me, which after all was mostly contributed by analysts who came to analysis on account of some difficulty—but I am almost inclined to believe that indeed most counter-transference difficulties are of the permanent type. It is obvious that the acute ones are much easier to deal with than the others. Frequently a bit of self-analysis can reveal what is going on and bring about a complete solution of the conflict. The permanent and more generalized forms are consequences of deeply engrained personality difficulties of the analyst for which there is only one solution: thorough analysis. Freud, in his paper "Analysis terminable and interminable", advises that the analyst after some years of practice should have some more analysis, even when the difficulties he has to struggle with are not as serious as those described. This is something we really should bear in mind.

The two forms of counter-transference manifestations could be compared with incidental hysterical symptoms in contrast to permanent character distortions. The attempt to keep these two types of counter-transference clearly separated is of course schematic. As mentioned before, there are transitions from one form to the other.

It would be impossible to attempt to give a complete description and classification of even the most frequent forms of counter-transference only. This would amount to a survey of the

ON COUNTER-TRANSFERENCE   103

psychopathology of the analyst. We are most concerned with the effect these psychological mechanisms have on analytic technique. Nearly all the phenomena mentioned will interfere with the analyst's ability to understand, to respond, to handle the patient, to interpret in the right way. But on the other hand, the special talent and the pathologic are usually just two sides of the same; a slight shift in cathexis may transform an unconscious mechanism of the analyst from a living out of his own conflicts into a valuable sublimation. On the other hand, what is the preliminary condition for his psychological interest and skill may degenerate into acting out.

It appears to me highly desirable to reach a closer understanding about the conditions under which these unconscious elements do constitute a foundation for adequate or even outstanding functioning and when they serve to interfere with or at least to complicate the activity of analysing. We said before that the unconscious of the analyst is his tool. The readiness and faculty to use his own unconscious in that way obviously must have some deeper motivation in the analyst's psychological make-up.

The analysis of these deeper motives, which, as we said, are the necessary basis for the analyst's interest, leads us back to the unconscious drives which were sublimated into psychological talent. Sometimes this personal origin of the analyst's interest in his work is clearly discernible even without analysis. I know, for instance, a number of analysts who, after many years of work, are still fascinated by their being entitled to pry into other people's secrets; that is to say, they are voyeurs; they live out their infantile sexual curiosity. Curiosity is seriously considered by many analysts as an essential prerequisite for analysis, but this curiosity has to be of a special nature. It has to be desexualized. If it were still connected with sexual excitement, this would necessarily interfere with the analyst's functioning. It must be, furthermore, removed from the original objects and has to be used for an interest in understanding their psychology and their structure. In this way the whole process is lifted above the original level of conflict.

I give here a piece of case material from the analysis of an analyst that throws some light on the psychologic background of such a sublimation; this may permit a somewhat deeper understanding of the structure of such a sublimation. The example I am choosing comes from a person who was capable and successful and had good therapeutic results. The counter-transference in his case, in spite of the rather pathological origin, was, one might say, tamed and harnessed for the benefit of the work. I shall limit myself to a few important elements.

One of the special gifts of this analyst was his keenness of observation, his ability to grasp little peculiarities of behaviour in his patients and to understand them—correctly—as expressions of an unconscious conflict. He was deeply interested in his work, to the exclusion of extraneous intellectual inclinations.

The genesis of his psychological interest could be reconstructed in analysis as follows: Dr X. from early childhood was again and again an unwilling witness of violent fights between unhappily married parents, which frightened him and brought forth the wish to reconcile them and to undo whatever damage might have been done in their battles, which were misunderstood by the child as sadistic primal scenes. The father, strong and powerful, but intellectually the mother's inferior, was "tearing pieces out of mother", as she complained whenever she wished to ward off his affectionate approaches. This left mother, the boy felt, castrated, sick, complaining and, at the same time, overambitious and demanding recompensation for her own deficiencies from her son, who had to become "magnificent" to fill her narcissistic needs. Too frightened to identify with the father in his sadistic activities, the child rather early identified with the mother and felt passive and castrated like her. A mild attack of poliomyelitis during the height of the Oedipal period served to engrave the mother identification more deeply. He now began to observe his own body as he had been observed anxiously by his mother who had been looking for signs of the illness. Overstress was now laid on any spark of masculinity, strength and perfection to contradict the inner awareness of his passivity and his fear of castration. In a partial regression he now became interested in his anal functions, following his mother here, too, who overanxiously watched his anal productions, willing to give him ample praise when she was satisfied. He now overevaluated himself just as his mother overevaluated him. At that time a peculiar fantasy appeared: he is one with mother as if he and she were one body. He is her most precious part, that is, he is her penis. By being "magnificent" as she wants him to be, his whole body becomes a big penis and in this way he undoes her castration. Both together they are complete.

This fantasy remained the basis for his tendency to self-observation, which thenceforward continued to exist. In this self-observation he plays two roles. He is identified with the anxious, castrated mother who watches him and at the same time he exhibits himself in order to gratify her. This narcissistic play now becomes a new source of gratification for himself. He is proud of his keenness of observation, his intelligence and knowledge. His thoughts are his mental products, of which he is as proud as of his anal achievements. In this way he is reconstructing what mother has lost. By self-observation he heals her castration in a magic way.

When he was nine, a little brother, the only other sibling, was born. This was a fulfilment of a desire for a child of his own which had already come to the fore in connection with his anal interests. Now he develops a motherly interest in the baby and succeeds in turning away his interest to a large degree from his own body to the baby and later to other outside objects. The self-observation turns into observation of other people, and thus the original play between him and mother is re-enacted by him in projection on to outside objects and thus becomes unselfish and objective. A necessary preliminary step in the direction of sublimation was made.

Furthermore, another important development can be now noticed. His interest in the little brother becomes a psychological one. He remembers a scene when the little one, not yet two years of age, had a temper tantrum, in his rage biting into the wood of the furniture. The older brother was very concerned about the intensity of emotion in the child and wondered what to do about it. Thus the interest which originally had to do with physical intactness had turned towards emotional experiences. The psychological interest from now on played an important role in his life. The decision to study medicine and to choose psychoanalysis as his specialty impresses us as a natural development of these interests. Here he can build up a stable sublimation of his peculiar strivings. He can now continue to observe, not himself, but other people. He can unearth their hidden defects and signs of castration and can use the technique of analysis for healing them. He has a special talent for understanding other people's unconscious and their hidden resistance. In the relationship with the patient he relives his original interplay with mother. By curing the patient he himself becomes cured and his mother's castration is undone. The cured patient represents himself as a wonderful phallus that has returned to mother. It is obvious what tremendous narcissistic stress he laid on being a "good analyst". In this new position, as a "magnificent" analyst, he represents his deepest ego-ideal as fulfilled, he is a phallic mother.

On a higher level, the patient also represents his child, his little brother, whom he wants to understand, in order to educate and help him.

The analytic faculties of this analyst are obviously based on an originally rather pathologic and narcissistic self-interest. That he is interested in a patient is based on a projection of this self-interest; but what he observes remains objective and does not represent a projection of inner experiences and fantasies. This faculty for objective observation has to do with the fact that Dr X., in spite of the at some time unstable boundaries between him and his mother, had had a warm and affectionate relationship with her and was capable of real object libidinal relationships. He sees what is there and not what is within himself, though his motive for seeing and his ability to understand are based primarily upon his preoccupation with the mother's and his own intactness or deficiency; though deep down he wants to be a magic healer he is able to content himself with the slow process of interpreting resistances, removing defences and unearthing the unconscious. Thus one can say that though his need to understand is the result of his highly pathological mother fixation he has succeeded in sublimating these infantile needs into true psychological interest. That he wishes to understand and to heal is motivated by the past. What he understands and how he tries to heal is based on objective reality. This is essential, as it represents the difference between acting out and a true sublimation.

I am aware that in representing this bit of case material I am not being fully successful in really shedding light on the finer prerequisites of this accomplishment. The problem why a sublimation is successful or not depends to a large degree on economic factors, and these are beyond the scope of this discussion. This is a problem, by the way, which is by no means specific for this type of sublimation. The wish to heal and the psychological interest could be traced in this material to specific infantile set-ups. I do not feel entitled to assume that the wish to heal is typically based on a similar conflict situation. A further investigation of the origin of the interest in psychology and healing in a more general way would be a challenging problem.

What is of interest for us here is the similarity and the difference of the well-functioning sublimation and the aforementioned types of acting out. Here as well as there deep personal needs are fulfilled. But while in this sublimation the fulfilment is achieved via the route of desexualized psychological insight this transformation has not taken place in the pathological forms of counter-transference.

The double-edged character of such a sublimation is obvious. The intensity of interest, the special faculty of understanding lead to a high quality of work, but any disturbance of psychic equilibrium may bring about a breakdown of the sublimation and the satisfaction of personal needs may become over-important so that the objectivity in the relationship to the patient becomes disturbed.

What I should like to stress is that in this case of undisturbed functioning the psychological interest obviously is based on a very complicated "counter-transference", which is desexualized and sublimated in character, while in the pathological examples the conflict persisted in its original form and the analytic situation was used either for living out the underlying impulses or defending against them or for proving that no damage has occurred in consequence of them.

Maybe we might come to the following conclusion: Counter-transference is a necessary prerequisite of analysis. If it does not exist, the necessary talent and interest is lacking. But it has to remain shadowy and in the background. This can be compared to the role that attachment to the mother plays in the normal object choice of the adult man. Loving was learned with the mother, certain traits in the adult object may lead back to her—but normally the object can be seen in its real character and responded to as such. A neurotic person takes the object absolutely for his mother or suffers because she is not his mother.

In the normally functioning analyst we find traces of the original unconscious meaning of analysing, while the neurotic one still misunderstands analysis under the influence of his unconscious fantasies and reacts accordingly.

Note

1. Read at the Midwinter Meeting of the American Psychoanalytic Association, New York City, December, 1949.

Article citation

2. Reich, A. (1951) On counter-transference. *International Journal of Psycho-Analysis, 32:* 25–31.

CHAPTER SEVEN

Current concepts of transference[1]

Elizabeth R. Zetzel

There are few current problems concerning the problem of transference that Freud did not recognize either implicitly or explicitly in the development of his theoretical and clinical framework. For all essential purposes, moreover, his formulations, in spite of certain shifts in emphasis, remain integral to contemporary psychoanalytic theory and practice. Recent developments mainly concern the impact of an ego-psychological approach; the significance of object relations, both current and infantile, external and internal; the role of aggression in mental life, and the part played by regression and the repetition compulsion in the transference. Nevertheless, analysis of the infantile Oedipal situation in the setting of a genuine transference neurosis is still considered a primary goal of psychoanalytic procedure.

Originally, transference was ascribed to displacement on to the analyst of repressed wishes and fantasies derived from early childhood. The transference neurosis was viewed as a compromise formation similar to dreams and other neurotic symptoms. Resistance, defined as the clinical manifestation of repression, could be diminished or abolished by interpretation mainly directed towards the content of the repressed. Transference resistance, both positive and negative, was ascribed to the threatened emergence of repressed unconscious material in the analytic situation. Soon, with the development of a structural approach, the superego described as the heir to the genital Oedipal situation was also recognized as playing a leading part in the transference situation. The analyst was subsequently viewed not only as the object by displacement of infantile incestuous fantasies, but also as the substitute by projection for the prohibiting parental figures which had been internalized as the definitive superego. The effect of transference interpretation in mitigating undue severity of the superego has, therefore, been emphasized in many discussions of the concept of transference.

Certain expansions in the structural approach related to increased recognition of the role of early object relations in the development of both ego and superego have affected current concepts of transference. In this connection, the significance of the analytic situation as a repetition of the early mother–child relationship has been stressed from different points of view. An equally important development relates to Freud's revised concept of anxiety which not only led to theoretical developments in the field of ego psychology, but also brought about related clinical changes in the work of many analysts. As a result, attention was no longer mainly focused on the content of the unconscious. In addition, increasing importance was attributed to the defensive processes by means of which the anxiety which would be engendered if repression and other related mechanisms were broken down, was avoided in the analytic situation. Differences in the interpretation of the role of the analyst and the nature of transference developed from emphasis, on the one hand, on the importance of early object relations, and on the other, from primary attention to the role of the ego and its defences. These defences first emerged clearly in discussion of the technique of child analysis, in which Melanie Klein (1927) and Anna Freud (1926), the pioneers in this field, played leading roles.

From a theoretical point of view, discussion foreshadowing the problems which face us today was presented in 1934 in well-known papers by Richard Sterba and James Strachey, and further elaborated at the Marienbad Symposium at which Edward Bibring (1937) made an important contribution. The importance of identification with, or introjection of, the analyst in the transference situation was clearly indicated. Therapeutic results were attributed to the effect of this process in mitigating the need for pathological defences. Strachey, however, considerably influenced by the work of Melanie Klein, regarded transference as essentially a projection on to the analyst of the patient's own superego. The therapeutic process was attributed to subsequent introjection of a modified superego as a result of "mutative" transference interpretation. Sterba (1934) and Bibring (1937), on the other hand, intimately involved with development of the ego-psychological approach, emphasized the central role of the ego, postulating a therapeutic split and identification with the analyst as an essential feature of transference. To some extent, this difference of opinion may be regarded as semantic. If the superego is explicitly defined as the heir of the genital Oedipus conflict, then earlier intra-systemic conflicts within the ego, although they may be related retrospectively to the definitive superego, must, nevertheless, be defined as contained within the ego. Later divisions within the ego of the type indicated by Sterba and very much expanded by Edward Bibring in his concept of therapeutic alliance between the analyst and the healthy part of the patient's ego, must also be excluded from superego significance. In contrast, those who attribute pregenital intra-systemic conflicts within the ego primarily to the introjection of objects, consider that the resultant state of internal conflict resembles in all dynamic respects the situation seen in later conflicts between ego and superego. They, therefore, believe that these structures develop simultaneously and suggest that no sharp distinction should be made between pre-Oedipal, Oedipal, and post-Oedipal superego.

The differences, however, are not entirely verbal, since those who attribute superego formation to the early months of life tend to attribute a significance to early object relations which differs from the conception of those who stress control and neutralization of instinctual energy as primary functions of the ego. This theoretical difference necessarily implies some disagreement as to the dynamic situation both in childhood and in adult life, inevitably reflected in the concept of transference and in hypotheses as to the nature of the therapeutic process. From one point of view, the role of the ego is central and crucial at every phase of analysis. A differentiation is made between transference as therapeutic alliance and the transference neurosis, which, on the whole, is considered a manifestation of resistance. Effective analysis depends on a sound therapeutic alliance, a prerequisite for which is the existence, before analysis, of a degree of mature ego functions, the absence of which in certain severely disturbed patients and in young children may preclude traditional psychoanalytic procedure.

Whenever indicated, interpretation must deal with transference manifestations, which means, in effect, that the transference must be analysed. The process of analysis, however, is not exclusively ascribed to transference interpretation. Other interpretations of unconscious material, whether related to defence or to early fantasy, will be equally effective provided they are accurately timed and provided a satisfactory therapeutic alliance has been made. Those, in contrast, who stress the importance of early object relations emphasize the crucial role of transference as an object relationship, distorted though this may be, by a variety of defences against primitive unresolved conflicts. The central role of the ego, both in the early stages of development and in the analytic process, is definitely accepted. The nature of the ego is, however, considered at all times to be determined by its external and internal objects. Therapeutic progress indicated by changes in ego function results, therefore, primarily from a change in object relations through interpretation of the transference situation. Less differentiation is made between transference as therapeutic alliance and the transference neurosis as a manifestation of resistance. Therapeutic progress depends almost exclusively on transference interpretation. Other interpretations, although indicated at times, are not, in general, considered an essential feature of the analytic process. From this point of view, the pre-analytic maturity of the patient's ego is not stressed as a prerequisite for analysis; children and relatively disturbed patients are considered potentially suitable for traditional psychoanalytic procedure.

These differences in theoretical orientation are not only reflected in the approach to children and disturbed patients. They may also be recognized in significant variations of technique in respect to all clinical groups, which inevitably affect the opening phases, under-standing of the inevitable regressive features of the transference neurosis, and handling of the terminal phases of analysis. I shall try to underline the main problems by emphasizing contrast, rather than similarity. I shall also try to avoid too detailed discussion of controversial theory regarding the nature of early ego development by a somewhat arbitrary differentiation between those who relate ego analysis to the analysis of defences and those who stress the primary significance of object relations both in the transference, and in the development and definitive structure of the ego. Needless to say, this involves some over-simplification. I hope, however, that it may, at the same time, clarify certain important issues. To take up first the analysis of patients generally agreed to be suitable for classical analytic procedure, the transference neuroses.

Those who emphasize the role of the ego and the analysis of defences, not only maintain Freud's conviction that analysis should proceed from surface to depth, but also consider that early material in the analytic situation derives, in general, from defensive processes rather than from displacement on to the analyst of early instinctual fantasies. Deep transference interpretation in the early phases of analysis will, therefore, either be meaningless to the patient since its unconscious significance is so inaccessible, or, if the defences are precarious, will lead to premature and possibly intolerable anxiety. Premature interpretation of the equally unconscious automatic defensive processes by means of which instinctual fantasy has been kept unconscious is also ineffective and undesirable. There are, however, differences of opinion within this group, as to how far analysis of defence can be separated from analysis of content. Waelder (1954), for example, has stressed the impossibility of such separation. Fenichel (1941), however, considered that at least theoretical separation should be made and indicated that, as far as possible, analysis of defence should precede analysis of unconscious fantasy. It is, nevertheless, generally agreed that the transference neurosis develops, as a rule, after ego defences have been sufficiently undermined to mobilize previously hidden instinctual conflict. During both the early stages of analysis, and at frequent points after the development of the transference neurosis, defence against the transference will become a main feature of the analytic situation.

This approach, as already indicated, is based on certain definite premises regarding the nature and function of the ego in respect to the control and neutralization of instinctual energy and unconscious fantasy. While the importance of early object relations is not neglected, the conviction that early transference interpretation is ineffective and potentially dangerous is related to the hypothesis that the instinctual energy available to the mature ego has been neutralized and is, for all effective purposes, relatively or absolutely divorced from its unconscious fantasy meaning at the beginning of analysis. In contrast, there are a number of analysts of differing theoretical orientation who do not view the development of the mature ego as a relative separation of ego functions from unconscious sources, but consider that unconscious fantasy continues to operate in all conscious mental activity. These analysts also tend on the whole to emphasize the crucial significance of primitive fantasy in respect to the development of the transference situation. The individual entering analysis will inevitably have unconscious fantasies concerning the analyst derived from primitive sources. This material, although deep in one sense, is, nevertheless, strongly current and accessible to interpretation. Mrs Klein (1948, 1952), in addition, relates the development and definitive structure of both ego and superego to unconscious fantasy determined by the earliest phases of object relationship. She emphasizes the role of early introjective and projective processes in relation to primitive anxiety ascribed to the death instinct and related aggressive fantasies. The unresolved difficulties and conflicts of the earliest period continue to colour object relations throughout life. Failure to achieve an essentially satisfactory object relationship in this early period, and failure to master relative loss of that object without retaining its good internal representative, will not only affect all object relations and definitive ego function, but more specifically determine the nature of anxiety-provoking fantasies on entering the analytic situation. According to this point of view, therefore, early transference interpretation, even though it may relate to fantasies derived from an early period of life, should result not in an increase, but a decrease of anxiety.

In considering next problems of transference in relation to analysis of the transference neurosis, two main points must be kept in mind. First, as already indicated, those who emphasize the analysis of defence tend to make a definite differentiation between transference as therapeutic alliance and the transference neurosis as a compromise formation which serves the purposes of resistance. In contrast, those who emphasize the importance of early object relations view the transference primarily as a revival or repetition, sometimes attributed to symbolic processes of early struggles in respect to objects. Here, no sharp differentiation is made between the early manifestations of transference and the transference neurosis. In view, moreover, of the weight given to the role of unconscious fantasy and internal objects in every phase of mental life, healthy and pathological functions, though differing in essential respects, do not differ with regard to their direct dependence on unconscious sources.

In the second place, the role of regression in the transference situation is subject to wide differences of opinion. It was, of course, one of Freud's earliest discoveries that regression to earlier points of fixation is a cardinal feature, not only in the development of neurosis and psychosis, but also in the revival of earlier conflicts in the transference situation. With the development of psychoanalysis and its application to an ever increasing range of disturbed personalities, the role of regression in the analytic situation has received increased attention. The significance of the analytic situation as a means of fostering regression as a prerequisite for the therapeutic work has been emphasized by Ida Macalpine (1950) in a recent paper. Differing opinions as to the significance, value, and technical handling of regressive manifestations form the basis of important modifications of analytic technique which will be considered presently. In respect, however, to the transference neuroses, the view recently expressed by Phyllis Greenacre (1954) that regression, an indispensable feature of the transference situation, is to be resolved by traditional technique would be generally accepted. It is also a matter of general agreement that a prerequisite for successful analysis is revival and repetition in the analytic situation of the struggles of primitive stages of development. Those who emphasize defence analysis, however, tend to view regression as a manifestation of resistance; as a primitive mechanism of defence employed by the ego in the setting of the transference neurosis. Analysis of these regressive manifestations with their potential dangers depends on the existing and continued functioning of adequate ego strength to maintain therapeutic alliance at an adult level. Those, in contrast, who stress the significance of transference as a revival of the early mother–child relationship do not emphasize regression as an indication of resistance or defence. The revival of these primitive experiences in the transference situation is, in fact, regarded as an essential prerequisite for satisfactory psychological maturation and true genitality. The Kleinian school, as already indicated, stress the continued activity of primitive conflicts in determining essential features of the transference at every stage of analysis. Their increasingly overt revival in the analytic situation, therefore, signifies a deepening of the analysis, and in general, is regarded as an indication of diminution rather than increase of resistance. The dangers involved according to this point of view are determined more by failure to mitigate primitive anxiety by suitable transference interpretation, than by failure to achieve, in the early phases of analysis, a sound therapeutic alliance based on the maturity of the patient's essential ego characteristics.

In considering, briefly, the terminal phases of analysis, many unresolved problems concerning the goal of therapy and definition of a completed psychoanalysis must be kept in mind. Distinction must also be made between the technical problems of the terminal phase and evaluation of transference resolution after the analysis has been terminated. There is widespread agreement as to the frequent revival in the terminal phases of primitive transference manifestations apparently resolved during the early phase of analysis. Balint (1952), and those who accept Ferenczi's concept of primary passive love, suggest that some gratification of primitive passive needs may be essential for successful termination. To Mrs Klein (1950) the terminal phases of analysis also represent a repetition of important features of the early mother–child relationship. According to her point of view, this period represents, in essence, a revival of the early weaning situation. Completion depends on a mastery of early depressive struggles culminating in successful introjection of the analyst as a good object. Although, in this connection, emphasis differs considerably, it should be noted that those who stress the importance of identification with the analyst as a basis for therapeutic alliance, also accept the inevitability of some permanent modifications of a similar nature. Those, however, who make a definite differentiation between transference and the transference neurosis stress the importance of analysis and resolution of the transference neurosis as a main prerequisite for successful termination. The identification based on therapeutic alliance must be interpreted and understood, particularly with reference to the reality aspects of the analyst's personality. In spite, therefore, of significant important differences, there are, as already indicated in connection with the earlier papers of Sterba and Strachey, important points of agreement in respect to the goal of psychoanalysis.

The differences already considered indicate some basic current problems of transference. So far, however, discussion has been limited to variations within the framework of a traditional technique. We must now consider problems related to overt modifications. Here it is essential to distinguish between variations introduced in respect to certain clinical conditions, often as a preliminary to classical psychoanalysis, and modifications based on changes in basic approach which lead to significant alterations with regard both to the method and to the aim of therapy. It is generally agreed that some variations of technique are indicated in the treatment of certain character neuroses, borderline patients, and the psychoses. The nature and meaning of such changes is, however, viewed differently according to the relative emphasis placed on the ego and its defences, on underlying unconscious conflicts, and on the significance and handling of regression in the therapeutic situation. In "Analysis terminable and interminable" (1937), Freud suggested that certain ego attributes may be inborn or constitutional and, therefore, probably inaccessible to psychoanalytic procedure. Hartmann (1946, 1950, 1952) has suggested that in addition to these primary attributes, other ego characteristics, originally developed for defensive purposes, and the related neutralized instinctual energy at the disposal of the ego, may be relatively or absolutely divorced from unconscious fantasy. This not only explains the relative inefficacy of early transference interpretation, but also hints at possible limitations in the potentialities of analysis attributable to secondary autonomy of the ego which is considered to be relatively irreversible. In certain cases, moreover, it is suggested that analysis of precarious or seriously pathological defences—particularly those concerned with the control of aggressive impulses—may be not only ineffective, but dangerous. The relative failure of ego development in such cases not only precludes the development of a genuine therapeutic alliance, but also raises the risk of a serious regressive, often predominantly hostile transference situation. In certain cases, therefore, a preliminary period of psychotherapy is recommended in order to explore the capacities of the patient to tolerate traditional psychoanalysis. In others, as Robert Knight (1954) in his paper on "Borderline states", and as many analysts working with psychotic patients have suggested, psychoanalytic procedure is not considered applicable. Instead, a therapeutic approach based on analytic understanding which, in essence, utilizes an essentially implicit positive transference as a means of reinforcing, rather than analysing the precarious defences of the individual, is advocated. In contrast, Herbert Rosenfeld (1952) has approached even severely disturbed psychotic patients with minimal modifications of psychoanalytic technique. Only changes which the severity of the patient's condition enforces are introduced. Here, the dangers of regression in therapy are not emphasized since primitive fantasy is considered to be active under all circumstances. The most primitive period is viewed in terms of early object relations with special stress on persecutory anxiety related to the death instinct. Interpretation of this primitive fantasy in the transference situation, as already indicated, is considered to diminish rather than to increase psychotic anxiety and to offer the best opportunity of strengthening the severely threatened psychotic ego. Other analysts, Dr Winnicott (1955), for example, attribute psychosis mainly to severe traumatic experiences, particularly of deprivation in early infancy. According to this point of view, profound regression offers an opportunity to fulfil, in the transference situation, primitive needs which had not been met at the appropriate level of development. Similar suggestions have been proposed by Margolin (1953) and others, in the concept of anaclitic treatment of serious psychosomatic disease. This approach is also based on the premise that the inevitable regression shown by certain patients should be utilized in therapy, as a means of gratifying, in an extremely permissive transference situation, demands which had not been met in infancy. It must, in this connection, be noted that the gratifications recommended in the treatment of severely disturbed patients are determined by the conviction that these patients are incapable of developing transference as we understand it in connection with neuroses and must therefore be handled by a modified technique.

The opinions so far considered, however much they may differ in certain respects, are nonetheless all based on the fundamental premise that an essential difference between analysis and other methods of therapy depends on whether or not interpretation of transference is an integral feature of technical procedure. Results based on the effects of suggestion are to be avoided, as far as possible, whenever traditional technique is employed. This goal has, however, proved more difficult to achieve than Freud expected when he first discerned the significance of symptomatic recovery based on positive transference. The importance of suggestion, even in the most strict analytic methods, has been repeatedly stressed by Edward Glover and others (1954, 1955).

Widespread and increasing emphasis as to the part played by the analyst's personality in determining the nature of the individual transference also implies recognition of unavoidable suggestive tendencies in the therapeutic process. Many analysts today believe that the classical conception of analytic objectivity and anonymity cannot be maintained. Instead, thorough analysis of reality aspects of the therapist's personality and point of view is advocated as an essential feature of transference analysis and an indispensable prerequisite for the dynamic changes already discussed in relation to the termination of analysis. It thus remains the ultimate goal of psychoanalysts, whatever their theoretical orientation, to avoid, as far as is humanly possible, results based on the unrecognized or unanalysed action of suggestion, and to maintain, as a primary goal, the resolution of such results through consistent and careful interpretation.

There are, however, a number of therapists, both within and outside the field of psychoanalysis, who consider that the transference situation should not be handled only or mainly as a setting for interpretation even in the treatment or analysis of neurotic patients. Instead, they advocate utilization of the transference relationship for the manipulation of corrective emotional experience. The theoretical orientation of those utilizing this concept of transference may be closer to, or more distant from, a Freudian point of view according to the degree to which current relationships are seen as determined by past events. At one extreme, current aspects and cultural factors are considered of predominant importance; at the other, mental development is viewed in essentially Freudian terms and modifications of technique are ascribed to inherent limitations of the analytic method rather than to essentially changed conceptions of the early phases of mental development. Of this group, Alexander (1925) is perhaps the best example. It is thirty years since, in his Salzburg paper, he indicated the tendency for patients to regress, even after apparently successful transference analysis of the Oedipal situation to narcissistic dependent pregenital levels which prove stubborn and refractory to transference interpretation. In his more recent work, the role of regression in the transference situation has been increasingly stressed. The emergence and persistence of dependent, pregenital demands in a very wide range of clinical conditions, it is argued, indicates that the encouragement of a regressive transference situation is undesirable and therapeutically ineffective. The analyst, therefore should when this threatens, adopt a definite role explicitly differing from the behaviour of the parents in early childhood in order to bring about therapeutic results through a corrective emotional experience in the transference situation. This, it is suggested, will obviate the tendency to regression, thus curtailing the length of treatment and improving therapeutic results. Limitation of regressive manifestations by active steps modifying traditional analytic procedure in a variety of ways is also frequently indicated, according to this point of view.

It will be clear that to those who maintain the conviction that interpretation of all transference manifestations remains an essential feature of psychoanalysis, the type of modification here described, even though based on a Freudian reconstruction of the early phases of mental development, represents a major modification. It is determined by a conviction that psychoanalysis, as a therapeutic method, has limitations related to the tendency to regression, which cannot be resolved by traditional technique. Moreover, the fundamental premise on which the conception of corrective emotional experience is based minimizes the significance of insight and recall. It is, essentially, suggested that corrective emotional experience alone may bring about qualitative dynamic alterations in mental structure, which can lead to a satisfactory therapeutic goal. This implies a definite modification of the analytic hypothesis that current problems are determined by the defences against instinctual impulses and/or internalized objects which had been set up during the decisive periods of early development. An analytic result therefore depends on the revival, repetition and mastery of earlier conflicts in the current experience of the transference situation with insight an indispensable feature of an analytic goal.

Since certain important modifications are related to the concept of regression in the transference situation, I should like briefly to consider this concept in relation to the repetition compulsion. That transference, essentially a revival of earlier emotional experience, must be regarded as a manifestation of the repetition compulsion is generally accepted. It is, however, necessary to distinguish between repetition compulsion as an attempt to master traumatic experience and repetition compulsion as an attempt to return to a real or fantasied earlier state of rest or gratification. Lagache, in a recent paper, has related the repetition compulsion to an inherent need to return to any problem previously left unsolved. From this point of view, the regressive aspects of the transference situation are to be regarded as a necessary preliminary to the mastery of unresolved conflict. From the second point of view, however, the regressive aspects of transference are mainly attributed to a wish to return to an earlier state of rest or narcissistic gratification, to the maintenance of the status quo in preference to any progressive action, and finally, to Freud's original conception of the death instinct. There is a good deal to suggest that both aspects of the repetition compulsion may be seen in the regressive aspects of every analysis. To those who feel that regressive self-destructive forces tend to be stronger than progressive libidinal impulses, the potentialities of the analytic approach will inevitably appear to be limited. Those, in contrast, who regard the reappearance in the transference situation of earlier conflicts as an indication of tendencies to master and progress will continue to feel that the classical analytic method remains the optimal approach to psychological illness wherever it is applicable.

To conclude: I have tried in this paper to outline some current problems of transference both in relation to the history of psycho-analytic thought and in relation to the theoretical premises on which they are based. With regard to contemporary views which advocate serious modification of analytic technique, I cannot improve on the remarks made by Ernest Jones (1925) in his Introduction to the Salzburg Symposium thirty years ago. "Depreciation of the Freudian (infantile) factors at the expense of the pre-Freudian (pre-infantile and post-infantile) is a highly characteristic manifestation of the general human resistance against the former, being usually a flight from the Oedipus conflict which is the centre of infantile factors. We also note that the practice of psychoanalysis does not always insure immunity from this reaction". With regard, finally, to the important problems which arise from genuine scientific differences within the framework of traditional technique, I have tried to focus the issues for discussion by emphasizing as objectively as possible divergence rather than agreement. I should like, however, to close on a more personal note. I have had the unusual opportunity over the past ten years to observe at close quarters impressive achievements by analysts of widely divergent theoretical orientation. All of them are in complete agreement as to the primary importance of transference analysis. None have accepted any significant modifications of traditional technique as a means of either shortening analysis or accepting a modified analytic goal. All finally agree as to the basic importance of understanding the significance and possible dangers of counter-transference manifestations. Unfortunately, however, this vitally important unconscious reaction is not limited to the individual analytic situation. It may also be aroused in respect to scientific theories both within and outside our special field of knowledge. Just as, therefore, resolution of the individual transference situation depends on the analyst's understanding of his own counter-transference, so too, similar insight and objectivity on a wider scale may determine resolution of the problems I have outlined today.

Note

1. Contribution to the Discussion of Problems of Transference. 19th International Psycho-Analytical Congress at Geneva, 24–28 July, 1955.

References

Alexander, F. (1925). Contribution to the symposium held at the Eighth International Psycho-Analytic Congress, Salzburg, 21 April, 1924. In: *International Journal of Psycho-Analysis, 6*: 13–34.
Balint, M. (1952). *Primary Love and Psycho-Analytic Technique.* London: Hogarth.
Bibring, E. (1937). Therapeutic results of psycho-analysis. *International Journal of Psycho-Analysis, 18*: 170–189.

Fenichel, O. (1941). Problems of psychoanalytic technique. *Psychoanalytic Quarterly.*

Freud, A. (1926). *Introduction to the technique in the analysis of children* (Vienna): *The Psychoanalytic Treatment of Children.* Imago, 1945.

Freud, S. (1937). Analysis terminable and interminable. *Collected Papers V.* London: Hogarth.

Glover, E. (1954). Therapeutic criteria of psychoanalysis. *International Journal of Psycho-Analysis.*

Glover, E. (1955). *The Technique of Psychoanalysis.* New York: International Universities Press.

Greenacre, P. (1954). The role of transference. Practical considerations in relation to psycho-analytic therapy. *Journal of the American Psychoanalytic Association,* 2: 671–684.

Hartmann, H. (1950). Psychoanalysis and development psychology. *Psychoanal. Study Child V.* New York: International Universities Press.

Hartmann, H. (1952). The mutual influences in the development of ego and id. *Psychoanal. Study Child VII.* New York: International Universities Press.

Hartmann, H., Kris, E., & Loewenstein, R. (1946). Comments on the formation of psychic structure. *Psychoanal. Study Child II.* New York: International Universities Press.

Jones, E. (1925). Introduction to the symposium on theories of therapeutic results. *International Journal of Psycho-Analysis,* 6: 1–4.

Klein, M. (1927). Symposium on child analysis. In: *Contributions to Psychoanalysis 1941–1945.* London: Hogarth, 1948.

Klein, M. (1948). *Contribution to Psychoanalysis 1941–1945.* London: Hogarth.

Klein, M. (1950). On the criteria for the termination of an analysis. *International Journal of Psycho-Analysis,* 31: Part 3.

Klein, M., et al. (1952). *Developments in Psychoanalysis.* London: Hogarth.

Knight, R. (1954). Borderline States. *Psychoanalytic Psychiatry and Psychology,* 1: 97–109.

Lagache, D. Quelques aspects du transfert (Some aspects of transference). *Revue Française de Psychanalyse,* 15: 407–424.

Macalpine, I. (1950). The Development of the transference. *Psychoanalytic Quarterly,* 19: 501–519.

Margolin, S. (1958). Genetic and dynamic psycho-physiological determinants of pathophysiological processes. In: F. Deutsch (Ed.), *The Psychosomatic Concept in Psychoanalysis* (pp. 8–35). New York: International Universities Press.

Rosenfeld, H. (1952). Transference-phenomena and transference-analysis in an acute catatonic schizophrenic patient. *International Journal of Psycho-Analysis, 33*: 457–464.

Sterba, R. (1934). The fate of the ego in analytic therapy. *International Journal of Psycho-Analysis, 15*: 117–126.

Strachey, J. (1934). The nature of the therapeutic action of psycho-analysis. *International Journal of Psycho-Analysis, 15*: 130–137.

Waelder, R. (1954). Contribution to panel on defence mechanisms and psychoanalytic technique. Mid-Winter meeting of the American Psychoanalytic Association 1953. *Journal of the American Psychoanalytic Association*.

Winnicott, D. W. (1955). Metapsychological and clinical aspects of regression within the psycho-analytical set-up. *International Journal of Psycho-Analysis, 36*: 16–26.

Article citation

Zetzel, E. (1956). Current concepts of transference. *International Journal of Psycho-Analysis, 37*: 369–375.

CHAPTER EIGHT

Attacks on linking[1]

W. R. Bion

In previous papers (1957a) I have had occasion, in talking of the psychotic part of the personality, to speak of the destructive attacks which the patient makes on anything which is felt to have the function of linking one object with another. It is my intention in this paper to show the significance of this form of destructive attack in the production of some symptoms met with in borderline psychosis.

The prototype for all the links of which I wish to speak is the primitive breast or penis. The paper presupposes familiarity with Melanie Klein's descriptions of the infant's fantasies of sadistic attacks upon the breast (1934), of the infant's splitting of its objects, of projective identification, which is the name she gives to the mechanism by which parts of the personality are split off and projected into external objects, and finally her views on early stages of Oedipus complex (1928). I shall discuss phantasied attacks on the breast as the prototype of all attacks on objects that serve as a link and projective identification as the mechanism employed by the psyche to dispose of the ego fragments produced by its destructiveness.

I shall first describe clinical manifestations in an order dictated not by the chronology of their appearance in the consulting room, but by the need for making the exposition of my thesis as clear as I can. I shall follow this by material selected to demonstrate the order which these mechanisms assume when their relationship to each other is determined by the dynamics of the analytic situation. I shall conclude with theoretical observations on the material presented. The examples are drawn from the analysis of two patients and are taken from an advanced stage of their analyses. To preserve anonymity I shall not distinguish between the patients and shall introduce distortions of fact which I hope do not impair the accuracy of the analytic description.

Observation of the patient's disposition to attack the link between two objects is simplified because the analyst has to establish a link with the patient and does this by verbal communication and his equipment of psychoanalytical experience. Upon this the creative relationship depends and therefore we should be able to see attacks being made upon it.

I am not concerned with typical resistance to interpretations, but with expanding references which I made in my paper on "The differentiation of the psychotic from the non-psychotic part of the personality" (1957a) to the destructive attacks on verbal thought itself.

Clinical examples

I shall now describe occasions which afforded me an opportunity to give the patient an interpretation, which at that point he could understand, of conduct designed to destroy whatever it was that linked two objects together.

These are the examples:

(i) I had reason to give the patient an interpretation making explicit his feelings of affection and his expression of them to his mother for her ability to cope with a refractory child. The patient attempted to express his agreement with me, but although he needed to say only a few words his expression of them was interrupted by a very pronounced stammer which had the effect of spreading out his remark over a period of as much as a minute and a half. The actual sounds emitted bore resemblance to gasping for breath; gaspings were interspersed with gurgling sounds as if he were immersed in water. I drew his attention to these sounds and he agreed that they were peculiar and himself suggested the descriptions I have just given.

(ii) The patient complained that he could not sleep. Showing signs of fear, he said, "It can't go on like this". Disjointed remarks gave the impression that he felt superficially that some catastrophe would occur, perhaps akin to insanity, if he could not get more sleep. Referring to material in the previous session I suggested that he feared he would dream if he were to sleep. He denied this and said he could not think because he was wet. I reminded him of his use of the term "wet" as an expression of contempt for somebody he regarded as feeble and sentimental. He disagreed and indicated that the state to which he referred was the exact opposite. From what I knew of this patient I felt that his correction at this point was valid and that somehow the wetness referred to an expression of hatred and envy such as he associated with urinary attacks on an object. I therefore said that in addition to the superficial fear which he had expressed he was afraid of sleep because for him it was the same thing as the oozing away of his mind itself. Further associations showed that he felt that good interpretations from me were so consistently and minutely split up by him that they became mental urine which then seeped uncontrollably away. Sleep was therefore inseparable from unconsciousness, which was itself identical with a state of mindlessness which could not be repaired. He said, "I am dry now". I replied that he felt he was awake and capable of thought, but that this good state was only precariously maintained.

(iii) In this session the patient had produced material stimulated by the preceding week-end break. His awareness of such external stimuli had become demonstrable at a comparatively recent stage of the analysis. Previously it was a matter for conjecture how much he was capable of appreciating reality. I knew that he had contact with reality because he came for analysis by himself, but that fact could hardly be deduced from his behaviour in the sessions. When I interpreted some associations as evidence that he felt he had been and still was witnessing an intercourse between two people, he reacted as if he had received a violent blow. I was not then able to say just where he had experienced the assault and even in retrospect I have no clear impression. It would seem logical to suppose that the shock had been administered by my interpretation and that therefore the blow came from without, but my impression is that he felt it as delivered from within; the patient often experienced what he described as a stabbing attack from inside. He sat up and stared intently into space. I said that he seemed to be seeing something. He replied that he could not see what he saw. I was able from previous experience to interpret that he felt he was "seeing" an invisible object and subsequent experience convinced me that in the two patients on whose analysis I am depending for material for this paper, events occurred in which the patient experienced invisible–visual hallucinations. I shall give my reasons later for supposing that in this and the previous example similar mechanisms were at work.

(iv) In the first twenty minutes of the session the patient made three isolated remarks which had no significance for me. He then said that it seemed that a girl he had met was understanding. This was followed at once by a violent, convulsive movement which he affected to ignore. It appeared to be identical with the kind of stabbing attack I mentioned in the last example. I tried to draw his attention to the movement, but he ignored my intervention as he ignored the attack. He then said that the room was filled with a blue haze. A little later he remarked that the haze had gone, but said he was depressed. I interpreted that he felt understood by me. This was an agreeable experience, but the pleasant feeling of being understood had been instantly destroyed and ejected. I reminded him that we had recently witnessed his use of the word "blue" as a compact description of vituperative sexual conversation. If my interpretation was correct, and subsequent events suggested that it was, it meant that the experience of being understood had been split up, converted into particles of sexual abuse and ejected. Up to this point I felt that the interpretation approximated closely to his experience. Later interpretations, that the disappearance of the haze was due to reintrojection and conversion into depression, seemed to have less reality for the patient, although later events were compatible with its being correct.

(v)   The session, like the one in my last example, began with three
      or four statements of fact such as that it was hot, that his train
      was crowded, and that it was Wednesday; this occupied thirty
      minutes. An impression that he was trying to retain contact
      with reality was confirmed when he followed up by saying that
      he feared a breakdown. A little later he said I would not
      understand him. I interpreted that he felt I was bad and would
      not take in what he wanted to put into me. I interpreted in these
      terms deliberately because he had shown in the previous
      session that he felt that my interpretations were an attempt to
      eject feelings that he wished to deposit in me. His response to
      my interpretation was to say that he felt there were two
      probability clouds in the room. I interpreted that he was trying
      to get rid of the feeling that my badness was a fact. I said it
      meant that he needed to know whether I was really bad or
      whether I was some bad thing which had come from inside
      him. Although the point was not at the moment of central
      significance I though the patient was attempting to decide
      whether he was hallucinated or not. This recurrent anxiety in
      his analysis was associated with his fear that envy and hatred
      of a capacity for understanding was leading him to take in a
      good, understanding object to destroy and eject it—a procedure
      which had often led to persecution by the destroyed and ejected
      object. Whether my refusal to understand was a reality or
      hallucination was important only because it determined what
      painful experiences were to be expected next.

(vi) Half the session passed in silence; the patient then announced
      that a piece of iron had fallen on the floor. Thereafter he made a
      series of convulsive movements in silence as if he felt he was
      being physically assaulted from within. I said he could not
      establish contact with me because of his fear of what was going
      on inside him. He confirmed this by saying that he felt he was
      being murdered. He did not know what he would do without
      the analysis as it made him better. I said that he felt so envious
      of himself and of me for being able to work together to make
      him feel better that he took the pair of us into him as a dead
      piece of iron and a dead floor that came together not to give
      him life but to murder him. He became very anxious and said
      he could not go on. I said that he felt he could not go on because

he was either dead, or alive and so envious that he had to stop good analysis. There was a marked decrease of anxiety, but the remainder of the session was taken up by isolated statements of fact which again seemed to be an attempt to preserve contact with external reality as a method of denial of his phantasies.

Features common to the above illustrations

These episodes have been chosen by me because the dominant theme in each was the destructive attack on a link. In the first the attack was expressed in a stammer which was designed to prevent the patient from using language as a bond between him and me. In the second sleep was felt by him to be identical with projective identification that proceeded unaffected by any possible attempt at control by him. Sleep for him meant that his mind, minutely fragmented, flowed out in an attacking stream of particles.

The examples I give here throw light on schizophrenic dreaming. The psychotic patient appears to have no dreams, or at least not to report any, until comparatively late in the analysis. My impression now is that this apparently dreamless period is a phenomenon analogous to the invisible–visual hallucination. That is to say, that the dreams consist of material so minutely fragmented that they are devoid of any visual component. When dreams are experienced which the patient can report because visual objects have been experienced by him in the course of the dream, he seems to regard these objects as bearing much the same relationship to the invisible objects of the previous phase as faeces seem to him to bear to urine. The objects appearing in experiences which we call dreams are regarded by the patient as solid and are, as such, contrasted with the contents of the dreams which were a continuum of minute, invisible fragments.

At the time of the session the main theme was not an attack on the link but the consequences of such an attack, previously made, in leaving him bereft of a state of mind necessary for the establishment of a satisfying relationship between him and his bed. Though it did not appear in the session I report, uncontrollable projective identification, which was what sleep meant to him, was thought to be a destructive attack on the state of mind of the coupling parents. There was therefore a double anxiety; one arising from his fear that he was being rendered mindless, the other from his fear that he was unable to control his hostile attacks, his mind providing the ammunition, on the state of mind that was the link between the parental pair. Sleep and sleeplessness were alike unacceptable.

In the third example in which I described visual hallucinations of invisible objects, we witness one form in which the actual attack on the sexual pair is delivered. My interpretation, as far as I could judge, was felt by him as if it were his own visual sense of a parental intercourse; this visual impression is minutely fragmented and ejected at once in particles so minute that they are the invisible components of a continuum. The total procedure has served the purpose of forestalling an experience of feelings of envy for the parental state of mind by the instantaneous expression of envy in a destructive act. I shall have more to say of this implicit hatred of emotion and the need to avoid awareness of it.

In my fourth example, the report of the understanding girl and the haze, my understanding and his agreeable state of mind have been felt as a link between us which could give rise to a creative act. The link had been regarded with hate and transformed into a hostile and destructive sexuality rendering the patient–analyst couple sterile.

In my fifth example, of the two probability clouds, a capacity for understanding is the link which is being attacked, but the interest lies in the fact that the object making the destructive attacks is alien to the patient. Furthermore, the destroyer is making an attack on projective identification which is felt by the patient to be a method of communication. In so far as my supposed attack on his methods of communication is felt as possibly secondary to his envious attacks on me, he does not dissociate himself from feelings of guilt and responsibility. A further point is the appearance of judgement, which Freud regards as an essential feature of the dominance of the reality principle, among the ejected parts of the patient's personality. The fact that there were two probability clouds remained unexplained at the time, but in subsequent sessions I had material which led me to suppose that what had originally been an attempt to separate good from bad survived in the existence of two objects, but they were now similar in that each was a mixture of good and bad. Taking into consideration material from later sessions, I can draw conclusions which were not possible at the time; his capacity for judgment, which had been split up and destroyed with the rest of his ego and then ejected, was felt by him to be similar to other bizarre objects of the kind which I have described in my paper on "The differentiation of the psychotic from the non-psychotic parts of the personality". These ejected particles were feared because of the treatment he had accorded them. He felt that the alienated judgment—the probability clouds—indicated that I was probably bad. His suspicion that the probability clouds were persecutory and hostile led him to doubt the value of the guidance they afforded him. They might supply him with a correct assessment or a deliberately false one, such as that a fact was an hallucination or *vice versa*; or would give rise to what, from a psychiatric point of view, we would call delusions. The probability clouds themselves had some qualities of a primitive breast and were felt to be enigmatic and intimidating.

In my sixth illustration, the report that a piece of iron had fallen on the floor, I had no occasion for interpreting an aspect of the material with which the patient had by this time become familiar. (I should perhaps say that experience had taught me that there were times when I assumed the patient's familiarity with some aspect of a situation with which we were dealing, only to discover that, in spite of the work that had been done upon it, he had forgotten it.) The familiar point that I did not interpret, but which is significant for the understanding of this episode, is that the patient's envy of the parental couple had been evaded by his substitution of himself and myself for the parents. The evasion failed, for the envy and hatred were now directed against him and me. The couple engaged in a creative act are felt to be sharing an enviable, emotional experience; he, being identified also with the excluded party, has a painful, emotional experience as well. On many occasions the patient, partly through experiences of the kind which I describe in this episode, and partly for reasons on which I shall enlarge later, had a hatred of emotion, and therefore, by a short extension, of life itself. This hatred contributes to the murderous attack on that which links the pair, on the pair itself and on the object generated by the pair. In the episode I am describing, the patient is suffering the consequences of his early attacks on the state of mind that forms the link between the creative pair and his identification with both the hateful and creative states of mind.

In this and the preceding illustration there are elements that suggest the formation of a hostile persecutory object, or agglomeration of objects, which expresses its hostility in a manner which is of great importance in producing the predominance of psychotic mechanisms in a patient; the characteristics with which I have already invested the agglomeration of persecutory objects have the quality of a primitive, and even murderous, superego.

Curiosity, arrogance and stupidity

In the paper I presented at the International Congress of 1957 (1957b) I suggested that Freud's analogy of an archaeological investigation with a psychoanalysis was helpful if it were considered that we were exposing evidence not so much of a primitive civilization as of a primitive disaster. The value of the analogy is lessened because in the analysis we are confronted not so much with a static situation that permits leisurely study, but with a catastrophe that remains at one and the same moment actively vital and yet incapable of resolution into quiescence. This lack of progress in any direction must be attributed in part to the destruction of a capacity for curiosity and the consequent inability to learn, but before I go into this I must say something about a matter that plays hardly any part in the illustrations I have given.

Attacks on the link originate in what Melanie Klein calls the paranoid–schizoid phase. This period is dominated by part-object relationships (8). If it is borne in mind that the patient has a part-object relationship with himself as well as with objects not himself, it contributes to the understanding of phrases such as "it seems" which are commonly employed by the deeply disturbed patient on occasions when a less disturbed patient might say "I think" or "I believe". When he says "it seems" he is often referring to a feeling— an "it seems" feeling—which is a part of his psyche and yet is not observed as part of a whole object. The conception of the part-object as analogous to an anatomical structure, encouraged by the patient's employment of concrete images as units of thought, is misleading because the part-object relationship is not with the anatomical structures only but with function, not with anatomy but with physiology, not with the breast but with feeding, poisoning, loving, hating. This contributes to the impression of a disaster that is dynamic and not static. The problem that has to be solved on this early, yet superficial, level must be stated in adult terms by the question, "What is something?" and not the question "Why is something?" because "why" has, through guilt, been split off. Problems, the solution of which depends upon an awareness of causation, cannot therefore be stated, let alone solved. This produces a situation in which the patient appears to have no problems except those posed by the existence of analyst and patient. His preoccupation is with what is this or that function, of which he is aware though unable to grasp the totality of which the function is a part. It follows that there is never any question why the patient or the analyst is there, or why something is said or done or felt, nor can there be any question of attempting to alter the causes of some state of mind. ... Since "what?" can never be answered without "how?" or "why?" further difficulties arise. I shall leave this on one side to consider the mechanisms employed by the infant to solve the problem "what?" when it is felt in relation to a part-object relationship with a function.

Denial of normal degrees of projective identification

I employ the term "link" because I wish to discuss the patient's relationship with a function rather than with the object that subserves a function; my concern is not only with the breast, or penis, or verbal thought, but with their function of providing the link between two objects.

In her Notes on Some Schizoid Mechanisms (1946) Melanie Klein speaks of the importance of an excessive employment of splitting and projective identification in the production of a very disturbed personality. She also speaks of "the introjection of the good object, first of all the mother's breast" as a "precondition for normal development". I shall suppose that there is a normal degree of projective identification, without defining the limits within which normality lies, and that associated with introjective identification this is the foundation on which normal development rests.

This impression derives partly from a feature in a patient's analysis which was difficult to interpret because it did not appear to be sufficiently obtrusive at any moment for an interpretation to be supported by convincing evidence. Throughout the analysis the patient resorted to projective identification with a persistence suggesting it was a mechanism of which he had never been able sufficiently to avail himself; the analysis afforded him an opportunity for the exercise of a mechanism of which he had been cheated. I did not have to rely on this impression alone. There were sessions which led me to suppose that the patient felt there was some object that denied him the use of projective identification. In the illustrations I have given, particularly in the first, the stammer, and the fourth, the understanding girl and the blue haze, there are elements which indicate that the patient felt that parts of his personality that he wished to repose in me were refused entry by me, but there had been associations prior to this which led me to this view.

When the patient strove to rid himself of fears of death which were felt to be too powerful for his personality to contain he split off his fears and put them into me, the idea apparently being that if they were allowed to repose there long enough they would undergo modification by my psyche and could then be safely reintrojected. On the occasion I have in mind the patient had felt, probably for reasons similar to those I give in my fifth illustration, the probability clouds, that I evacuated them so quickly that the feelings were not modified, but had become more painful.

Associations from a period in the analysis earlier than that from which these illustrations have been drawn showed an increasing intensity of emotions in the patient. This originated in what he felt was my refusal to accept parts of his personality. Consequently he strove to force them into me with increased desperation and violence. His behaviour, isolated from the context of the analysis, might have appeared to be an expression of primary aggression. The more violent his phantasies of projective identification, the more frightened he became of me. There were sessions in which such behaviour expressed unprovoked aggression, but I quote this series because it shows the patient in a different light, his violence a reaction to what he felt was my hostile defensiveness. The analytic situation built up in my mind a sense of witnessing an extremely early scene. I felt that the patient had experienced in infancy a mother who dutifully responded to the infant's emotional displays. The dutiful response had in it an element of impatient "I don't know what's the matter with the child". My deduction was that in order to understand what the child wanted the mother should have treated the infant's cry as more than a demand for her presence. From the infant's point of view she should have taken into her, and thus experienced, the fear that the child was dying. It was this fear that the child could not contain. He strove to split it off together with the part of the personality in which it lay and project it into the mother. An understanding mother is able to experience the feeling of dread, that this baby was striving to deal with by projective identification, and yet retain a balanced outlook. This patient had had to deal with a mother who could not tolerate experiencing such feelings and reacted either by denying them ingress, or alternatively by becoming a prey to the anxiety which resulted from introjection of the infant's feelings. The latter reaction must, I think, have been rare: denial was dominant.

To some this reconstruction will appear to be unduly fanciful; to me it does not seem forced and is the reply to any who may object that too much stress is placed on the transference to the exclusion of a proper elucidation of early memories.

In the analysis a complex situation may be observed. The patient feels he is being allowed an opportunity of which he had hitherto been cheated; the poignancy of his deprivation is thereby rendered the more acute and so are the feelings of resentment at the deprivation. Gratitude for the opportunity coexists with hostility to the analyst as the person who will not understand and refuses the patient the use of the only method of communication by which he feels he can make himself understood. Thus the link between patient and analyst, or infant and breast, is the mechanism of projective identification. The destructive attacks upon this link originate in a source external to the patient or infant, namely the analyst or breast. The result is excessive projective identification by the patient and a deterioration of his developmental processes.

I do not put forward this experience as the cause of the patient's disturbance; that finds its main source in the inborn disposition of the infant as I described it in my paper on "The differentiation of the psychotic from the non-psychotic part of the personality" (1957a). I regard it as a central feature of the environmental factor in the production of the psychotic personality.

Before I discuss this consequence for the patient's development, I must refer to the inborn characteristics and the part that they play in producing attacks by the infant on all that links him to the breast, namely, primary aggression and envy. The seriousness of these attacks is enhanced if the mother displays the kind of unreceptiveness which I have described, and is diminished, but not abolished, if the mother can introject the infant's feelings and remain balanced (Klein, 1957); the seriousness remains because the psychotic infant is overwhelmed with hatred and envy of the mother's ability to retain a comfortable state of mind although experiencing the infant's feelings. This was clearly brought out by a patient who insisted that I must go through it with him, but was filled with hate when he felt I was able to do so without a breakdown. Here we have another aspect of destructive attacks upon the link, the link being the capacity of the analyst to introject the patient's projective identifications. Attacks on the link, therefore, are synonymous with attacks on the analyst's, and originally the mother's, peace of mind. The capacity to introject is transformed by the patient's envy and hate into greed devouring the patient's psyche; similarly, peace of mind becomes hostile indifference. At this point analytic problems arise through the patient's employment (to destroy the peace of mind that is so much envied) of acting out, delinquent acts and threats of suicide.

Consequences

To review the main features so far: the origin of the disturbance is twofold. On the one hand there is the patient's inborn disposition to excessive destructiveness, hatred, and envy: on the other the environment which, at its worst, denies to the patient the use of the mechanisms of splitting and projective identification. On some occasions the destructive attacks on the link between patient and environment, or between different aspects of the patient's personality, have their origin in the patient; on others, in the mother, although in the latter instance and in psychotic patients, it can never be in the mother alone. The disturbances commence with life itself.

The problem that confronts the patient is: What are the objects of which he is aware? These objects, whether internal or external, are in fact part-objects and predominantly, though not exclusively, what we should call functions and not morphological structures. This is obscured because the patient's thinking is conducted by means of concrete objects and therefore tends to produce, in the sophisticated mind of the analyst, an impression that the patient's concern is with the nature of the concrete object. The nature of the functions which excite the patient's curiosity he explores by projective identification. His own feelings, too powerful to be contained within his personality, are amongst these functions. Projective identification makes it possible for him to investigate his own feelings in a personality powerful enough to contain them. Denial of the use of this mechanism, either by the refusal of the mother to serve as a repository for the infant's feelings, or by the hatred and envy of the patient who cannot allow the mother to exercise this function, leads to a destruction of the link between infant and breast and consequently to a severe disorder of the impulse to be curious on which all learning depends. The way is therefore prepared for a severe arrest of development. Furthermore, thanks to a denial of the main method open to the infant for dealing with his too powerful emotions, the conduct of emotional life, in any case a severe problem, becomes intolerable. Feelings of hatred are thereupon directed against all emotions including hate itself, and against external reality which stimulates them. It is a short step from hatred of the emotions to hatred of life itself. As I said in my paper on "The differentiation of the psychotic from the non-psychotic part of the personality" (1957a), this hatred results in a resort to projective identification of all the perceptual apparatus including the embryonic thought which forms a link between sense impressions and consciousness. The tendency to excessive projective identification when death instincts predominate is thus reinforced.

Superego

The early development of the superego is effected by this kind of mental functioning in a way I must now describe. As I have said, the link between infant and breast depends upon projective identification and a capacity to introject projective identifications. Failure to introject makes the external object appear intrinsically hostile to curiosity and to the method, namely projective identification, by which the infant seeks to satisfy it. Should the breast be felt as fundamentally understanding, it has been transformed by the infant's envy and hate into an object whose devouring greed has as its aim the introjection of the infant's projective identifications in order to destroy them. This can show in the patient's belief that the analyst strives, by understanding the patient, to drive him insane. The result is an object which, when installed in the patient, exercises the function of a severe and ego-destructive superego. This description is not accurate applied to any object in the paranoid–schizoid position because it supposes a whole-object. The threat that such a whole-object impends contributes to the inability, described by Melanie Klein and others (Segal, 1950), of the psychotic patient to face the depressive position and the developments attendant on it. In the paranoid–schizoid phase the bizarre objects composed partially of elements of a persecutory superego which I described in my paper on "The differentiation of the psychotic from the non-psychotic part of the personality" (1957a) are predominant.

Arrested development

The disturbance of the impulse of curiosity on which all learning depends, and the denial of the mechanism by which it seeks expression, makes normal development impossible. Another feature obtrudes if the course of the analysis is favourable; problems which in sophisticated language are posed by the question "Why?" cannot be formulated. The patient appears to have no appreciation of causation and will complain of painful states of mind while persisting in courses of action calculated to produce them. Therefore when the appropriate material presents itself the patient must be shown that he has no interest in why he feels as he does. Elucidation of the limited scope of his curiosity issues in the development of a wider range and an incipient preoccupation with causes. This leads to some modification of conduct which otherwise prolongs his distress.

Conclusions

The main conclusions of this paper relate to that state of mind in which the patient's psyche contains an internal object which is opposed to, and destructive of, all links whatsoever from the most primitive (which I have suggested is a normal degree of projective identification) to the most sophisticated forms of verbal communication and the arts. In this state of mind emotion is hated; it is felt to be too powerful to be contained by the immature psyche, it is felt to link objects and it gives reality to objects which are not self and therefore inimical to primary narcissism.

The internal object, which in its origin was an external breast that refused to introject, harbour, and so modify the baneful force of emotion, is felt, paradoxically, to intensify, relative to the strength of the ego, the emotions against which it initiates the attacks. These attacks on the linking function of emotion lead to an over-prominence in the psychotic part of the personality of links which appear to be logical, almost mathematical, but never emotionally reasonable. Consequently the links surviving are perverse, cruel, and sterile.

The external object which is internalized, its nature, and the effect when so established on the methods of communication within the psyche and with the environment, are left for further elaboration later.

Note

1. Paper read before the British Psycho-Analytical Society on 20 October, 1957.

References

Bion, W. R. (1954). Notes on the theory of schizophrenia. *International Journal of Psycho-Analysis*, 35(pt II).

Bion, W. R. (1956). Development of schizophrenic thought. *International Journal of Psycho-Analysis*, 37.

Bion, W. R. (1957). The differentiation of the psychotic from the non-psychotic part of the personality. *International Journal of Psycho-Analysis*, 38(pts III–IV).

Bion, W. R. (1957). On arrogance. *Int. Psycho-An. Congress*, 1957.

Klein, M. (1928). *Early Stages of the Oedipus Conflict.*

Klein, M. (1934). A contribution to the psychogenesis of manic-depressive states. *13th Int. Psycho-An. Congress*, 1934.

Klein, M. (1946). *Notes on some Schizoid Mechanisms.*

Klein, M. (1948). The theory of anxiety and guilt. *International Journal of Psycho-Analysis*, 29.

Klein, M. (1957). *Envy and Gratitude*, Chapter II. Tavistock Publications, 1957.

Rosenfeld, H. (1952). Notes on the superego conflict in an acute schizophrenic patient. *International Journal of Psycho-Analysis*, 33.

Segal, H. (1950). Some aspects of the analysis of a schizophrenic. *International Journal of Psycho-Analysis*, 31(pt IV).

Segal, H. (1956). Depression in the schizophrenic. *International Journal of Psycho-Analysis*, 37(pts IV–V).

Segal, H. (1957). Notes on symbol formation. *International Journal of Psycho-Analysis*, 38(pt VI).

Article citation

Bion, W. (1959). Attacks on linking. *International Journal of Psycho-Analysis*, 40: 308–315.

CHAPTER NINE

Notes on symbol formation[1]

Hanna Segal

The understanding and interpretation of unconscious symbolism is one of the main tools of the psychologist. Often he is faced with the task of understanding and recognizing the meaning not only of a particular symbol but also of the whole process of symbol formation. This applies particularly to work with patients who show a disturbance or inhibition in the formation or free use of symbols, as for instance, psychotic or schizoid patients.

To give a very elementary example from two patients. One—whom I will call A—was a schizophrenic in a mental hospital. He was once asked by his doctor why it was that since his illness he had stopped playing the violin. He replied with some violence: "Why? do you expect me to masturbate in public?"

Another patient, B, dreamt one night that he and a young girl were playing a violin duet. He had associations to fiddling, masturbating, etc., from which it emerged clearly that the violin represented his genital and playing the violin represented a masturbation phantasy of a relation with the girl. Here then are two patients who apparently use the same symbols in the same situation—a violin representing the male genital, and playing the violin representing masturbation. The way in which the symbols function, however, is very different. For A, the violin had become so completely equated with his genital that to touch it in public became impossible. For B, playing the violin in his waking life was an important sublimation. We might say that the main difference between them is that for A the symbolic meaning of the violin was conscious, for B unconscious. I do not think, however, that this was the most important difference between the two patients. In the case of B, the fact that the meaning of the dream became completely conscious had in no way prevented him from using his violin. In A, on the other hand, there were many symbols operating in his unconscious in the same way in which the violin was used on the conscious level.

Taking another example—this time from a schizophrenic patient in an analytical situation: one session, in the first weeks of his analysis, he came in blushing and giggling, and throughout the session would not talk to me. Subsequently we found out that previous to this hour he had been attending an occupational therapy class in which he was doing carpentry, making a stool. The reason for his silence, blushing, and giggling was that he could not bring himself to talk to me about the work he was doing. For him, the wooden stool on which he was working, the word "stool" which he would have to use in connexion with it, and the stool he passed in the lavatory were so completely felt as one and the same thing that he was unable to talk to me about it. His subsequent analysis revealed that this equation of the three "stools", the word, the chair, and the faeces, was at the time completely unconscious. All he was consciously aware of was that he was embarrassed and could not talk to me. The main difference between the first and second patient quoted in their use of the violin as the symbol for the male genital was not that in the one case the symbol was conscious and in the other unconscious, but that in the first case it was felt to be the genital, and in the second to represent it. According to Ernest Jones's (1916) definition, the violin of A, the schizophrenic, would be considered a symbol. Similarly in the dream of B. But it would not be a symbol in B's waking life when it was used in sublimation.

In his paper written in 1916, Jones differentiated unconscious symbolism from other forms of "indirect representation", and made the following statements about true unconscious symbolism:

(i)   A symbol represents what has been repressed from conscious-
      ness, and the whole process of symbolization is carried on
      unconsciously.
(ii) All symbols represent ideas of "the self and of immediate blood
      relations and of the phenomena of birth, life and death".
(iii) A symbol has a constant meaning. Many symbols can be used
      to represent the same repressed idea, but a given symbol has a
      constant meaning which is universal.
(iv) Symbolism arises as the result of intrapsychic conflict between
      the "repressing tendencies and the repressed". Further: "Only
      what is repressed is symbolized; only what is repressed needs
      to be symbolized".

He further distinguishes between sublimation and symbolization.
"Symbols," he says, "arise when the affect investing the symbolized
idea has not, as far as the symbol is concerned, proved capable of that
modification in quality which is denoted by the term sublimation".

Summarizing Jones's points, one might say that when a desire
has to be given up because of conflict and repressed, it may express
itself in a symbolical way, and the object of the desire which had to
be given up can be replaced by a symbol.

Further analytical work, and particularly play analysis with
young children, has fully confirmed some main points of Jones's
formulation. The child's first interests and impulses are directed to
his parents' bodies and his own, and it is those objects and impulses
existing in the unconscious which give rise to all further interests by
way of symbolization. Jones's statement, however, that symbols are
formed where there is no sublimation soon gave rise to disagreement. In fact, Jones himself as well as Freud wrote many interesting
papers analysing the content of works of art. In 1923, in her paper
on infant analysis, Melanie Klein did not agree with this view on the
relation between symbolization and sublimation. She tried to show
that children's play—a sublimated activity—is a symbolic expression of anxieties and wishes.

We might consider it as a question of terminology, and accept
Jones's view that we should call symbols only those substitutes
which replace the object without any change of affect. On the other
hand, there are very great advantages in extending the definition to
cover symbols used in sublimation. In the first place the wider

definition corresponds better to common linguistic usage. Jones's concept excludes most of that which is called "symbol" in other sciences and in everyday language. Secondly, and I shall elaborate this point later, there seems to be a continuous development from the primitive symbols as described by Jones to the symbols used in self-expression, communication, discovery, creation, etc. Thirdly, it is difficult to establish a connexion between the early primitive desires and processes in the mind and the later development of the individual, unless the wider concept of symbolism is admitted. In the analytical view, the child's interest in the external world is determined by a series of displacements of affect and interests from the earliest to ever new objects. And, indeed, how could such a displacement be achieved otherwise than by way of symbolization?

In 1930, Melanie Klein raised the problem of inhibition in symbol formation. She described an autistic little boy of four, Dick, who could not talk or play; he showed no affection or anxiety, and took no interest in his surroundings apart from door-handles, stations, and trains, which seemed to fascinate him. His analysis revealed that the child was terrified of his aggression towards his mother's body, and of her body which he felt had turned bad because of his attacks on it; because of the strength of his anxieties he had erected powerful defences against his phantasies about her. There resulted a paralysis of his phantasy life and of symbol formation. He had not endowed the world around him with any symbolic meaning and therefore took no interest in it. Melanie Klein came to the conclusion that if symbolization does not occur, the whole development of the ego is arrested.

If we accept this view it follows that the processes of symbolization require a new and more careful study. To begin with, I find it helpful, following C. Morris, to consider symbolizing as a three-term relation, i.e. a relation between the thing symbolized, the thing functioning as a symbol, and a person for whom the one represents the other. In psychological terms, symbolism would be a relation between the ego, the object, and the symbol.

Symbol formation is an activity of the ego attempting to deal with the anxieties stirred by its relation to the object. That is primarily the fear of bad objects and the fear of the loss or inaccessibility of good objects. Disturbances in the ego's relation to objects are reflected in disturbances of symbol formation. In particular, disturbances in differentiation between ego and object lead to disturbances in differentiation between the symbol and the object symbolized and therefore to concrete thinking characteristic of psychoses.

Symbol formation starts very early, probably as early as object relations, but changes its character and functions with the changes in the character of the ego and object relations. Not only the actual content of the symbol, but the very way in which symbols are formed and used seem to me to reflect very precisely the ego's state of development and its way of dealing with its objects. If symbolism is seen as a three-term relation, problems of symbol formation must always be examined in the context of the ego's relation with its objects.

I shall try to describe briefly some basic attitudes of the ego to the objects, and the way in which I think they influence the processes of symbol formation and the functioning of symbolism. My description is based here on Melanie Klein's (1930) concept of the paranoid–schizoid position and of the depressive position. According to her, the oral stage of development falls into two phases, the earlier being the point of fixation of the schizophrenic group of illnesses, the later that of the manic-depressive. In my description, which will of necessity be very schematic, I shall select only those points which are directly relevant to the problem of symbol formation.

The chief characteristics of the infant's first object relations are the following. The object is seen as split into an ideally good and a wholly bad one. The aim of the ego is total union with the ideal object and total annihilation of the bad one, as well as of the bad parts of the self. Omnipotent thinking is paramount and reality sense intermittent and precarious. The concept of absence hardly exists. Whenever the state of union with the ideal object is not fulfilled, what is experienced is not absence; the ego feels assailed by the counterpart of the good object—the bad object, or objects. It is the time of the hallucinatory wish-fulfilment, described by Freud, when the thought creates objects which are then felt to be available. According to Melanie Klein, it is also the time of the bad hallucinosis when, if the ideal conditions are not fulfilled, the bad object is equally hallucinated and felt as real.

A leading defence mechanism in this phase is projective

identification. In projective identification, the subject in phantasy projects large parts of himself into the object, and the object becomes identified with the parts of the self that it is felt to contain. Similarly, internal objects are projected outside and identified with parts of the external world which come to represent them. These first projections and identifications are the beginning of the process of symbol formation.

The early symbols, however, are not felt by the ego to be symbols or substitutes, but to be the original object itself. They are so different from symbols formed later that I think they deserve a name of their own. In my paper of 1950 I suggested the term "equation". This word, however, differentiates them too much from the word "symbol" and I would like to alter it here to "symbolic equation".

The symbolic equation between the original object and the symbol in the internal and the external world is, I think, the basis of the schizophrenic's concrete thinking where substitutes for the original objects, or parts of the self, can be used quite freely, but, as in the two examples of schizophrenic patients which I quoted, they are hardly different from the original object: they are felt and treated as though they were identical with it. This non-differentiation between the thing symbolized and the symbol is part of a disturbance in the relation between the ego and the object. Parts of the ego and internal objects are projected into an object and identified with it. The differentiation between the self and the object is obscured. Then, since a part of the ego is confused with the object, the symbol—which is a creation and a function of the ego—becomes, in turn, confused with the object which is symbolized.

Where such symbolic equations are formed in relation to bad objects, an attempt is made to deal with them as with the original object, that is by total annihilation and scotomization. In Melanie Klein's paper quoted above (1930), it seemed as though Dick had formed no symbolic relations to the external world. The paper was written very early on in Dick's analysis, and I wonder, on the basis of my own experience with schizophrenics, whether it did not, perhaps, subsequently transpire that Dick had formed numerous symbolic equations in the external world. If so, then these would have carried the full anxiety experienced in relation to the original persecutory or guilt-producing object: his mother's body, so that he had had to deal with them by annihilation, that is by total withdrawal of interest. Some of the symbols which he had formed as his analysis progressed, and he started to show an interest in certain objects in the consulting room, seemed to have had the characteristics of such symbolic equations. For instance, when he saw some pencil shavings he said: "Poor Mrs Klein". To him the shavings were Mrs Klein cut into bits.

This was the case in the analysis of my patient Edward (Segal, 1955). At one stage in the analysis a certain degree of symbol formation on a symbolic equation basis had occurred, so that some anxiety was displaced from the person of his analyst, felt as a bad internal object, on to substitutes in the external world. Thereupon the numerous persecutors in the external world were dealt with by scotomization. That phase of his analysis, which lasted several months, was characterized by an extreme narrowing of his interests in the external world. At that point also his vocabulary became very poor. He forbade himself and me the use of many words which he felt had the power to produce hallucinations and therefore had to be abolished. This is strikingly similar to the behaviour of a Paraguayan tribe, the Abipones, who cannot tolerate anything that reminds them of the dead. When a member of the tribe dies, all words having any affinity with the names of the deceased are immediately dropped from the vocabulary. In consequence, their language is most difficult to learn, as it is full of blocks and neologisms replacing forbidden words.

The development of the ego and the changes in the ego's relation to its objects are gradual, and so is the change from the early symbols, which I called symbolic equations, to the fully formed symbols in the depressive position. It is therefore only for the sake of clarity that I shall make here a very sharp differentiation between the ego's relations in the paranoid–schizoid position and in the depressive position respectively, and an equally sharp differentiation between the symbolic equations and the symbols which are formed during and after the depressive position.

When the depressive position has been reached, the main characteristic of object relation is that the object is felt as a whole object. In connexion with this there is a greater degree of awareness and differentiation of the separateness between the ego and the object. At the same time, since the object is recognized as a whole, ambivalence is more fully experienced. The ego in this phase is struggling with its ambivalence and its relation to the object is characterized by guilt, fear of loss or actual experience of loss and mourning, and a striving to re-create the object. At the same time, processes of introjection become more pronounced than those of projection, in keeping with the striving to retain the object inside as well as to repair, restore and re-create it.

In favourable circumstances of normal development, after repeated experiences of loss, recovery, and re-creation, a good object is securely established in the ego. Three changes in relation to the object, as the ego develops and integrates, affect fundamentally the ego's reality sense. With an increased awareness of ambivalence, the lessening of the intensity of projection, and the growing differentiation between the self and the object, there is a growing sense of reality both internal and external. The internal world becomes differentiated from the external world. Omnipotent thinking, characteristic of the earlier phase, gradually gives way to more realistic thinking. Simultaneously, and as part of the same process, there is a certain modification of the primary instinctual aims. Earlier on, the aim was to possess the object totally if felt as good, or to annihilate it totally if felt as bad. With the recognition that the good and the bad objects are one, both these instinctual aims are gradually modified. The ego is increasingly concerned with saving the object from its aggression and possessiveness. And this implies a certain degree of inhibition of the direct instinctual aims, both aggressive and libidinal.

This situation is a powerful stimulus for the creation of symbols, and symbols acquire new functions which change their character. The symbol is needed to displace aggression from the original object, and in that way to lessen the guilt and the fear of loss. The symbol is here not an equivalent of the original object, since the aim of the displacement is to save the object, and the guilt experienced in relation to it is far less than that due to an attack on the original object. The symbols are also created in the internal world as a means of restoring, re-creating, recapturing and owning again the original object. But in keeping with the increased reality sense, they are now felt as created by the ego and therefore never completely equated with the original object.

Freud postulates that a modification of instinctual aims is the basic precondition of sublimation. In my view the formation of symbols in the depressive position necessitates some inhibition of direct instinctual aims in relation to the original object and therefore the symbols become available for sublimation. The symbols, created internally, can then be reprojected into the external world, endowing it with symbolic meaning.

The capacity to experience loss and the wish to re-create the object within oneself gives the individual the unconscious freedom in the use of symbols. And as the symbol is acknowledged as a creation of the subject, unlike the symbolic equation, it can be freely used by the subject.

When a substitute in the external world is used as a symbol it may be used more freely than the original object, since it is not fully identified with it. Insofar, however, as it is distinguished from the original object it is also recognized as an object in itself. Its own properties are recognized, respected, and used, because no confusion with the original object blurs the characteristics of the new object used as a symbol.

In an analysis we can sometimes follow very clearly the changes in the symbolic relations in the patient's attitude to his faeces. On the schizoid level the patient expects his faeces to be the ideal breast; if he cannot maintain this idealization his faeces become persecutory, they are ejected as a bitten-up, destroyed and persecuting breast. If the patient tries to symbolize his faeces in the external world the symbols in the external world are felt to be faeces—persecutors. No sublimation of anal activities can occur under these conditions.

On the depressive level, the feeling is that the introjected breast has been destroyed by the ego and can be re-created by the ego. The faeces may then be felt as something created by the ego out of the object and can be valued as a symbol of the breast and at the same time as a good product of the ego's own creativity.

When this symbolic relation to faeces and other body products has been established a projection can occur on to substances in the external world such as paint, plasticine, clay, etc., which can then be used for sublimation.

When this stage of development has been achieved, it is of course not irreversible. If the anxieties are too strong, a regression to a paranoid–schizoid position can occur at any stage of the individual's development and projective identification may be resorted to as a defence against anxiety. Then symbols which have been developed and have been functioning as symbols in sublimation, revert to concrete symbolic equations. This is mainly due to the fact that in massive projective identification the ego becomes again confused with the object, the symbol becomes confused with the thing symbolized and therefore turns into an equation.

In the example of the schizophrenic patient A quoted at the beginning of this paper, there was a breakdown of an already established sublimation. Prior to his schizophrenic breakdown, the violin had been functioning as a symbol and used for purposes of sublimation. It had only become concretely equated to the penis at the time of his illness. Words which had certainly developed at the time when the ego is relatively mature, become equated with the objects that they should represent, and become experienced as concrete objects when projective identification occurs with the resulting confusion between the symbols created by the ego: the word, or even the thought, and the object that they were to symbolize.

I should like at this point to summarize what I mean by the terms "symbolic equation" and "symbol" respectively, and the conditions under which they arise. In the symbolic equation, the symbol-substitute is felt to be the original object. The substitute's own properties are not recognized or admitted. The symbolic equation is used to deny the absence of the ideal object, or to control a persecuting one. It belongs to the earliest stages of development.

The symbol proper, available for sublimation and furthering the development of the ego, is felt to represent the object; its own characteristics are recognized, respected, and used. It arises when depressive feelings predominate over the paranoid–schizoid ones, when separation from the object, ambivalence, guilt, and loss can be experienced and tolerated. The symbol is used not to deny but to overcome loss. When the mechanism of projective identification is used as a defence against depressive anxieties, symbols already formed and functioning as symbols may revert to symbolic equations.

Symbol formation governs the capacity to communicate, since all communication is made by means of symbols. When schizoid disturbances in object relations occur, the capacity to communicate is similarly disturbed: first because the differentiation between the subject and the object is blurred, secondly because the means of communication are lacking since symbols are felt in a concrete fashion and are therefore unavailable for purposes of communication. One of the ever-recurring difficulties in the analysis of psychotic patients is this difficulty of communication. Words, for instance, whether the analyst's or the patient's, are felt to be objects or actions, and cannot be easily used for purposes of communication.

Symbols are needed not only in communication with the external world, but also in internal communication. Indeed, it could be asked what is meant when we speak of people being well in touch with their unconscious. It is not that they have consciously primitive phantasies, like those which become evident in their analyses, but merely that they have some awareness of their own impulses and feelings. However, I think that we mean more than this; we mean that they have actual communication with their unconscious phantasies. And this, like any other form of communication, can only be done with the help of symbols. So that in people who are "well in touch with themselves" there is a constant free symbol-formation, whereby they can be consciously aware and in control of symbolic expressions of the underlying primitive phantasies. The difficulty of dealing with schizophrenic and schizoid patients lies not only in that they cannot communicate with us, but even more in that they cannot communicate with themselves. Any part of their ego may be split off from any other part with no communication available between them.

The capacity to communicate with oneself by using symbols is, I think, the basis of verbal thinking—which is the capacity to communicate with oneself by means of words. Not all internal communication is verbal thinking, but all verbal thinking is an internal communication by means of symbols—words. An important aspect of internal communication is the integration of earlier desires, anxieties, and phantasies into the later stages of development by symbolization. For instance, in the fully developed genital function, all the earlier aims—anal, urethral, oral—may by symbolically expressed and fulfilled, a point beautifully described in Ferenczi's Thalassa.

And this takes me to the last point of my paper. I think that one of the important tasks performed by the ego in the depressive position is that of dealing not with depressive anxieties alone, but also with unresolved earlier conflicts. A new achievement belonging to the depressive position; the capacity to symbolize and in that way to lessen anxiety and resolve conflict, is used in order to deal with the earlier unresolved conflicts by symbolizing them. Anxieties, which could not be dealt with earlier on, because of the extreme concreteness of the experience with the object and the object-substitutes in symbolic equations, can gradually be dealt with by the more integrated ego by symbolization, and in that way they can be integrated. In the depressive position and later, symbols are formed not only of the whole destroyed and re-created object characteristic of the depressive position, but also of the split object—extremely good and extremely bad—and not only of the whole object but also of part-objects. Some of the paranoid and ideal object relations and anxieties may be symbolized as part of the integrative process in the depressive position.

The fairy tale is an example in point. It deals basically with the witch and the fairy godmother, Prince Charming, the ogre, etc., and has in it a great deal of schizophrenic content. It is, however, a highly integrated product, an artistic creation which very fully symbolizes the child's early anxieties and wishes. I should like to illustrate the function of the fairy tale by some material from the analysis of an adolescent schizophrenic. This girl had been hallucinated and openly schizophrenic since the age of four. She had, however, a great many depressive features and there were in her life phases of relatively greater integration. In these phases, when she felt less persecuted, and, as she told me, could experience some longing for her parents, she used to write fairy tales. In the bad phases, the bad figures of her fairy tales came to life and persecuted her. One day, after many weeks of silence, when she was obviously hallucinated in a very persecutory way she suddenly turned round to me and asked with great fear "What are the Lancashire witches?" I had never heard of the Lancashire witches, she had never mentioned them before, but I knew that she herself came from Lancashire. After some interpretations she told me that when she was about 11 (she had at that time actually a whole year free of hallucinations), she had written a fairy tale about Lancashire witches. The phase of her analysis following this session has been very revealing. It turned out that the Lancashire witches repres-ented both herself and her mother. The anxiety situation went right back to early childhood, when she saw herself and her mother as devouring one another or devouring father. When a greater degree of integration was achieved and she established a more realistic relation to her parents, the earlier situation was dealt with by symbol formation: by writing the fairy tale about the Lancashire witches. In the subsequent deterioration of her health, the early persecutory situation recurred with concrete intensity but in a new form. The fairy tale come to life: the Lancashire witches—the fairy-tale figures which she had created, had become a concrete external reality. In the consulting room it was quite clear how this concretization of the fairy tale depended on projective identification. She turned to me and asked me about the Lancashire witches. She expected me to know who they were. In fact, she thought that I was a Lancashire witch. She had unconsciously phantasied that she had put into me the part of herself which had invented the Lancashire witches, and she had lost contact with this part. She lost all sense of reality in this projection and all memory that she had created this symbol, the "Lancashire witches". Her symbol became confused with me, an actual external object, and so became for her a concrete external reality—I had turned into a Lancashire witch.

The way in which the maturing ego, in the process of working through the depressive position, deals with the early object relations, is of paramount importance. Some integration and whole object relations can be achieved in the depressive position, accompanied by the splitting off of earlier ego experiences. In this situation, something like a pocket of schizophrenia exists isolated in the ego and is a constant threat to stability. At worst, a mental breakdown occurs and earlier anxieties and split-off symbolic equations invade the ego. At best, a relatively mature but restricted ego can develop and function.

However, if the ego in the depressive position is strong enough and capable of dealing with anxieties, much more of the earlier situations can be integrated into the ego and dealt with by way of symbolization, enriching the ego with the whole wealth of the earlier experiences.

The word "symbol" comes from the Greek term for throwing together, bringing together, integrating. The process of symbol formation is, I think, a continuous process of bringing together and integrating the internal with the external, the subject with the object, and the earlier experiences with the later ones.

Notes

1. Paper read at the meeting of the Medical Section, the British Psychological Society, in May 1955, based on an earlier paper presented at a Symposium on Symbolism at St. Anne's House, London, in November 1954.
2. No reference is made in this paper to the papers by Rodriguez and Rycroft, as these and the paper by Morris were written and read almost concurrently.

References

Freud, S. The ego and the id.

Jones, E. (1916). The theory of symbolism. *Papers on Psycho-Analysis*.

Klein, M. (1930). On the importance of symbol formation in the development of the ego. *Contributions to Psycho-Analysis, 1921–1945*.

Morris, C. Foundations of the theory of signs. *International Encyclopedia of Unified Science, 2*.

Rodriguez, E. Notes on symbolism. *International Journal of Psycho-Analysis, 37*.[2]

Rycroft, C. Symbolism and its relation to primary and secondary processes. *International Journal of Psycho-Analysis, 37*.[2]

Segal, H. (1950). Some aspects of the analysis of a schizophrenic. *International Journal of Psycho-Analysis, 31*.

Segal, H. (1952). A psycho-analytic contribution to aesthetics. *International Journal of Psycho-Analysis, 33*.

Segal, H. (1955). Depression in the schizophrenic. *International Journal of Psycho-Analysis, 36*.

Article citation

Segal, H. (1957). Notes on symbol formation. *International Journal of Psycho-Analysis, 38* :39–397.

CHAPTER TEN

Autism and symbiosis, two extreme disturbances of identity[1]

Margaret Schoenberger Mahler[2]

My hypothesis of infantile psychoses is based upon two of Freud's fundamental concepts. It is a quasi-sociobiological proposition. Freud emphasized that whereas the animal has an instinctual faculty for sensing danger in the outside world which enables it to take appropriate action to cope with such danger, this faculty has atrophied in the human being. In the human being the ego has to take over the reality testing which the id neglects (Freud, 1923). The predicament of the human young is immensely increased by still another biological circumstance—namely, by the fact that he is born at an earlier, less matured stage of physical development than any other mammal. These two interrelated circumstances, namely (i) the atrophy of the instinct of self-preservation, and (ii) the immaturity of apparatuses at birth, result in the human infant's absolute dependence for his very survival on the nursing care of a mother or a mother substitute for a long period. Long after the child has been born, a species-characteristic social symbiosis between the infant and mother is necessary. I shall try to demonstrate that the syndromes of early infantile psychoses, both the autistic as well as the symbiotic type, represent fixations at, or regressions to, the first two developmental stages of "undifferentiation" within this early mother–child unity. Within that twilight stage of early life which Freud designated as primary narcissism, the infant shows hardly any sign of perceiving anything beyond his own body. He seems to live in a world of inner stimuli. The first weeks of extrauterine life are characterized by what (according to Ferenczi) we call the stage of hallucinatory wish-fulfilment. Whereas (the coenesthetic) the enteroceptive system functions from birth, the perceptual conscious system, the sensorium, is not yet cathected. This lack of peripheral sensory cathexis only gradually gives way to perception, particularly to distance perception, of the outside world. However, most babies are born with an appropriate signal equipment for dealing with instinctual tensions when they mount beyond a tolerable degree. Their affectomotor reactions serve automatically to summon and use the mother as external executive ego (Spitz, 1951). Furthermore, as early as the first day of extra-uterine life the full term neonate displays a discriminatory grasping reflex (Stirnimann, 1949) which proves that he has a significant innate endowment for distinguishing in a sensori-motor way between the living part-object and lifeless matter. This primal ability to discriminate between animate and inanimate was given the name *Urunterscheidung*: *Protodiakrisis*, by von Monakow (Stirnimann, 1949).

The pre-symbiotic, normal-autistic phase of the mother–infant unity gives way to the symbiotic phase proper (from about the age of three months on). During his wakeful hungry periods of the day the three–four-months-old baby seems to perceive, temporarily at least, and, in a Gestalt kind of perception, that small part of external reality which is represented by the mother's breast, face, and hands, the Gestalt of her ministrations as such. This occurs in the matrix of the oral gratification–frustration sequences of the normal nursing situation. This phase of dim awareness of the "need-satisfying object" marks the beginning of the phase of symbiosis in which the infant behaves and functions as though he and his mother were an omnipotent system (a dual unity) within one common boundary (a symbiotic membrane as it were). The symbiotic phase is followed by the so-called separation-individuation phase proper. This occurs parallel with the maturation and consolidation of such autonomous ego functions as locomotion, and the beginning of language (Mahler-Gosliner, 1955).

Two conditions are requisite for structuralization of the ego and neutralization of drives in order to achieve individuation, that is to say, a sense of individual entity and identity: (i) the enteroceptive–proprioceptive stimuli must not be so persistent and so intense as to prevent formation of structure; (ii) in the absence of an "inner organizer" in the human infant (Spitz, 1945) the symbiotic partner must be able to serve as a buffer against inner and outer stimuli, gradually organizing them for the infant and orienting it to inner *versus* outer world, i.e. to boundary formation and sensory perception. Freud (1923) emphasized, "Perceptions may be said to have the same significance for the ego as instincts have for the id". Hartmann has pointed out that formation of structure and neutralization of drives is a circular process: structure is formed by perceptual turning toward the outside world, and *vice versa*. If the two afore-mentioned conditions are not met, the ego's perceptual faculty cannot gain ascendancy nor can the ego's integrative and synthetic function develop (Hartmann, 1953; Hartmann & Loewenstein, 1946).

Hermann's (1936) and Bak's (1939) theories of schizophrenia indicate that predisposition to psychosis has its origin in those early physiological distress situations which are connected with or ensue from psychophysiological incompatibility of the mother–infant unit in the first weeks of life in which these overflow assimilatory processes take place. There are situations in early infancy in which entero-proprioceptive overstimulation due to illness, or an adverse maternal (symbiotic) milieu generate great quantities of unneutralized explosive and, therefore, disorganizing aggressive drive-energy. These are the situations in which neutralization or counter-cathexis cannot be effected by the usual contact perceptual libidinizing process of the mother's nursing care (Hoffer, 1950). In certain cases the severity of the physiological upheaval not only impairs the perceptual activity of the sensorium and thus formation of structure (ego), but even the faculty of primal discrimination (protodiakrisis) between living and inanimate may be lost.

Such catastrophic shifts and reactions seem to be the pathogenic agents in early infantile autism. The pivotal disturbance lies in these children's inability to perceive the Gestalt of the mother and the Gestalt of her vital functioning on their behalf. There seems no perceptual awareness of an inside *versus* an outside world, no awareness of the child's own self as distinct from the inanimate environment.[3]

From our sociobiological point of view these infants remain fixated or regress to the autistic phase of extrauterine life or (as far as protodiakrisis is concerned) to an even more archaic foetal stage of functioning. Among the clinical findings bearing out the above-described dynamics are the grossly inadequate peripheral pain-sensitivity in these children and also the signs pointing to the insufficiency of the peripheral blood circulation. Concurrent with this cathectic deficiency of the sensorium is a lack of hierarchic stratification of zonal libidinization and sequence. This is evident from the relative paucity of auto-erotic activities on the one hand, and a facility for libidinal positions substituting for each other. Instead of auto-erotic activities these children show auto-aggressive habits such as head-knocking, self-biting, or other self-hurting activities. Auto-aggressive activities in a quasi-restitutive attempt serve to sharpen the awareness of the body–self boundaries, often at the expense, or at the actual sacrifice of parts of the body image (Szasz, 1957). As a consequence of this lack of cathexis of the PCPT-Cs-System, these children are completely impervious to their mother's voice and commands, nor do they seem to see you; they look through you. It is an open question whether this turning a deaf ear toward mother and, consequently, toward the outside world is inborn or an acquired defence. Their inability to use the symbiotic partner makes it necessary for these children to find substitute adaptive mechanisms for survival, and these substitutive formations represent the symptomatology of early infantile autism (Kanner, 1942, 1949).

The symbiotic psychotic syndrome (Mahler, 1951, Amsterdam) represents fixation at or regression to the second undifferentiated stage of the mother–child unity, which is the stage of delusional omnipotent symbiotic fusion with the need-satisfying object.

Primary autism gradually becomes manifest as sequelae of the autistic isolation become more and more apparent with the maturational growth of the organism. But the symbiotic psychotic picture in contrast develops, more often than not, with crises of catastrophic and panic reactions marking its course. Unlike the persistent imperviousness of the autistic cases, the anamnesis of these symbiotic psychotics show unequivocal signs of a defective stimulus barrier, an insufficiency of the protective counter-cathexis of the PCPT-Cs-System with hypersensitivity, labile homeostasis, increased vulnerability of the ego, and impairment of many functions, but particularly the repressive defensive function of the ego (Jacobson, 1957; Mahler-Elkisch, 1953; Mahler-Gosliner, 1955). The slightest additional trauma causes the rudimentary brittle ego structure to fragmentate. One of the characteristics of the symbiotic psychotic ego structure, in contradistinction to that of the autistic one, is its great incohesive interpermeability with the id. The lack of distinction between the primary and secondary process and the dominance of the pleasure principle persist. Inner and outer reality are fused because of the incohesive boundary formation of the self: hence, the original common symbiotic boundary of self and object world, of the child and mother, is maintained beyond the symbiotic age, and the ego cannot perform those developmental tasks which would result in further self-differentiation and separation from the mother. In consequence, these children do not attain the separation–individuation phase which is the first level of the normal child's subjective, but all-important, sense of individual entity and identity. Very little is known in psychoanalytic (and other) literature about this all-important cohesive cathectic state which gives us our sense of identity (Mahler, 1957). Those who work with psychotic children are impressed by the most pervasive feature of this disorder, namely, a partial or complete loss of personal identity, which seems to usher in alienation and withdrawal from reality.

The sense of self-identity

The sense of individual identity is mediated by our bodily sensations. Its core is the body image which consists of a fairly stabilized, predominantly libidinal cathexis of the body in its central and peripheral parts (Greenacre, 1953). "The infant's body is both internal and external at the same time. By virtue of this characteristic, it stands out for him from the rest of the world and thereby enables him to work out the distinction between self and non-self". (Hartmann, 1950; Hartmann & Loewenstein, 1946). Proprioceptive inner stimuli, as well as contact perceptions, deep pressure sensitivity and thermal interchange, in addition to kinesthetic experiences (equilibrium) in the nursing situation contribute much more importantly and immediately to the core of our feeling of identity, to our body image, than the later maturing distance-perceptive visual and auditory images. The latter contribute primarily and most importantly to the recognition of and distinction from the object world. Integration of our bodily feelings, and unconscious phantasies about the body self, especially its contents, with visual, auditory, and kinesthetic data about it are a relatively late acquisition of the ego. It coincides with the first level of integration of the sense of identity which is dependent on separation–individuation and which is characterized by a negativistic phase (5).

The maturational spurt which takes place in the second year puts the (normal) toddler in the position of a relatively advanced physical autonomy. Locomotion is one of the autonomous ego functions whose maturation may become the most conspicuous paradigm of discrepancy between the rate of maturational and the developmental growth of the personality (Hartmann & Loewenstein, 1946).[4] Locomotion enables the child to separate, physically to move away from the mother, when emotionally he may be quite unprepared to do so. The two-year-old child very soon experiences his separateness in many other ways. He enjoys his independence and exercises mastery with great tenacity, and thus large quantities of libido and aggression are utilized by the ego. On the other hand there are junior toddlers who show adverse reactions and increased clinging to the mother in reaction to their own autonomy. The awareness of separate functioning may elicit intense anxiety in these vulnerable toddlers, who then try desperately to deny the fact of separateness, on the one hand, and struggle against re-engulfment by increased opposition to the adults.

Experimental and academic psychologists also found the phase of individuation in which the child develops "self-awareness" an uneasy period in his life. Wallon and his pupil, Zazzo, have studied the young child's recognition of his own image in three different situations: in the mirror, on photos, and in films. It was found that recognition of the mirror image does not occur until two years and two or three months.[5] A few weeks before this occurs the observers "noticed a kind of disorganization, as if a sudden state of awareness of self had caused an affective upset". (Zazzo, 1953). Up to the end of the third year the child displays a certain fearfulness and at the same time a certain pleasure in looking at himself in the mirror. At about two years and ten months the image has become familiar and no longer causes uneasiness. It is at the same time, that is, two years and ten months to three years of age, that the personal pronoun "I" begins to be used without hesitation and grammatically.

The normal negativistic phase of the toddler is the accompanying behavioural reaction of this process of individuation, of disengagement from the mother–child symbiosis. The fear of re-engulfment threatens a recently and barely started individual differentiation which must be defended. The less satisfactory or the more parasitic the symbiotic phase has been, the more prominent and exaggerated will be this negativistic reaction (1951; Lowald, 1951; Mahler-Gosliner, 1955). An ego which is unable to function separately from the symbiotic partner tries to re-entrench itself in the delusional phantasy of oneness with the omnipotent mother, by coercing her into functioning as an extension of the self. This device of course usually fails to halt the process of alienation from reality (a reality still represented almost exclusively by the mother).

The separation–individuation phase is vulnerable in any child's life. If the struggle is lost, as in symbiotic psychosis, fragmentation of his ego has as its consequence a complete breakdown of integrative functions on all levels. To begin with, proprioceptive perception may be mistaken for and confused with sensory perception: inner intentions are attributed to outside factors, biodynamics are taken for mechanical dynamics (Mahler *et al.*, 1949). The ego-regression seems to be aimed in particular at de-differentiation of function and contents because the fragmented ego cannot cope with complexities. De-differentiation seems to be the adaptive mechanism serving survival under these circumstances with secondary autistic mechanisms. If this process is complete, the clinical picture may show superficial resemblance to primary autism. Let me give a clinical example:

George was the firstborn of his parents. Immediately after his birth, the father left for the Navy. Among many interesting data, I mention only that mother and infant saw practically no one but each other and that the mother treated the child as though he were a vegetative appendage of her own self, e.g. there was hardly any verbal communication between mother and baby. When the child was approximately two years old the father returned, but he was always morose and uninterested in the boy. In his third year of life George's behaviour clearly demonstrated an overgrowth of unchecked and unmitigated (unconscious) aggressive phantasies. There was evidence of his utter misunderstanding of the affective meaning of social situations, in terms of projection of his unneutralized aggression. For example, he would cry like an infant of eight months when greeted by an unfamiliar person with a friendly hello. If friends or relatives patted him on the shoulder or head, he became terrified, stated that they hit him, and seemed frightened that they would harm him. The momentum of his pent-up aggression broke through the patient's hitherto mute behaviour. At the age two and a half to three, George's mutism abruptly changed to flighty and panic-stricken language of the primary process variety which his mother aptly described and called "talking tantrums". When frustrated, but also without apparent cause, he would pace around the room, talking angrily to himself about something which seemed entirely unintelligible and irrelevant to his environment. During the second half of his third year, in the separation individuation phase of George's development, the mother again became pregnant. George began to have night terrors. When he was past three, his baby sister was born and George became acutely disturbed. During the last months of his mother's pregnancy he developed an absorbing, exclusive interest in examining his inanimate environment by touching objects. Regression to contact—perceptual as well as olfactory and gustatory reality testing—is often found in infantile psychosis. George became conspicuous during his mother's pregnancy by his strange compulsive interest in barrels, beer barrels in particular (they lived near a brewery). He would stop and touch each barrel and examine it with care. Following this preoccupation with barrels he became fascinated by pipes of all sorts, which, again, he would have to touch, size up, stroke, etc., commenting on their size, shape, or other characteristics. After a few months he developed a similar preoccupation with electrical appliances; he would endlessly pretend to be plugging a flex into a socket. Still later George developed an intense interest in fires, and this was predominant at the time of his hospitalization at six and a half years of age.

Two aspects of this frantic reality testing in the wake of the symbiotic psychotic process are characteristic and deserve discussion. First, we can see the slipping away of the living object world

(through withdrawal of the libidinal cathexis) so that an estrange-
ment in terms of de-animation and de-differentiation takes place.
With the de-cathexis of the living object world, the child's own
body, the body feelings deriving directly from instinctual processes
not sifted by the ego gain ascendancy. These feelings usurp the
place of the "not me" object world. The body and the feelings it
conveys are the only remaining objects of the patient's ego! The
second aspect to be discussed is the alienation from the child's own
body, the fragmentation of the body image, the parts of which are
cathected with grossly aggressivized energy. This second aspect of
the symbiotic–psychotic break hangs together or is the counterpart
of the delibidinization of the object world. It becomes manifest as
the psychotic elaboration of the bisexual conflict which in George's
case coincided with the sister's birth (and his phallic phase). The
second level of integration of the sense of identity is the resolution
of the bisexual identification. Psychosexual maturation is also
biologically predetermined and thus proceeds even though object
relationship and reality testing may not. It seems that the phallic
phase brings with it a most consequential maturational event,
massive concentration of libido in the sexual parts of the body
image. This process occurs regardless of what environmental
influences there are. Normally, it inevitably causes important shifts
of cathexis in terms of body image representations emerging via
pregenital libidinal phases, and bisexual identifications to firm
establishment of sexual identity. This second phase of integration
of the body image and feeling of identity seems to be dependent on
a number of important conditions: (i) on the successful integration
of pregenital phases of development; (ii) on the successful
identification with the parental figure of the same sex in which
both parents' emotional attitude toward the child's sexual identity
is of the utmost importance; and (iii) the ability of the ego to
organize the memories, ideas, and feelings about the self into a
hierarchically stratified, firmly cathected organization of self-
representations.

The dissociation of the constituents of the feeling of identity is
ushered in by the loss of the innate human faculty of discrimination
between the animate and the inanimate, the living and the dead.
This primal discrimination, this *"protodiakrisis"* (Monakow) seems
to depend on and consists of impressions of warmth, resiliency,

turgor, deep tactile sensations between two living higher organisms at contact with one another.

George demonstrated this utter confusion of animate and inanimate. For example, he was panic-stricken when he had to pass a certain picket-fence for fear that the holes might swallow him; he also demonstrated confusion of anything moving. He became frantic about and later obsessed with the workings of electrical appliances (which obviously symbolized his body and particularly his genital). The symbolic oral connotation of the fence holes, the barrel bellies; the anal meaning of George's interest in the shapes of the pipes and the plumbing, etc.; and the phallic meaning of the machines, are quite obvious. My emphasis, however, is on the pathognomonic significance of the animation of the inanimate and de-animation of the living environment in the wake of the psychotic process. When gradual transition from primary to secondary identification with the love object has failed, it seems that all the libido is suddenly withdrawn from the object world.

The clinical manifestations must be regarded as restitution attempts. Shortly after baby sister came, George wanted to wear her clothes, and often also his mother's dresses. This was not like a normal child's make-believe play, for these psychotic children believe that they become the mother or the sister by wearing their clothes (29). He spoke to everybody of his sister and again and again of his pet kitten: "I have a cat at home. It's a girl cat. I like my cat. I am a girl cat".

George's parasitic-symbiosis was suddenly terminated by several factors: (i) the father's reappearance and hostility; (ii) soon afterward, the mother's pregnancy; (iii) the birth of a female sibling; and (iv) the father's preference for, as well as the mother's preoccupation with, the baby sister. George was suddenly faced, in a hostile Oedipal atmosphere, with separateness in the functional–maturational sense, without being emotionally at all prepared to give up the delusion of omnipotent fusion with the mother. We may assume that neither were his self-boundaries cathected with neutralized energy, nor was his body image differentiated beyond confused bisexual self-representations and object representation. George seemed to have tried frantically to adopt counter-cathectic devices against fragmentation of his brittle ego. He tried to counteract the threatening loss of the libidinal object world by attempting to recapture it in a concrete sense through the contact-perceptive faculties of his ego. George compulsively and feverishly tried to finger, "to feel" things around him; he obviously tried to distinguish between, to compare, beer barrels and his pregnant mother's body. After his baby sister's birth, George compared, in this tactile way, concrete symbols of male and female anatomy, and at the same time perhaps endeavoured to distinguish the semi-animate and inanimate shapes and phenomena of oral and anal experiences.

The bisexual problem augmented to a spectacular degree this boy's struggle to regain his symbiotic completeness with the "lost mother". Castration fear and envy of the intimate relationship of the girl-baby and the mother seemed to drive George into intense body hallucinations which were characterized by psychotically destructive contents.

George's outstanding hallucination during hospitalization was of seeing a fire destroying his little sister. At first George used to verbalize during these fire-hallucinations, and hence we knew how to read his agitated behaviour when it betrayed these visions.

It seemed that his hallucinatory and delusional restitution attempts consisted of incorporative and destructive tendencies toward his sister and mother. In his clearer periods he would state: "I'm afraid of killing my mother. I have ideas of wanting to kill her. Yes, I think of killing her, and these thoughts upset me so. That gives me bad feelings in my head. It makes me so upset when I am home. Doctor, you are supposed to take that out".

Defusion of instincts seems to result in uneven aggressivization of bodily part images, and a confusion of object representations with the introjects. The fragments of the self-images are secondarily recathected although with grossly instinctualized energy. The result is the frequently found body delusions and hallucinations observable in the schizophrenic child. After withdrawal from the object world, he recreates in his own internal reality both the subject and the object, the mother and himself. He may alternately take the outside object or parts of his own body, an eroticized hand or the aggressivized skin of his arm, or an inanimate object as symbol for the introject. He may show outward rage and destruction or all kinds of self-mutilating and self-destructive tendencies. That George's hallucinations served restitution as well, the following example will illustrate: While sitting next to the nurse whom George loved and also hated most, he appeared to hallucinate the big fire. During the conflagration George unzipped his overalls and began pulling at the nurse's skirt as though gathering up the ashes. He then put his hands in his overalls as if pouring in what he had gathered. This went on for a short time, then he zipped up his overalls and sat there smiling. "I've got a Hollinger (name of the nurse) in there ... that's what I've got in there". George was hilariously elated for the rest of the day and sat away in a corner, communicating with the introjected beloved (Klein, 1932; Klein *et al.*, 1952).

By this behaviour and the resulting affect we saw that George introjected the loved object and by so doing succeeded in restoring his former symbiotic unity with mother.

Summary

Research in child schizophrenia points to

(i)   an inborn or very early acquired basic defect of the ego,

    a. one of the manifestations of which in autistic children is the inability of perceptual discrimination of animate and inanimate, and of the mother as a living being in particular,

    b. whereas in the symbiotic psychotic child the most important manifestation of this basic defect is the insufficiency of the stimulus barrier (which prevents the mother's acting as efficient buffer against over-stimulation from without).

(ii) In consequence of these defects, the mother is either not perceived at all (as in autism) or remains undifferentiated from the self (symbiotic syndrome). Hence, all relations to the object world, to the child's own body as well as the concepts of the self are altered.

(iii) Apart from the basic defect, additional problems are created by virtue of the fact that maturation proceeds while development lags.

(iv) One of the most momentous maturational thrusts occurs in the phallic phase. The concentration of psychic energy in the sexual organs (and in the child's own body) leads to further depletion of the already precarious object cathexis. This phase resembles in many respects the picture of pre- or pseudo-psychosis in puberty (in which grave subjectively registered disturbance of the sense of identity is so conspicuous), of which it seems to be the forerunner.

(v) In order to survive the child has to develop several restitutive devices which I have tried to illustrate in one such case.

Notes

1. Paper prepared for the 20th Congress of the International Psycho-analytical Association, Paris, July–August, 1957. The author was prevented from attending the Congress. Mme Marie Bonaparte kindly offered a paper (in French) "Psycho-analysis in its relation to religion, science, and society", which will be published in the next issue (Ed.).
2. Clinical Professor of Psychiatry, Albert Einstein College of Medicine, New York City.
3. Compare Buytendijk as quoted by Werner.
4. According to Hartmann & Loewenstein (1946, p. 18) maturation indicates the processes of growth that occur relatively independent of environmental influences; development indicates the processes of growth in which environment and maturation interact more closely.
5. There seem, however, to be some exceptions to the rule of timing of this self-identity-recognition. Such an exception (premature recognition) was observed by me in the case of a monozygotic twin (Mahler & Silberpfennig, 1938).

References

Bak, R. (1939). Regression of ego-orientation and libido in schizophrenia. *International Journal of Psycho-Analysis, 20.*

Bak, R. (1954). The schizophrenic defence against aggression. *International Journal of Psycho-Analysis, 35.*

Bergman & Escalona (1949) Unusual sensitivities in very young children. *Psychoanal. Study Child, 3–4.*

Fliess, R. (1957). *Erogeneity and Libido.* New York: International Universities Press.

(1951). Negativism and emotional surrender. Paper read at the 17th Congress of the International Psycho-Analytic Association, Amsterdam, Holland (not published).

Freud, A. (1952). The role of bodily illness in the mental life of children. *Psychoanal. Study Child, 7.*

Freud, A. (1953). Some remarks on infant observation. *Psychoanal. Study Child, 8.*

Freud, S. (1923). The ego and the id.

Freud, S. (1939). An outline of psychoanalysis.

Greenacre, P. (1945). The biological economy of birth. *Psychoanal. Study Child. 1.*

Greenacre, P. (1953). Certain relationships between fetishism and the faulty development of the body image. *Psychoanal. Study Child, 8.*

Hartmann, H. (1950). Comments on the psychoanalytic theory of the ego. *Psychoanal. Study Child, 5.*

Hartmann, H. (1953). The metapsychology of schizophrenia. *Psychoanal. Study Child, 8.*

Hartmann, K., & Loewenstein (1946). Formation of psychic structure. *Psychoanal. Study Child, 2.*

Hermann, I. (1934). Urwahrnehmungen insb. Augenleuchten und Lautwerden des Inneren. *Int. Z. f. Psa., 20.*

Hermann, I. (1936). Sich Anklammern, auf Suche Gehen. *Int. Z. f. Psa., 22.*

Hoffer, W. (1950). Development of the body ego. *Psychoanal. Study Child, 5.*

Hoffer, W. (1951). Oral aggressiveness and ego development. *International Journal of Psycho-Analysis, 32.*

Jacobson, E. (1954). The self and the object world. *Psychoanal. Study Child, 9.*

Jacobson, E. (1957). Denial and repression. *Amer. J. Psa., 5.*

Kanner, L. (1942). Autistic disturbances of affective contact. *Am. J. Orthopsych., 12.*

Kanner, L. (1949). Early infantile autism. *Am. J. Orthopsych., 19.*

Klein, M. (1932). *The Psychoanalysis of Children.* London: Hogarth.

Klein, M. et al., (1952). *Developments in Psychoanalysis.* London: Hogarth.

Kris, E. (1950). Notes on the development and on some current problems of psychoanalytic child psychology. *Psychoanal. Study Child, 5.*

Linn, L. (1955). Some developmental aspects of the body-image. *International Journal of Psycho-Analysis, 36.*

Lowald, H. W. (1951). Ego and reality. *International Journal of Psycho-Analysis, 32.*

Mahler, M. S. (1952). On child psychosis and schizophrenia (autistic and symbiotic infantile psychosis). *Psychoanal. Study Child, 7.*

Mahler, M. S. (1957). Contribution to the panel on problems of identity. To be published in *Am. J. Psa.*

Mahler, R., & De Fries (1949). Clinical studies in benign and malignant cases of childhood psychosis (schizophrenia-like). *Am. J. Orthopsych.*, 19.

Mahler-Elkisch (1953). Disturbances of the ego in a case of infantile psychosis. *Psychoanal. Study Child*, 8.

Mahler-Gosliner (1955). On symbiotic child psychosis. *Psychoanal. Study Child*, 10.

Mahler-Schoenberger & Silberpfennig (1938). Schweizer Archiv für Neurologie und Psychiatrie 40 fasc. 2.

Piaget-Inhelder (1953). *Geneva, World Health Organization's Discussion on Child Development*, Vol. 1. New York: International Universities Press.

Ribble, M. (1941). Disorganizing factors in infant personality. *Am. J. Psychiatry*, 98.

Sechehaye (1956). The transference in symbolic realization. *International Journal of Psycho-Analysis*, 37.

Spitz, R. A. (1945). Diacritic and coenesthetic organizations. *Psa. Review.*

Spitz, R. A. (1951). The psychogenic diseases in infancy. *Psychoanal. Study Child*, 6.

Stirnimann (1949). Das Kind und seine früheste Umwelt. *Psychologische Praxis 6*. Basel: Karger.

Szasz, T. (1957). *Pain and Pleasure. A Study of Bodily Feelings.*

Weil, A. (1952). Clinical data and dynamic considerations in certain cases of childhood schizophrenia. *Am. J. Orthopsych.*

Werner, H. (1948). *Comparative Psychology of Mental Development*. New York: Follett.

Winnicott, D. W. (1953). Transitional objects and transitional phenomena. *International Journal of Psycho-Analysis*, 34.

Zazzo (1953). *Geneva, World Health Organization's Discussions on Child Development*, Vol. 1. New York: International Universities Press.

Article citation

Mahler, M. (1958). Autism and symbiosis, two extreme disturbances of identity. *International Journal of Psycho-Analysis, 39*: 77–82.

CHAPTER ELEVEN

New beginning and the paranoid and the depressive syndromes

Michael Balint

Editorial note

Nearly all the papers in this number of the Journal are by those of Mrs Klein's colleagues or pupils whose approach to psychoanalysis is known to be strongly influenced by her theoretical conclusions, so that their work will be widely taken as representative of hers. We are glad to include this paper by one old colleague and friend who had appreciated her work from the beginning. But we feel it should be made clear that his views on certain basic points are not the same as hers.

The divergence concerns the role of unconscious phantasy and early development, and so naturally also affects psychoanalytic procedure. It may be illustrated by one example:

Dr Balint, unlike Mrs Klein, believes there is a phase of primary object love in which aggressiveness, and the persecutory anxieties aroused by it, do not yet play an important role. But it is perhaps less about the priority than about the distorting influence of aggression that, in our view, far reaching differences lie. To Mrs Klein, aggression inevitably distorts the child's picture of the world, making him feel attacked with hatred whenever he is at all thwarted or deprived. Early environment may do much to increase, or lessen, this sense of persecution; but a "bad" home does not create it, nor does a good one prevent it from appearing.

To Dr Balint, however, persecutory feelings seem to be something which, in a good home, would hardly arise at all.

A more extreme form of this view, and of the technique which corresponds to it, was originally adopted by Ferenczi. And, although Dr Balint does not go as far as he did, the same objections would we think be made by Mrs Klein to both: namely, that there is an overemphasis on external factors which leads to an underrating of internal ones, and so to an underrating of the power of primary unconscious phantasies.

It follows from Mrs Klein's views on the primary importance of the paranoid–schizoid position that with every patient it will reappear in the transference, and that the success of every analysis depends on the extent to which its origin in the projection of aggression can then be made conscious by transference interpretations. But reassurance tends to prevent or obscure its reappearance in this form. Therefore, in her view, psychoanalytic procedure depends solely upon interpretations and reassurances are to be avoided. Now the indulgences on the forepleasure level which Dr Balint describes in this paper, and which he feels to be helpful to analysis, cannot be small in their effects on the patient's unconscious. We therefore believe that they must operate as reassurances which disturb the transference situation, and which, for this reason, would be avoided by Mrs Klein and other analysts practising her methods.

But while we have felt bound to draw attention to these differences in theory and technique, we welcome Dr Balint's paper as an original and stimulating exposition of divergent views.
P. H. R. M-K.

I

I felt greatly honoured when I was asked to contribute a paper to this number as I cannot consider myself Mrs Klein's pupil in the ordinary sense of the word. My justification for inclusion is a long-standing interest in her work, and—if I may call it so—a friendship dating back to our bygone Berlin days when both of us were still under analysis and by good luck for me we lived for some time only a few doors away from each other. In every other respect our positions were wholly different. I was a real beginner, fresh from the University, while Mrs Klein was already an analyst of repute who was listened to attentively, even though at times ironically. She still had an uphill fight to face, being the only non-academic and the only child analyst in the midst of a very academic and very "learned" German society. Time and again she brought her clinical material, using very courageously and for the sake of greater faithfulness the same naïve expressions of the nursery as her child patients did, often causing in her learned and reluctant audience embarrassment, incredulity or even sardonic laughter. Yet, despite this ambivalent reception she remained steadfast in her primary aim of showing that neurotic symptoms and defensive mechanisms found in adults can be observed also in young children and very often, in quite relevant respects, can be studied better in children than in adults. Both Mrs Klein and the analytic world have travelled a long way since those days. Many—certainly not all—of her then hotly disputed ideas have since become an integral part of the body of accepted analytic knowledge.

As my tribute to her birthday I wish to show how her ideas helped me to understand an impasse in my work and gave me hope that in the future this impasse might be avoided by better knowledge and skill. In 1932 I described[1] a peculiar phase in the analytic treatment of patients. Since then on several occasions I have returned to the same theme trying to describe it more and more exactly.

My clinical experience was briefly this: at times when the analytic work has already progressed a long way, i.e. towards the end of a cure, my patients began—very timidly at first—to desire, to expect, even to demand certain simple gratifications mainly though not exclusively from their analyst. On the surface these wishes appeared unimportant: to give a present to the analyst or—more frequently—to get one from him, to be allowed to touch or stroke him or to be touched or stroked by him, etc., and most frequently of all: to be able to hold his hand or just one of his fingers. Two highly important characteristics of these wishes are easily seen. First: they can be satisfied only by another human being, an autoerotic satisfaction is simply impossible. Second: the level of gratification never goes beyond that of mild forepleasure. Correspondingly[2] a really full satisfaction followed by an anticlimax can hardly ever be observed, only a more or less complete saturation. Thus, if satisfaction arrives at the right moment and with the right intensity, it leads to reactions which can be observed and recognized only with difficulty, as the level of pleasure amounts only to a tranquil quiet sense of well being.

This leads me to a very difficult technical problem: what the analyst should do about these wishes. The first task is obvious: both he and his patient must recognize them and understand their essentially primitive nature. This is a difficult task because these wishes—like all other material produced by the patient—are overdetermined, and all the overlying determinants must first be resolved by the analytic work before their primitiveness can clearly emerge. In most cases this much is sufficient. There are, however, some patients whose analysis—in my experience—demands more. They belong to a class which can be described either as deeply disturbed, or as people, whose ego development was distorted by early traumas. These patients have the ability—or compulsion, or symptom—of regressing to a state of infantile helplessness in which they do not seem to be able to comprehend intellectual considerations, i.e. interpretations couched in words. These states are, of course, overdetermined; they are a sign of strong resistance, an expression of intense fear, a bitter reproach, a way of demonstrating the disastrous effects of the trauma, a means of getting masochistic pleasure by repeating the surrender to the trauma and by inviting through helplessness another traumatic attack, etc., etc. In some such cases—encouraged by Ferenczi's experiments[3]—my patient and I agreed that some of the primitive wishes belonging to such a state should be satisfied in so far as they were compatible with the analytic situation. The terms of such "agreement" are naturally very elastic, but in the mutually trusting atmosphere of this period they have proved quite workable.

To maintain this mutually trusting atmosphere between patient and analyst requires very great tact and careful skill. On one side lies the precipice of addiction-like states. If the analyst is incautiously indulgent, the patients develop an almost insatiable greediness, they can never have enough. On the other side are the horrors of the state of frustration. Perhaps the most striking feature of this state is the overwhelming flood of sadistic tendencies. Session after session may be completely taken up with the most cruel phantasies of how the analyst should be treated as a retaliation for his indifferent and thus frustrating behaviour, and/or equally cruel phantasies about what the patient must expect as the well merited punishment of his aggressiveness. Similarly intense but well disguised aggressiveness can also be demonstrated in the addiction-like states; the form of the disguise is usually inhibited masochistic pleasure in one's own sufferings. In both states—of frustration and of addiction alike—in contrast to the silent signs of well timed and spaced satisfactions, one encounters vehement and noisy reactions caused by very painful, almost unbearable tensions in the patients. It is anything but easy to steer an even course through all these difficulties and pitfalls. However, if one succeeds, this period proves to be very fruitful; rigid ego structures, character traits and defensive mechanisms, ossified behaviour patterns and ever-repeated forms of object relations become analysable, understandable to both patient and analyst and finally adaptable to reality which then usually leads to a true termination of the analysis. I had two reasons for calling these phenomena new beginning. The main reason was psychological. The whole, very dramatic, process struck one as if the patient—though only very cautiously—gave up bit by bit his accustomed automatic forms of object relation, or in other words: his hitherto unchangeable, fateful, ways of loving and hating. Simultaneously he made timid attempts at trying out new ways which, however, could easily be proved to be really old ones which in their time had been spoilt for him by his frustrating, unresponsive, or merely indifferent early environment. His ever-recurring bad experiences amounting in some cases to real traumas forced him at that time to start his neurotic ways of loving and hating. Now, in the safety of the analytical transference, he seemed to give up tentatively his defences, to regress to an—as yet—undefended, naïve, i.e. pre-traumatic state, and to begin anew to love and to hate in a primitive way, which was then speedily followed by the development of a mature, well adapted, non-neurotic (as far as such a state is thinkable) way of loving and hating.

A piece of theory is the corollary of this train of thought. I consider this period of primitive, or archaic object love (at first—under the influence of Ferenczi—I used the term: passive object love) to be the *fons et origo* of human libido-development. The original and everlasting aim of all object relations is the primitive wish: I must be loved without any obligation on me and without any expectation of return from me. All "adult" ways of object relation, i.e. of loving and hating, are compromise formations between this original wish and the acceptance of an unkind, unpleasant, indifferent reality. If a neurotic compromise (i.e. one economically much too expensive) is resolved by analysis, the original primitive form of love emerges again. This has to be realized and the patient be allowed to go back, to "regress", to this archaic, pre-traumatic state. The more the patient is able to divest himself of his acquired forms of object relation, the more he is able to begin anew to love, the greater is the probability of his developing a non-neurotic "adult" way of loving.

My additional reason for calling these phenomena new beginning came from biology.[4] In highly unfavourable external circumstances only those living beings can survive who are able to give up their well differentiated organization and regress to primitive stages in their development, in order to begin the process of adaptation anew. Highly developed forms are more efficient but also more dependent on a special set of environmental factors. Primitive, undifferentiated states are elastic, capable of new adaptation in various directions. The similarity is striking: Highly differentiated forms both in biology and in psychology are rigid unadaptable; if a radical new adaptation becomes necessary, the highly differentiated organization must be reduced to its primitive undifferentiated form from which a new beginning may then issue.

II

Looking through my case material, i.e. all the patients who continued their analyses beyond the trial period, I find that a proper period of new beginning leading to a true termination of the analysis could be achieved only in about 20 per cent of my cases.[5] Another 20 per cent could be described as practically cured and another 30 to 40 per cent as considerably improved (the uncertainty is due to the interpretation of the adverb "considerably"), while 20 to 30 per cent must be considered as uninfluenced or not materially improved.

All these figures deserve thorough discussion. On this occasion I propose to examine what happened to the patients who achieved only a practical (not a theoretical) cure and to those who could be improved but not cured. If my idea about the importance of the new beginning is correct, the first question in this examination must be: what happened to the patients during this period? I mentioned this problem already in my first paper on this subject, in 1934, but in spite of constant attention and endeavour ever since, I have not been able to arrive at a satisfactory theoretical clarification. Using some of Mrs Klein's ideas, I think I can now take an important step towards solution.

My clinical experience has been that all patients proceed very cautiously towards what I call "new beginning". This cautiousness I interpreted—to myself but also to my patients—as a precipitate of all the frustrations suffered during their development, on the lines of "a burnt child dreads the fire". Often we discovered that the patient's early environment was anything but loving, in fact quite often deliberately and maliciously frustrating. In other cases the environment apparently was not malicious, only careless or indifferent which, however, was interpreted by the patient's phantasies as malicious or hostile—sometimes probably correctly. All this, naturally, was worked through both in the recollection and in the repetition, i.e. in the transference to the analytical situation.

Even so, in some cases the mutually trusting atmosphere of the new beginning would not develop. The patients remained suspicious and mistrustful towards their analyst in spite of honest endeavour on both sides. And although they could speak as a possibility about their awakening primitive wishes—so characteristic of the period of new beginning—they could never relax, i.e. abandon their suspicious adult selves to the extent of feeling these wishes as an actual reality. They remained even in their most relaxed states split adults who "took care of themselves", they could not reach the state when they were "one with themselves".[6]

This state is—I think—reminiscent of that described by Mrs Klein as the "paranoid position".[7] The patients, in their innermost selves, are convinced that everybody else is bad, hostile, malicious, an evil-wisher who grudges any happiness to anybody—and they readily admit that they too are hostile, bad and grudging. According to them the only true, the only possible relation between them and their environment, in fact between any two human beings, is that of guarded suspicion and never relaxing watchfulness. People do not love each other and if anybody says he does, or merely tries to show sincere interest (e.g. the analyst), it is the easiest thing for these patients to prove that all this is only hypocritical pretence, a make-believe, a clumsy attempt at misleading a fool in order to take advantage of him after lulling him into relaxing his guard. It is amazing how often these people succeed in creating a world around themselves in which all this is really true. And still more amazing, that sometimes they can trap their analyst as well. In spite of keeping constant watch on counter-transference—I must admit—I have not always been able to keep completely clear of this world of general suspicion.

Is one justified in calling this world of suspicion which the patient creates around himself out of his transference and of the systematically provoked and nursed counter-transferences of practically all of his objects, a world of persecutory anxieties? Mrs Klein uses these two terms—paranoid and persecutory—as synonyms, perhaps even preferring the latter as a more general notion. As far as my experience goes, in the phase described above, which precedes the relaxation and abandonment of the period of new beginning, the attitude of the patients can be best described in terms of delusions of reference (*Beziehungswahn*). Everything, the most everyday happening, will inevitably be referred to the patient's own person, everything has some hidden meaning and almost always this deep, the "true" meaning is inconsiderateness and lovelessness. The question, therefore, is: can persecution on the one hand, and loveless, careless indifference on the other, be considered as meaning the same thing? Or, is this meticulous distinction only a late development without any meaning for the primitive unconscious mind?

Even if I am inclined to accept this latter possibility for the patient's (and the child's) unconscious, I cannot do so for our terminology. Words have their inevitable associations, not only for the patient but also for the analyst; using one word instead of another of necessity summons up a whole cluster of associations, creates a very definite atmosphere in our minds—and in our discussions. That is why I wish, when describing this kind of environment, to stick to careless loveless indifference, creating in turn fear and suspicion in the patient. This state of affairs is adequately described by "paranoid" attitude or position and I propose to use "persecutory" and "persecution" only in their proper sense, not as general notions.

Some people seem to be unable to overcome completely this barrier of suspicion. With my present technique at least I have not been able to resolve this world of suspicion in all my patients. With the patients who finished their analyses in the stage when they could admit—as a possibility—that they were feeling those primitive wishes but could not abandon themselves to break down the barrier between themselves and these wishes, the analytic cure usually achieved quite commendable results. After analysis these people could, as a rule, maintain a good social adaptation, achieve social and financial success and show hardly any neurotic symptoms. They have no serious difficulty with their sexual life, usually no impotence or frigidity. But somehow their love life is cool and colourless. They can never accept their partners as true equals; the partners though quite attractive and pleasant people, do not mean much. The patients themselves remain all their lives independent, unattached, lonely people, somewhat suspicious, hypercritical and overbearing. Characteristically their criticisms though never unjustified or incorrect, are always exaggerated, somehow out of proportion. Another interesting feature is that they do not feel ill and in fact they cannot be called ill.

If I was able to help my patients out of this paranoid position, another state developed; and here too, Mrs Klein's work has helped me a great deal towards its proper evaluation. Before describing this state, I wish to add that the change from the suspicious state to this new one is a very gradual process fraught with several real relapses and with still more that threaten, but do not materialize. This new state is best described as depression. As a rule the patients say in so many words: I am worthless, unlovable; I know I ought to be different; I see it would be better for me and for everyone if I were different; I would be a much better man in every way, more pleasant, more lovable, perhaps even happy—but I cannot change, it is totally impossible. Sometimes they can even admit that they do not want to change or dare not.

Behind all that façade, however, there is the feeling of a deep, painful, narcissistic wound which, as a rule, can be made conscious without serious difficulty, somehow in this way: It is terrifying and dreadfully painful that I am not loved for what I am, time and again I cannot avoid seeing that people are critical of me; it is an irrefutable fact that no one loves me as I want to be loved. From here it is an easy step for the patient to get back into the paranoid state by projecting the real cause of this ever present experience on the general loveless indifference between man and man. If this can be prevented by correct and timely interpretations, the patient cannot but admit that he—or at least parts of himself—are not really lovable, or using Mrs Klein's word: not really good. In this way a long-standing but carefully covered up split becomes apparent and a very painful process starts in which one part of the patient's mind—the healthy part of his ego—has to struggle with the rest of his ego and his old superego—with some help, it is true, from the analyst.

This is a very hard and painful fight, giving up consciously parts of ourselves as unlovable and unacceptable to our fellow men—or using again Mrs Klein's word: as bad. By now the patient knows the history of these parts, that they have been developed mainly as defences against an environment felt to be cruel, indifferent, etc.; but at the same time he knows also that those parts represent, albeit in a distorted way, the people most important and dearest to him and— last but not least—these parts have been for many, many years and still are important parts of himself which he valued highly. An additional reason for the high emotional value of these parts to the patient is that they are, so to speak, the last survivors of his archaic object relation, they are the remnants of the eternal wish that he may live without the strain of constantly testing the reality, and without any obligation of regard or consideration for the wishes and sensitivities of people around him. All these wishes have become incorporated in the introjected archaic objects or, using another metaphor, the introjection of the archaic objects has enabled these wishes to survive in great force. The stronger these wishes, the greater is the task of renouncing them consciously. During this very bitter struggle the patients show all the features described so poignantly by Freud:[8] "A profoundly painful dejection, abrogation of interest in the outside world, loss of capacity to love, inhibition of all activity, and a lowering of the self-regarding feelings, ... culminating in expectations of punishment".

Is one to call this syndrome melancholia or depression? Here I am fully on the side of Mrs Klein who hardly ever calls this state melancholia, but speaks of depressive position and depressive anxieties.[9] In my opinion the clinical observations reported above have a significantly different mechanism from that studied and described by Abraham and Freud[10] for which I propose to reserve the term melancholia, while depression could be used in a wider sense which should include the classical melancholia, the early states described by Mrs Klein, my clinical observations and very likely many more others.[11] I think it can be accepted that one condition, perhaps the distinguishing one of every depression is a very painful split leading to one part of the personality rejecting the other part and trying to discard it altogether, even to annihilate it. (In paranoid states this fight seems to be successfully terminated, all the bad things have been projected outside, the ego feels whole, clever, superior and often overbearing—in fact like a true conqueror. Like every conqueror, however, the paranoiac, too, has to organize a police state around himself in which suspicion reigns supreme.) In classical melancholia—according to Fenichel[12] it is either the ego that fights against the superego and the introjects or the superego that fights against the ego and the introjects. Neither of these two descriptions fits my case.

To show what I mean I shall start with the every-day adaptation to reality. In every such process giving up part of our personality (certain of our wishes) for some time or even for good is unavoidably involved. As we know from Freud,[13] a very instructive example of this is mourning. Conversely every adaptation can be described as, and perhaps is, in fact, mourning. From here an interesting line of thought leads to the general problem of the acceptance of unpleasure;[14] certainly a most important facet of adaptation. All this—mourning, adaptation, the classical melancholia, in fact every form of depression—show very strong secondary narcissistic features, usually taking the form of a bitter resentment about an undeserved unfair and unjust injury—a mixture of paranoid and depressive mechanisms. Mourning, again, is a good example. Under the pressure of the feeling of an unjust injury quite often markedly paranoid features develop, as can be often observed after the death of a beloved person: assuming hostile intentions in the doctors who did not treat our beloved with proper skill and care, or even accusing the dead partner of not taking enough care of himself, etc.—obvious projections of one's own unconscious tendencies.

The depressive states, preceding the new-beginning, in many points differ considerably from these forms. There is undoubtedly the fight of one part of the personality against the other (the precondition of every depression) but this time the aim is not to create or to widen a split but to remove it, to enable the patient to be "one with himself". The parts against which the patient's ego has to fight are not rejected, condemned or hated (although these feelings may be, and often are, present) but above all mourned for, and—*sit venia verbo*—buried with full honours. And lastly, the whole process happens all the time on two planes simultaneously; on a narcissistic plane in the patient's mind and on the plane of transference, i.e. in an object relation. In my opinion, this last quality constitutes the crucial difference between all the other depressive states and the therapeutic depression, of which the phenomena in the new-beginning period are but one example. In this benign form of depression the patient in his newly won courage allows himself to experience the actual revival of old, primitive, object relations; he admits them not only as mere possibilities but as actual wishes and feelings, although he is in no doubt that the analytical situation permits at best only very partial gratifications and even these only for a very limited period; he does not shut himself off from the painful sweetness of these desires, i.e. does not repress them. In this way he may remain "unsplit", the memory of these gratifications remains accessible and even further gratifications of these infantile, primitive longings by a real object remain potentially possible, although admittedly somewhat comical because of their often very primitive nature.

I must add that my knowledge of these phenomena is still not so well founded as it is of the paranoid state, and consequently most of my mistakes used to happen here. Perhaps an added difficulty is the very high vulnerability of patients in the depressive period which is far beyond that of the paranoid period, in fact it surpasses all expectation. Time and again I was surprised that in spite of every precaution and—as far as I know—the best of wills, one or the other of my patients felt deeply and unjustly hurt by an interpretation or even by a "neutral" remark or an "everyday" gesture of mine.

As in the paranoid state, it happens that some patients cannot be helped—by my present technique—through the depressive state, and so finish their analysis with a partial result. And similarly, although the therapeutic result is quite commendable, it is not as good as one would wish. These patients, too, usually show a good social adaptation, a good measure of success in life, but somehow they remain discontented, they cannot enjoy their laurels. For them there is always some flaw in everything, fate is never as kind to them as to others. Despite this they are well liked, though often considered difficult and awkward; lots of people are willing to go out of their way to help them to quite a considerable degree which these patients accept and even demand as a matter of course. Their love life runs on similar lines; they are usually fairly successful, people fall for them often quite unexpectedly, still their basic ambivalent attitude remains unchanged. They accept the love offered to them, even demand more and more of it and then go on wondering about the true motives of the partner for choosing them, whether these motives are sound and trustworthy enough. The same applies to their physical sexuality; as a rule they are not impotent or frigid but never quite certain of it. Their whole sexuality seems to be rather precarious but somehow it works. In contrast to the patients who left analysis during the paranoid period who do not feel ill and hardly ever complain, the patients leaving analysis before the depressive state could be resolved usually complain a lot, try to raise guilt feelings in their environment (and in their former analyst) by exhibiting and even flaunting their shortcomings, but they hardly ever want to make real efforts towards a basic change. Apparently they cannot renounce their right to expect miraculous help from their environment—a clear remnant of the archaic object love.

III

To sum up my clinical experience (leaving out the technical difficulties): new beginning means the capacity for an unsuspicious, trusting self-abandoned and relaxed object-relation. There are two clinically necessary conditions without which a proper phase of new beginning cannot develop. These are: (1) the relinquishing of the paranoid attitude, the realization that the paranoid anxieties were unfounded or at least grossly exaggerated, (2) the acceptance without undue anxiety of a certain amount of depression as an inevitable condition of life, the confidence that it is possible—nay certain—to emerge from this kind of depression a better man.[15]

Is it justified to assume that the sequence: paranoid attitude—depression—archaic object love, occurring regularly in the end phases of my analyses, is significant? i.e. that it is determined by some principle of repetition? Or is this sequence accidental, caused merely by the peculiarity of my technique? In a paper recently reprinted in English[16] I discussed in detail the reasons for preferring the first assumption with regard to the archaic object love. But if we accept the view that the occurrence of primitive forms of object love in the transference situation has the significance of repetition, the same must be assumed of its concomitant syndromes: the paranoid attitude and the depression.

The next objection will likely be: the sequence—paranoid attitude–depression–primary object love—observed in adult patients, though perhaps of repetitive nature, is probably so distorted that any inference to early states of development is unjustified without careful validation by direct observation of the child. This—on the surface—appears to be a legitimate argument which can be, and is in fact often, used against any inference from adult to infant—except against the classical theory of primary narcissism. In the paper just quoted, I think, I showed the fallacy in this argument.

But if we accept the view that the clinical observations described in this paper are, at least partly, determined by repetition of early states of human development, we have to face a very old and very vexed problem of psychoanalysis, that of chronology. The clinical sequence is doubtless: paranoia–depression–new-beginning. Moreover, till the full development of the last phase, the therapeutic situation remains precarious and the patient may relapse at any moment into either of the two previous states. Can one conclude that the above sequence describes the line of development of the human mind? It is a weighty argument that Mrs Klein and her school think, in fact, that the first phase of the human mind is dominated by paranoid anxieties and mechanisms and that this is followed by the depressive position.

If I were to accept this chronology, I should have to give up the idea of the archaic object love as the first phase; it is true, however, that even in this case the archaic object love might be retained as a focal point of all later forms of object love but it would be preceded by the paranoid and the depressive phases. In other words: The sequence: paranoid attitude–depression–archaic form of love, as observed in adult patients, corresponds to the sequence of early stages of the human mind. Mrs Klein's theory of the persecutory phase followed by depression is correct; one has only to insert the archaic object love between these two earlier phases and any later form of object relation.

There are, however, several important clinical facts that speak against this conception. I have mentioned already that both the paranoid and the depressive states preceding the period of new beginning show many narcissistic features. According to my experience narcissism is always secondary.[17] (If I am right, Mrs Klein has recently come very near to this idea. In any case she has stressed time and again the presence of early object relations, an inevitable corollary of which is that narcissism is secondary—unless it is assumed that object relations and a narcissistic attitude coexist right from the beginning of extra-uterine life which, however, is contrary to my clinical observations discussed in the paper just mentioned.) If we accept the secondary nature of all narcissistic features, then it is very probable that syndromes incorporating many narcissistic traits are also secondary phenomena, forms of reaction, and not primary phases.

A second, still weightier argument is provided by the different fate of these three phases during analytic treatment under my technique. All three must be interpreted and worked through, none of them can be carried over unchanged into adult life. As I have mentioned, the paranoid phantasies must be worked through, recognized as originating from a greatly distorted picture of the reality, i.e. from faulty reality testing, and then be given up. The depression—caused by the realization that the environment is largely indifferent towards us (or as someone said to me recently: "has not been cut to fit us") and that we must renounce certain of our wishes if we want any favour from our environment—must be accepted as inevitable and the attempts at circumventing it largely given up. Or in other words: removing the paranoid anxieties enables the patient to evaluate the every day hardship of life in their proper proportion, while removing the depressive anxieties enables him to accept a certain amount of depression as caused by common frustrations and to arrange his life better by taking full account of them.

The fate of the archaic object love is quite different. Although the difference is great, I find it difficult to express it in words. Both the paranoid and the depressive attitude, preceding the period of new-beginning appear to be markedly pathological, they must be overcome, put right; the archaic form of object love is only undeveloped, and the healthy adult way of love life may grow out of it in a straight line. The task of analytic therapy is only to assist this development. From another angle the same difference may be described in this way: both the paranoid and the depressive attitude are fraught with anxieties; analysis can reduce the intensity of these anxieties and then these attitudes lose their importance. There is no fear inherent in the archaic object love—only naïve confidence and unsuspicious self-abandonment; the more paranoid and depressive anxieties and fears have been removed by analysis, the more clearly the phenomena of the archaic object love—the new-beginning in an adult patient—develop before our eyes.

I find it difficult to reconcile these clinical facts with the theory that the very first extra-uterine phase of the human mind is characterized by the paranoid attitude, out of which then the depressive position develops. The next argument, I expect, will be worded somehow in this way: there is no need to reconcile my observation with those of Mrs Klein and her school, the two sets of observations are—because of the different techniques used—incommensurable. Although very plausible, I think this argument is unacceptable as it is only a pusillanimous, and at the same time stealthily supercilious, attempt at avoiding the real issue, admittedly a very difficult one. The real issue is this: how far does the analyst's individual technique, i.e. his attitude in the analytical situation, his theoretical expectations, the set of technical terms used by him, etc., etc., influence among other things: (a) the patient's reactions and associations, (b) the analyst's observations, and (c) the analyst's description of his observations. As may be expected, most analysts (including myself) superciliously admit the possibility, or rather the certainty, of such a "distorting" influence by the technique of any one not belonging to their own school while pusillanimously stating that their own technique exerts no, or only negligible, influence of this kind.

In my Zurich Congress paper[18] I dealt with some aspects of this cardinal problem, especially with the importance to the analyst of using his own accustomed ways of thinking and speaking, i.e. his familiar set of technical terms. I am fully aware that by this only the very fringe of the problem has been reached and that it will not be easy to penetrate further. But what are we to do in the meanwhile? i.e. before we know with some certainty how far the analyst's honest account of his experience in the analytical situation is biased by his technique?

I wish to propose two interim working principles. First: for the time being we should accept every positive finding by an analyst as something that must be evaluated by, and then allotted some place in, any theoretical construction. A theory which cannot explain and place a clinical observation satisfactorily should be considered with due scepticism. On the other hand, negative findings need not necessarily be given such weight. The reason for this discrimination is that it is not impossible for one to miss this or that event in the long process of analysis, or not to attribute to it the weight it deserves, because of some emotional blind spot not yet dealt with by one's own training analysis or the subsequent self-analysis. On the other hand, it is not very likely that one could be misled to the extent of reporting something non-existent. Secondly: as long as we have hardly any well-founded knowledge of the dynamisms governing the relation of the various technical approaches to their respective theoretical findings, we have no choice but to accept most analytic techniques as peers. I wish I could add to this frighteningly sweeping statement: "except a few obviously faulty ones"! The reason why I abstain from including this rider, is that for the present I cannot see any criteria which would enable us to decide objectively what is an "obviously faulty" technique and what is not, although, like every other analyst, subjectively I am convinced that doubtless there are some "obviously faulty" techniques.

Honouring these two working principles let us now return to the differing descriptions of our analytical experiences. Among the new terms introduced by Mrs Klein we find a very important notion which must have been based on clinical experiences very similar to, if not identical with, those which lead me to the idea of the primitive object relation. This notion is the phantasy of the "idealized object". Such an object is inviolate and inviolable, it has no needs and no demands, is eternal and never changing and it can and does give bountifully everything that one can wish for. Obviously a very near description of what I would call an archaic or primitive object, though equally obviously it has a much richer content. The first question we have to decide is, is this "idealized object" a primary or a secondary phenomenon, or in other words has it or has it not a history? I think it is correct to say that the general view is that the "idealized object" is the result of a split, the other split off part being the persecutory object. But, if we accept this, we must ask ourselves what was the original, the unsplit, the primary object? what was its history before the split? and what will its fate be in later life? e.g. does it disappear altogether in the turmoil of the archaic splitting? The present literature—if I am right—does not give answers to any of these questions, in fact, it has not even asked these questions.

Apparently we have reached a problem not yet solved, perhaps not even noticed. In my view there are two trains of thought which point to a possible solution; both of them are based on the fact that the concept of the "idealized object" is much richer than that of the "archaic object". First the "idealised object" contains a very important element of denial, especially the denial of aggressive intentions against it. The true meaning of being inviolate and inviolable is, very likely, the bitter experience that the most violent aggressiveness has proved of no avail against it. This characteristic alone points irrefutably to its comparative lateness, to its secondary nature. In contradistinction there is no quality of aggressivity or its denial in the concept of archaic object relation, only confidence and self-abandonment.

A second train of thought makes use of the interrelation between the development of libidinous object relation, on the one hand, and that of reality testing, on the other.[19] Primary, archaic, object relation hardly demands any reality testing, there is no need to account for the object. A change is brought about by the experience of being frustrated or being compelled to wait for satisfaction by an indifferent, insufficiently considerate, or even hostile environment. This enforces upon the child a very primitive kind of reality testing, resulting in splitting the object into a frustrating bad, and into a gratifying good, part object. Out of the former develop the phantasies about the hostile, persecutory or depressing objects, out of the latter—as a kind of reaction-formation or reparation—the phantasy of the "idealized object". It is certain that there are many more phases in this complicated interrelation of two parallel developments (that of object relations and that of testing the reality); the last rung of which is the mature form of object relation with a fully developed sense of reality enabling the individual to accept a certain measure of unpleasure as unavoidable, or in other words, to accept reality as real and even to enjoy it as far as it is enjoyable. But, behind every one of the many forms of object relation there remains practically unchanged the eternal archaic wish: I shall be loved for every little bit that I am, by every one of my objects, for whom I need not care, whose interests and sensitivity I need not consider, who shall be just there when I want them, and shall not bother me after my needs have been satisfied.[20]

Considering all this, I think that the unsuspicious, naïve, archaic object love should be considered as the first postnatal phase in the development of the human mind; it is a centre or a nodal point from which all later developments radiate. One such development is narcissism: if I am not loved by the world (in the way I want it), I must love myself. Another direction of development is depression and the paranoid attitude. These two are closely interlinked, each of them can be used as a defence against the other; quite often—even after the termination of an analysis—I remained in doubt whether to consider the change over from one position to the other in that particular case as a progression or a regression. Several of these baffling clinical experiences have been mentioned in this paper, e.g. that patients who left the analysis without working through their paranoid attitudes usually appear healthier and feel better than those who went through their paranoid position but left the analysis before fully coping with their depressive attitude. All this prompts me to leave the chronology of these two phases undecided for the time being. Yet another direction of development, mainly due to certain educational influences, is what analysis describes as anal-sadistic object-relation. And last, but not least, there is that very complicated and rather precarious direction which we call adult sexuality and genital object-love.

Unfortunately the different lines of development are neither straight, nor cleanly separated one from the others. I pointed out that both the paranoid and the depressive positions show many markedly narcissistic features; conversely in the clinical picture of very narcissistic patients strong paranoid and depressive features are always present.

If we accept the view that a real adaptation—the acceptance of unpleasure—is only possible if one can face depression without undue anxiety, then the depressive position must be considered as a second focus through which every line of development associated with adaptation must pass. The relation between these two nodal points of development—archaic object-love and normal depression—is far from being clear; on the basis of my scanty knowledge I expect that they have a profound influence on each other. I could quote many more examples of such entanglement of directions of development or—using another metaphor—of overlapping.

I do not think, however, that a similar overall importance can be attributed to the paranoid position, which then perhaps means that the depressive position must be considered more fundamental, more primitive than the paranoid.

I wish to mention one more complication. My experiences concern only adults and thus the conclusions reported here are inferences, based on the assumption that these processes, these positions or syndromes, have a fairly similar dynamism, stay in a fairly similar chronological and structural relation to each other in adults and in children. Although as far as we know there is no proof against this assumption, it is only a plausibility, not a certainty. On the other hand, it must not be forgotten that practically all our knowledge about the infantile mind was acquired when analysing adults. The only exception of which I know are Mrs Klein's ideas and theories which originated mostly—though not exclusively—in her work with children. Despite all these complications I think that a theory of human development starting with the state of archaic object love is worth considering and worth examining again after more clinical material has been collected.

It is fair to say that the value of any new contribution to scientific theory or practice can best be assessed by the quality and number of problems that have emerged under its impact. Measured by this standard the value of Mrs Klein's contribution is high indeed. It is no exaggeration to say that her ideas are at present perhaps the most hotly discussed topics in our psychoanalysis. This is only the natural consequence of her dauntless courage in directing her research towards the very roots of human nature, in consequence of which her ideas cannot be but challenging.

In my tribute to her birthday I have tried to show her how the challenge of her ideas has helped me to solve some of my old problems and led me to find many more new ones.

Notes

1. In "Charakteranalyse und Neubeginn", read at the 12th Congress of the International Psycho-Analytic Association, published: *Int. Zeitschr. f. Psa.* (1934), *20*, 54.
2. M. Balint (1936). Eros and Aphrodite, *Int. Zeitschr. f. Psa.*, 22, 453; *International Journal of Psycho-Analysis* (1938), *19*, 199.
3. S. Ferenczi (1930). The principle of relaxation and neocatharsis, *International Journal of Psycho-Analysis*, 11, 428. Child analysis in the analysis of adults, (1931), *International Journal of Psycho-Analysis*, 12, 468. Confusion of tongues between the adults and the child (1949, originally in 1933), *International Journal of Psycho-Analysis*, 30, 225.
4. M. Balint (1932). Psychosexuelle Parallelen zum biogenetischen Grundgesetz, *Imago*, 18, 14.
5. Being abstract, i.e. lifeless, figures are a dangerous matter. Quoted by themselves, without relation to experience on which they are based, i.e. life, they can be very misleading. That is why I wish to add that my case material includes all sorts of patients from a short-lived monosymptomatic psychosomatic illness to very severe paranoias, schizophrenias and depressions, cases with good prognoses and so-called "hopeless" cases; the ages range from sixteen to over sixty and there are a number of training analyses amongst them. In short: the very mixed bag of a general psychoanalytic practice.
6. Ferenczi (1949). Notes and fragments, integration and splitting. *International Journal of Psycho-Analysis*, 30, 241. (Originally written in 1932.)
7. E.g. in Klein (1946). Notes on some schizoid mechanisms, *International Journal of Psycho-Analysis*, 27, 99.
8. Mourning and melancholia, in *S.E.*, 4: 153.
9. E.g. in Klein (1935). A contribution to the psychogenesis of manic depressive states, *International Journal of Psycho-Analysis*, 16, 145; Mourning and its relation to manic-depressive states, (1940) *International Journal of Psycho-Analysis*, 21, 125. The Oedipus Complex in the light of early anxieties, (1945) *International Journal of Psycho-Analysis*, 26, 11.
10. Freud, e.g. in A Contribution to the psychogenesis of manic depressive states, Abraham: Development of the libido, in *S.E.*, p. 418 ff. London: Hogarth Press.

11. Cf. M. Balint (1951) On punishing offenders, In: *Psychoanalysis and Culture*. New York.

12. *The Psychoanalytic Theory of Neuroses* (1945), p. 398. New York: Norton & Co.

13. Mourning and melancholia, in *S.E.*, *4*: 153.

14. Ferenczi: Bausteine zur Psychoanalyse, 1, p. 84. Further Contributions, p. 366.

15. Professor Lagache who kindly read the MS, suggested that the idea of new beginning should not be restricted to the events occurring towards the end of a treatment but to use it also in relation to all the occasions during an extended analysis when a patient gives up some complicated defensive mechanism for the first time. In this experience—which I can fully confirm—each time the patient first develops some form of the paranoid and depressive syndromes described in this paper, overcomes it and then starts some new attitude, usually of a primitive nature. Further analysis proves in all such cases that the newly begun attitudes or activities are in fact repetitions of early forms. Such an extension is probably legitimate and I think it will prove to be fruitful as it will almost certainly lead to a better understanding of the all important problem of tolerating unpleasure and through it to the general problem of adaptation to reality, especially to the reality of one's objects. I see, however, a number of complications and must therefore content myself with this short note.

16. M. Balint (1937) Early developmental states of the ego. primary object love, *Imago*, *23*: 270; (1949) *International Journal of Psycho-Analysis*, *30*: 265.

17. *Ibid*.

18. M. Balint (1950) Changing therapeutical aims and techniques in psychoanalysis. *International Journal of Psycho-Analysis*, *31*: 121–122.

19. Cf. Alice Balint (1949) Love for the mother and mother-love, *International Journal of Psycho-Analysis*, *30*: 251–259.

20. Attention was called to a very important new field for studying clinical phenomena closely linked with this idea by D. W. Winnicott in a paper: "Transitional objects and transitional phenomena" read before the British Psycho-Analytic Society on 30 May, 1951.

Article citation

Balint, M. (1952). New beginning and the paranoid and the depressive syndromes. *International Journal of Psycho-Analysis*, *33*: 214–224.

CHAPTER TWELVE

On transference[1]

D. W. Winnicott

My contribution to this Symposium on Transference deals with one special aspect of the subject. It concerns the influence on analytical practice of the new understanding of infant care which has, in turn, derived from analytical theory.

There has often, in the history of psychoanalysis, been a delay in the direct application of analytical metapsychology in analytical practice. Freud was able to formulate a theory of the very early stages of the emotional development of the individual at a time when theory was being applied only in the treatment of the well-chosen neurotic case. (I refer to the period of Freud's work between 1905, the "Three contributions", and 1914, "Narcissism".)

For instance, the part of theory that concerns the primary process, primary identification, and primary repression appeared in analytical practice only in the form of a greater respect that analysts had, as compared with others, for the dream and for psychic reality.

As we look back now we may say that cases were well chosen as suitable for analysis if in the very early personal history of the patient there had been good enough infant-care. This good enough adaptation to need at the beginning had enabled the individual's ego to come into being, with the result that the earlier stages of the establishment of the ego could be taken for granted by the analyst. In this way it was possible for analysts to talk and write as if the human infant's first experience was the first feed, and as if the object-relationship between mother and infant that this implied was the first significant relationship. This was satisfactory for the practising analyst, but it could not satisfy the direct observer of infants in the care of their mothers.

At that time theory was groping towards a deeper insight into this matter of the mother with her infant, and indeed the term "primary identification" implies an environment that is not yet differentiated from that which will be the individual. When we see a mother holding an infant soon after birth, or an infant not yet born, at this same time we know that there is another point of view, that of the infant if the infant were already there; and from this point of view the infant is either not yet differentiated out, or else the process of differentiation has started and there is absolute dependence on the immediate environment and its behaviour. It has now become possible to study and use this vital part of old theory in a new and practical way in analytical work, work either with borderline cases or else with the psychotic phases or moments that occur in the course of the analyses of neurotic patients or normal people. This work widens the concept of transference since at the time of the analysis of these phases the ego of the patient cannot be assumed as an established entity, and there can be no transference neurosis for which, surely, there must be an ego, and indeed an intact ego, an ego that is able to maintain defences against anxiety that arises out of instinct the responsibility for which is accepted.

I have referred to the state of affairs that exists when a move is made in the direction of emergence from primary identification. Here at first is absolute dependence. There are two possible kinds of outcome: by the one environmental adaptation to need is good enough, so that there comes into being an ego which, in time, can experience id-impulses; by the other environmental adaptation is not good enough, and so there is no true ego establishment, but instead there develops a pseudo-self which is a collection of innumerable reactions to a succession of failures of adaptation. I would like here to refer to Anna Freud's paper: "The widening scope of indications for psychoanalysis".[2] The environment, when it successfully adapts at this early stage, is not recognized, or even recorded, so that in the original stage there is no feeling of dependence; whenever the environment fails in its task of making active adaptation, however, it automatically becomes recorded as an impingement, something that interrupts the continuity of being, that very thing which, if not broken up, would have formed itself into the ego of the differentiating human being.

There may be extreme cases in which there is no more than this collection of reactions to environmental failures of adaptation at the critical stage of emergence from primary identification. I am sure this condition is compatible with life, and with physical health. In the cases on which my work is based there has been what I call a true self hidden, protected by a false self. This false self is no doubt an aspect of the true self. It hides and protects it, and it reacts to the adaptation failures and develops a pattern corresponding to the pattern of environmental failure. In this way the true self is not involved in the reacting, and so preserves a continuity of being. This hidden true self suffers an impoverishment, however, that results from lack of experience.

The false self may achieve a deceptive false integrity, that is to say a false ego-strength, gathered from an environmental pattern, and from a good and reliable environment; for it by no means follows that early maternal failure must lead to a general failure of child-care. The false self cannot, however, experience life, and feel real.

In the favourable case the false self develops a fixed maternal attitude towards the true self, and is permanently in a state of holding the true self as a mother holds a baby at the very beginning of differentiation and of emergence from primary identification.

In the work that I am reporting the analyst follows the basic principle of psychoanalysis, that the patient's unconscious leads, and is alone to be pursued. In dealing with a regressive tendency the analyst must be prepared to follow the patient's unconscious process if he is not to issue a directive and so step outside the analyst's role. I have found that it is not necessary to step outside the analyst's role and that it is possible to follow the patient's unconscious lead in this type of case as in the analysis of neurosis. There are differences, however, in the two types of work.

Where there is an intact ego and the analyst can take for granted these earliest details of infant-care, then the setting of the analysis is unimportant relative to the interpretative work. (By setting, I mean the summation of all the details of management.) Even so there is a basic ration of management in ordinary analysis which is more or less accepted by all analysts.

In the work I am describing the setting becomes more important than the interpretation. The emphasis is changed from the one to the other.

The behaviour of the analyst, represented by what I have called the setting, by being good enough in the matter of adaptation to need, is gradually perceived by the patient as something that raises a hope that the true self may at last be able to take the risks involved in starting to experience living. Eventually the false self hands over to the analyst. This is a time of great dependence, and true risk, and the patient is naturally in a deeply regressed state. (By regression here I mean regression to dependence and to the early developmental processes.) This is also a highly painful state because the patient is aware, as the infant in the original situation is not aware, of the risks entailed. In some cases so much of the personality is involved that the patient must be in care at this stage. The processes are better studied, however, in those cases in which these matters are confined, more or less, to the time of the analytic sessions.

One characteristic of the transference at this stage is the way in which we must allow the patient's past to be the present. This idea is contained in Mme Sechehaye's book and in her title *Symbolic Realization*. Whereas in the transference neurosis the past comes into the consulting room, in this work it is more true to say that the present goes back into the past, and is the past. Thus the analyst finds himself confronted with the patient's primary process in the setting in which it had its original validity.

Good enough adaptation by the analyst produces a result which is exactly that which is sought, namely, a shift in the patient of the main site of operation from a false to a true self. There is now for the first time in the patient's life an opportunity for the development of an ego, for its integration from ego nuclei, for its establishment as a body ego, and also for its repudiation of an external environment with the initiation of a relatedness to objects. For the first time the ego can experience id-impulses, and can feel real in so doing, and also in resting from experiencing. And from here there can at last follow an ordinary analysis of the ego's defences against anxiety.

There builds up an ability of the patient to use the analyst's limited successes in adaptation, so that the ego of the patient becomes able to begin to recall the original failures, all of which were recorded, kept ready. These failures had a disruptive effect at the time, and a treatment of the kind I am describing has gone a long way when the patient is able to take an example of original failure and to be angry about it. Only when the patient reaches this point, however, can there be the beginning of reality-testing. It seems that something like primary repression overtakes these recorded traumata once they have been used.

The way that this change from the experience of being disrupted to the experience of anger comes about is a matter that interests me in a special way, as it is at this point in my work that I found myself surprised. The patient makes use of the analyst's failures. Failures there must be, and indeed there is no attempt to give perfect adaptation; I would say that it is less harmful to make mistakes with these patients than with neurotic patients. The analyst may be surprised as I was to find that while a gross mistake may do but little harm, a very small error of judgement may produce a big effect. The clue is that the analyst's failure is being used and must be treated as a past failure, one that the patient can perceive and encompass, and be angry about. The analyst needs to be able to make use of his failures in terms of their meaning for the patient, and he must if possible account for each failure even if this means a study of his unconscious counter-transference.

In these phases of analytic work resistance or that which would be called resistance in work with neurotic patients always indicates that the analyst has made a mistake, or in some detail has behaved badly; in fact, the resistance remains until the analyst has found out the mistake and has tried to account for it, and has used it. If he defends himself just here the patient misses the opportunity for being angry about a past failure just where anger was becoming possible for the first time. Here is a great contrast between this work and the analysis of neurotic patients with intact ego. It is here that we can see the sense in the dictum that every failed analysis is a failure not of the patient but of the analyst.

This work is exacting partly because the analyst has to have a sensitivity to the patient's needs and a wish to provide a setting that caters for these needs. The analyst is not, after all, the patient's natural mother.

It is exacting, also, because of the necessity for the analyst to look for his own mistakes whenever resistances appear. Yet it is only by using his own mistakes that he can do the most important part of the treatment in these phases, the part that enables the patient to become angry for the first time about the details of failure of adaptation that (at the time when they happened) produced disruption. It is this part of the work that frees the patient from dependence on the analyst.

In this way the negative transference of "neurotic" analysis is replaced by objective anger about the analyst's failures, so here again is an important difference between the transference phenomena in the two types of work.

We must not look for an awareness at a deep level of our adaptation successes, since these are not felt as such. Although we cannot work without the theory that we build up in our discussions, undoubtedly this work finds us out if our understanding of our patient's need is a matter of the mind rather than of the psychesoma.

I have discovered in my clinical work that one kind of analysis does not preclude the other. I find myself slipping over from one to the other and back again, according to the trend of the patient's unconscious process. When work of the special kind I have referred to is completed it leads naturally on to ordinary analytic work, the analysis of the depressive position and of the neurotic defences of a patient with an ego, an intact ego, an ego that is able to experience id-impulses and to take the consequences.

What I have described is only the beginning. For me it is the application of the statements I made in my paper "Primitive emotional development" (1945). What needs to be done now is the study in detail of the criteria by which the analyst may know when to work with the change of emphasis, how to see that a need is arising which is of the kind that I have said must be met (at least in a token way) by active adaptation, the analyst keeping the concept of Primary Identification all the time in mind.

Notes

1. Contribution to the Discussion of Problems of Transference. 19th International Psychoanalytical Congress, Geneva, 24–28 July, 1955.
2. *Journal of the American Psychoanalytic Association*, 2, 1954.

Article citation

Winnicott, D. (1956). On transference. *International Journal of Psycho-Analysis*, 37: 386–388.

CHAPTER THIRTEEN

Transitional objects and transitional phenomena[1]—a study of the first not-me possession[2]

D. W. Winnicott

It is well known that infants as soon as they are born tend to use fist, fingers, thumbs in stimulation of the oral erotogenic zone, in satisfaction of the instincts at that zone, and also in quiet union. It is also well known that after a few months infants of either sex become fond of playing with dolls, and that most mothers allow their infants some special object and expect them to become, as it were, addicted to such objects.

There is a relationship between these two sets of phenomena that are separated by a time interval, and a study of the development from the earlier into the later can be profitable, and can make use of important clinical material that has been somewhat neglected.

The first possession

Those who happen to be in close touch with mothers' interests and problems will be already aware of the very rich patterns ordinarily displayed by babies in their use of the first not-me possession. These patterns, being displayed, can be subjected to direct observation.

There is a wide variation to be found in a sequence of events which starts with the newborn infant's fist-in-mouth activities, and that leads eventually on to an attachment to a teddy, a doll or soft toy, or to a hard toy.

It is clear that something is important here other than oral excitement and satisfaction, although this may be the basis of everything else. Many other important things can be studied, and they include:

1. The nature of the object.
2. The infant's capacity to recognize the object as "not-me".
3. The place of the object—outside, inside, at the border.
4. The infant's capacity to create, think up, devise, originate, produce an object.
5. The initiation of an affectionate type of object relationship.

I have introduced the terms "transitional object" and "transitional phenomena" for designation of the intermediate area of experience, between the thumb and the teddy bear, between the oral erotism and true object-relationship, between primary creative activity and projection of what has already been introjected, between primary unawareness of indebtedness and the acknowledgement of indebtedness ("Say: ta!").

By this definition an infant's babbling or the way an older child goes over a repertory of songs and tunes while preparing for sleep come within the intermediate area as transitional phenomena, along with the use made of objects that are not part of the infant's body yet are not fully recognized as belonging to external reality.

Inadequacy of usual statement

It is generally acknowledged that a statement of human nature in terms of interpersonal relationships is not good enough even when the imaginative elaboration of function and the whole of fantasy both conscious and unconscious, including the repressed unconscious, are allowed for. There is another way of describing persons that comes out of the researches of the past two decades. Of every individual who has reached to the stage of being a unit with a limiting membrane and an outside and an inside, it can be said that there is an inner reality to that individual, an inner world which can be rich or poor and can be at peace or in a state of war. This helps, but is it enough?

My claim is that if there is a need for this double statement, there is also need for a triple one; the third part of the life of a human being, a part that we cannot ignore, is an intermediate area of experiencing, to which inner reality and external life both contribute. It is an area which is not challenged, because no claim is made on its behalf except that it shall exist as a resting-place for the individual engaged in the perpetual human task of keeping inner and outer reality separate yet interrelated.

It is usual to refer to "reality-testing", and to make a clear distinction between apperception and perception. I am here staking a claim for an intermediate state between a baby's inability and growing ability to recognize and accept reality. I am therefore studying the substance of illusion, that which is allowed to the infant, and which in adult life is inherent in art and religion, and yet becomes the hallmark of madness when an adult puts too powerful a claim on the credulity of others, forcing them to acknowledge a sharing of illusion that is not their own. We can share a respect for illusory experience, and if we wish we may collect together and form a group on the basis of the similarity of our illusory experiences. This is a natural root of grouping among human beings.

I hope it will be understood that I am not referring exactly to the little child's Teddy Bear nor to the infant's first use of the first (thumb, fingers). I am not specifically studying the first object of object-relationships. I am concerned with the first possession, and with the intermediate area between the subjective and that which is objectively perceived.

Development of a personal pattern

There is plenty of reference in psychoanalytic literature to the progress from "hand to mouth" to "hand to genital", but perhaps less to further progress to the handling of truly "not-me" objects. Sooner or later in an infant's development there comes a tendency on the part of the infant to weave other-than-me objects into the personal pattern. To some extent these objects stand for the breast, but it is not especially this point that is under discussion.

In the case of some infants the thumb is placed in the mouth while fingers are made to caress the face by pronation and supination movements of the forearm. The mouth is then active in relation to the thumb, but not in relation to the fingers. The fingers caressing the upper lip, or some other part, may be or may become more important than the thumb engaging the mouth. Moreover this caressing activity may be found alone, without the more direct thumb–mouth union.[3]

In common experience one of the following occurs, complicating an auto-erotic experience such as thumb-sucking: (1) with the other hand the baby takes an external object, say a part of a sheet or blanket, into the mouth along with the fingers; or (2) somehow or other the bit of cloth[4] is held and sucked, or not actually sucked. The objects used naturally include napkins and (later) handkerchiefs, and this depends on what is readily and reliably available; or (3) the baby starts from early months to pluck wool and to collect it and to use it for the caressing part of the activity.[5] Less commonly, the wool is swallowed, even causing trouble; or (4) mouthing, accompanied by sounds of "mummum", babbling,[6] anal noises, the first musical notes and so on.

One may suppose that thinking, or fantasying, gets linked up with these functional experiences. All these things I am calling transitional phenomena. Also, out of all this (if we study any one infant) there may emerge some thing or some phenomenon— perhaps a bundle of wool or the corner of a blanket or eiderdown, or a word or tune, or a mannerism, which becomes vitally important to the infant for use at the time of going to sleep,[7] and is a defence against anxiety, especially anxiety of depressive type. Perhaps some soft object or type of object has been found and used by the infant, and this then becomes what I am calling a transitional object. This object goes on being important. The parents get to know its value and carry it round when travelling. The mother lets it get dirty and even smelly, knowing that by washing it she introduces a break in continuity in the infant's experience, a break that may destroy the meaning and value of the object to the infant.

I suggest that the pattern of transitional phenomena begins to show at about 4–6–8–12 months. Purposely I leave room for wide variations.

Patterns set in infancy may persist into childhood, so that the original soft object continues to be absolutely necessary at bed-time or at time of loneliness or when a depressed mood threatens. In health, however, there is a gradual extension of range of interest, and eventually the extended range is maintained, even when depressive anxiety is near. A need for a specific object or a behaviour pattern that started at a very early date may reappear at a later age when deprivation threatens.

This first possession is used in conjunction with special techniques derived from very early infancy, which can include or exist apart from the more direct autoerotic activities. Gradually in the life of an infant Teddies and dolls and hard toys are acquired. Boys to some extent tend to go over to use hard objects, whereas girls tend to proceed right ahead to the acquisition of a family. It is important to note, however, that there is no noticeable difference between boy and girl in their use of the original not-me possession, which I am calling the transitional object.

As the infant starts to use organized sounds (mum, ta, da) there may appear a "word" for the transitional object. The name given by the infant to these earliest objects is often significant, and it usually has a word used by the adults partly incorporated in it. For instance, "baa" may be the name, and the "b" may have come from the adult's use of the word "baby" or "bear".

I should mention that sometimes there is no transitional object except the mother herself. Or an infant may be so disturbed in emotional development that the transition state cannot be enjoyed, or the sequence of objects used is broken. The sequence may nevertheless be maintained in a hidden way.

Summary of special qualities in the relationship

1. The infant assumes rights over the object, and we agree to this assumption. Nevertheless some abrogation of omnipotence is a feature from the start.
2. The object is affectionately cuddled as well as excitedly loved and mutilated.
3. It must never change, unless changed by the infant.
4. It must survive instinctual loving, and also hating, and, if it be a feature, pure aggression.

5. Yet it must seem to the infant to give warmth, or to move, or to have texture, or to do something that seems to show it has vitality or reality of its own.
6. It comes from without from our point of view, but not so from the point of view of the baby. Neither does it come from within; it is not an hallucination.
7. Its fate is to be gradually allowed to be decathected, so that in the course of years it becomes not so much forgotten as relegated to limbo. By this I mean that in health the transitional object does not "go inside" nor does the feeling about it necessarily undergo repression. It is not forgotten and it is not mourned. It loses meaning, and this is because the transitional phenomena have become diffused, have become spread out over the whole intermediate territory between "inner psychic reality" and "the external world as perceived by two persons in common", that is to say, over the whole cultural field.

At this point my subject widens out into that of play, and of artistic creativity and appreciation, and of religious feeling, and of dreaming, and also of fetishism, lying and stealing, the origin and loss of affectionate feeling, drug addiction, the talisman of obsessional rituals, etc.

Relationship of the transitional object to symbolism

It is true that the piece of blanket (or whatever it is) is symbolical of some part-object, such as the breast. Nevertheless the point of it is not its symbolic value so much as its actuality. Its not being the breast (or the mother) although real is as important as the fact that it stands for the breast (or mother).

When symbolism is employed the infant is already clearly distinguishing between fantasy and fact, between inner objects and external objects, between primary creativity and perception. But the term transitional object, according to my suggestion, gives room for the process of becoming able to accept difference and similarity. I think there is use for a term for the root of symbolism in time, a term that describes the infant's journey from the purely subjective to objectivity; and it seems to me that the transitional object (piece of blanket, etc.) is what we see of this journey of progress towards experiencing.

It would be possible to understand the transitional object while not fully understanding the nature of symbolism. It seems that symbolism can only be properly studied in the process of the growth of an individual, and that it has at the very best a variable meaning. For instance, if we consider the wafer of the Blessed Sacrament, which is symbolic of the body of Christ. I think I am right in saying that for the Roman Catholic community it is the body, and for the Protestant community it is a substitute, a reminder, and is essentially not, in fact, actually the body itself. Yet in both cases it is a symbol.

A schizoid patient asked me, after Christmas, had I enjoyed eating her at the feast? And then, had I really eaten her or only in fantasy? I knew that she could not be satisfied with either alternative. Her split needed the double answer.

Clinical description of a transitional object

For anyone in touch with parents and children, there is an infinite quantity and variety of illustrative clinical material.[8] The following illustrations are given merely to remind readers of similar material in their own experiences.

Two brothers; contrast in early use of possessions

(Distortion in use of transitional object.) X, now a healthy man, has had to fight his way towards maturity. The mother "learned how to be a mother" in her management of X when he was an infant and she was able to avoid certain mistakes with the other children because of what she learned with him. There were also external reasons why she was anxious at the time of her rather lonely management of X when he was born. She took her job as a mother very seriously and she breast-fed X for seven months. She feels that in his case this was too long and he was very difficult to wean. He never sucked his thumb or his fingers and when she weaned him "he had nothing to fall back on". He had never had the bottle or a dummy or any other form of feeding. He had a very strong and early attachment to her herself, as a person, and it was her actual person that he needed.

From twelve months he adopted a rabbit which he would cuddle and his affectionate regard for the rabbit eventually transferred to real rabbits. This particular rabbit lasted till he was five or six years old. It could be described as a comforter, but it never had the true quality of a transitional object. It was never, as a true transitional object would have been, more important than the mother, an almost inseparable part of the infant. In the case of this particular boy the kind of anxieties which were brought to a head by the weaning at seven months later produced asthma, and only gradually did he conquer this. It was important for him that he found employment far away from the home town. His attachment to his mother is still very powerful, although he comes within the wide definition of the term normal, or healthy. This man has not married.

(Typical use of transitional object.) X's younger brother, Y, has developed in quite a straightforward way throughout. He now has three healthy children of his own. He was fed at the breast for four months and then weaned without difficulty.[9] Y sucked his thumb in the early weeks and this again "made weaning easier for him than for his older brother". Soon after weaning at five to six months he adopted the end of the blanket where the stitching finished. He was pleased if a little bit of the wool stuck out at the corner and with this he would tickle his nose. This very early became his "Baa"; he invented this word for it himself as soon as he could use organized sounds. From the time when he was about a year old he was able to substitute for the end of the blanket a soft green jersey with a red tie. This was not a "comforter" as in the case of the depressive older brother, but a "soother". It was a sedative which always worked. This is a typical example of what I am calling a Transitional Object. When Y was a little boy it was always certain that if anyone gave him his "Baa" he would immediately suck it and lose anxiety, and in fact he would go to sleep within a few minutes if the time for sleep were at all near. The thumb-sucking continued at the same time, lasting until he was three or four years old, and he remembers thumb-sucking and a hard place on one thumb which resulted from it. He is now interested (as a father) in the thumb-sucking of his children and their use of "Baas".

		Thumb	Transitional Object		Type of Child
X	Boy	O	Mother	Rabbit (comforter)	Mother-fixated
Y	Boy	+	'Baa'	Jersey (soother)	Free
Twins { Girl		O	Dummy	Donkey (friend)	Late maturity
Twins { Boy		O	'Ee'	Ee (protective)	Latent psychopathic
Chil- { Girl		O	'Baa'	Blanket (reassurance)	Developing well
dren { Girl		+	Thumb	Thumb (satisfaction)	„ „
of Y { Boy		+	'Mimis'*	Objects (sorting)	„ „

* Innumerable similar soft objects distinguished by colour, length, width, and early subjected to sorting and classification.

The story of seven ordinary children in this family brings out the following points, arranged for comparison:

Value in history-taking

In consultation with a parent it is often valuable to get information about the early techniques and possessions of all the children of the family. This starts the mother off on a comparison of her children one with another, and enables her to remember and compare their characteristics at an early age.

The child's contribution

Information can often be obtained from a child in regard to transitional objects; for instance, Angus (11 years 9 months) told me that his brother "has tons of teddies and things" and "before that he had little bears", and he followed this up with a talk about his own history. He said he never had teddies. There was a bell rope which hung down, a tag end of which he would go on hitting, and so go off to sleep. Probably in the end it fell, and that was the end of it. There was, however, something else. He was very shy about this. It was a purple rabbit with red eyes. "I wasn't fond of it. I used to throw it around". "Jeremy has it now. I gave it to him. I gave it to Jeremy because it was naughty. It would fall off the chest of drawers. It still visits me. I like it to visit me". He surprised himself when he drew the purple rabbit. It will be noted that this eleven-year-old boy with the ordinary good reality-sense of his age spoke as if lacking in reality sense when describing the transitional object's qualities and activities. When I saw the mother later she expressed surprise that Angus remembered the purple rabbit. She easily recognized it from the coloured drawing.

Ready availability of examples

I deliberately refrain from giving more case material here, particularly as I wish to avoid giving the impression that what I am reporting is rare. In practically every case history there is something to be found that is interesting in the transitional phenomena, or in their absence. (It is my intention to give other examples and to develop subsidiary themes in future work.)

Theoretical study

There are certain comments that can be made on the basis of accepted psychoanalytic theory.

1. The transitional object stands for the breast, or the object of the first relationship.
2. The transitional object antedates established reality-testing.
3. In relation to the transitional object the infant passes from (magical) omnipotent control to control by manipulation (involving muscle erotism and co-ordination pleasure).
4. The transitional object may eventually develop into a fetish object and so persist as a characteristic of the adult sexual life. (See Wulff's development of the theme.)
5. The transitional object may, because of anal erotic organization, stand for faeces (but it is not for this reason that it may become smelly and remain unwashed).

Relationship to internal object (Klein)

It is interesting to compare the transitional object concept with Melanie Klein's concept of the internal object. The transitional object is not an internal object (which is a mental concept)—it is a possession. Yet it is not (for the infant) an external object either.

The following complex statement has to be made. The infant can employ a transitional object when the internal object is alive and real and good enough (not too persecutory). But this internal object depends for its qualities on the existence and aliveness and behaviour of the external object (breast, mother figure, general environmental care). Badness or failure of the latter indirectly leads to deadness or to a persecutory quality of internal object. After a persistence of failure of the external object the internal object fails to have meaning to the infant, and then, and then only, does the transitional object become meaningless too. The transitional object may therefore stand for the "external" breast, but indirectly, through standing for an "internal" breast.

The transitional object is never under magical control like the internal object, nor is it outside control as the real mother is.

Illusion–disillusionment

In order to prepare the ground for my own positive contribution to this subject I must put into words some of the things that I think are taken too easily for granted in many psychoanalytic writings on infantile emotional development, although they may be understood in practice.

There is no possibility whatever for an infant to proceed from the pleasure-principle to the reality principle or towards and beyond primary identification (see Freud, *The Ego and the Id*, p. 14),[10] unless there is a good enough mother.[11] The good enough "mother" (not necessarily the infant's own mother) is one who makes active adaptation to the infant's needs, an active adaptation that gradually lessens, according to the infant's growing ability to account for failure of adaptation and to tolerate the results of frustration. Naturally the infant's own mother is more likely to be good enough than some other person, since this active adaptation demands an easy and unresented preoccupation with the one infant; in fact, success in infant-care depends on the fact of devotion, not on cleverness or intellectual enlightenment.

The good enough mother, as I have stated, starts off with an almost complete adaptation to her infant's needs, and as time proceeds she adapts less and less completely, gradually, according to the infant's growing ability to deal with her failure.

The infant's means of dealing with this maternal failure include the following:

1. The infant's experience, often repeated, that there is a time limit to frustration. At first, naturally, this time limit must be short.
2. Growing sense of process.
3. The beginnings of mental activity.
4. Employment of auto-erotic satisfactions.
5. Remembering, reliving, fantasying, dreaming; the integrating of past, present, and future.

If all goes well the infant can actually come to gain from the experience of frustration, since incomplete adaptation to need makes objects real, that is to say hated as well as loved. The consequence of this is that if all goes well the infant can be disturbed by a close adaptation to need that is continued too long, not allowed its natural decrease, since exact adaptation resembles magic and the object that behaves perfectly becomes no better than an hallucination. Nevertheless at the start adaptation needs to be almost exact, and unless this is so it is not possible for the infant to begin to develop a capacity to experience a relationship to external reality, or even to form a conception of external reality.

Illusion and the value of illusion

The mother, at the beginning, by almost 100 per cent adaptation affords the infant the opportunity for the illusion that her breast is part of the infant. It is, as it were, under magical control. The same can be said in terms of infant care in general, in the quiet times between excitements. Omnipotence is nearly a fact of experience. The mother's eventual task is gradually to disillusion the infant, but she has no hope of success unless at first she has been able to give sufficient opportunity for illusion.

In another language, the breast is created by the infant over and over again out of the infant's capacity to love or (one can say) out of need. A subjective phenomenon develops in the baby which we call the mother's breast.[12] The mother places the actual breast just there where the infant is ready to create, and at the right moment.

From birth therefore the human being is concerned with the problem of the relationship between what is objectively perceived and what is subjectively conceived of, and in the solution of this problem there is no health for the human being who has not been started off well enough by the mother. The intermediate area to which I am referring is the area that is allowed to the infant between primary creativity and objective perception based on reality testing. The transitional phenomena represent the early stages of the use of illusion, without which there is no meaning for the human being in the idea of a relationship with an object that is perceived by others as external to that being.

The idea illustrated in Figure 1 is this: that at some theoretical point early in the development of every human individual an infant in a certain setting provided by the mother is capable of conceiving of the idea of something which would meet the growing need which arises out of instinctual tension. The infant cannot be said to know at first what is to be created. At this point in time the mother presents herself. In the ordinary way she gives her breast and her potential feeding urge. The mother's adaptation to the infant's needs, when good enough, gives the infant the illusion that there is an external reality that corresponds to the infant's own capacity to create. In other words, there is an overlap between what the mother supplies and what the child might conceive of. To the observer the child perceives what the mother actually presents, but this is not the whole truth. The infant perceives the breast only in so far as a breast could be created just there and then. There is no interchange between the mother and the infant. Psychologically the infant takes from a breast that is part of the infant, and the mother gives milk to an infant that is part of herself. In psychology, the idea of interchange is based on an illusion.

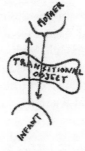

Figure 1   Figure 2

In Figure 2 a shape is given to the area of illusion, to illustrate what I consider to be the main function of the transitional object and of transitional phenomena. The transitional object and the transitional phenomena start each human being off with what will always be important for them, i.e. a neutral area of experience which will not be challenged. Of the transitional object it can be said that it is a matter of agreement between us and the baby that we will never ask the question "Did you conceive of this or was it presented to you from without?" The important point is that no decision on this point is expected. The question is not to be formulated.

This problem, which undoubtedly concerns the human infant in a hidden way at the beginning, gradually becomes an obvious problem on account of the fact that the mother's main task (next to providing opportunity for illusion) is disillusionment. This is preliminary to the task of weaning, and it also continues as one of the tasks of parents and educators. In other words, this matter of illusion is one which belongs inherently to human beings and which no individual finally solves for himself or herself, although a theoretical understanding of it may provide a theoretical solution. If things go well, in this gradual disillusionment process, the stage is set for the frustrations that we gather together under the word weaning; but it should be remembered that when we talk about the phenomena (which Mrs Klein has specifically illuminated) that cluster round weaning we are assuming the underlying process, the process by which opportunity for illusion and gradual disillusionment is provided. If illusion–disillusionment has gone astray the infant cannot get to so normal a thing as weaning, nor to a reaction to weaning, and it is then absurd to refer to weaning at all. The mere termination of breast feeding is not a weaning.

We can see the tremendous significance of weaning in the case of the normal child. When we witness the complex reaction that is set going in a certain child by the weaning process we know that this is able to take place in that child because the illusion–disillusionment process is being carried through so well that we can ignore it while discussing actual weaning.

Development of the theory of illusion–disillusionment

It is assumed here that the task of reality-acceptance is never completed, that no human being is free from the strain of relating inner and outer reality, and that relief from this strain is provided by an intermediate area of experience[13] which is not challenged (arts, religion, etc.). This intermediate area is in direct continuity with the play area of the small child who is "lost" in play.

In infancy this intermediate area is necessary for the initiation of a relationship between the child and the world, and is made possible by good enough mothering at the early critical phase. Essential to all this is continuity (in time) of the external emotional environment and of particular elements in the physical environment such as the transitional object or objects.

The transitional phenomena are allowable to the infant because of the parents' intuitive recognition of the strain inherent in objective perception, and we do not challenge the infant in regard to subjectivity or objectivity just here where there is the transitional object.

Should an adult make claims on us for our acceptance of the objectivity of his subjective phenomena we discern or diagnose madness. If, however, the adult can manage to enjoy the personal intermediate area without making claims, then we can acknowledge our own corresponding intermediate areas, and are pleased to find overlapping, that is to say common experience between members of a group in art or religion or philosophy.

Reference to Wulff's paper

I wish to draw particular attention to the paper by Wulff, referred to above, in which excellent clinical material is given illustrating exactly that which I am referring to under the heading of transitional objects and transitional phenomena. There is a difference between my point of view and that of Wulff which is reflected in my use of this special term and his use of the term "fetish object". A study of Wulff's paper seems to show that in using the word fetish he has taken back to infancy something that belongs in ordinary theory to the sexual perversions. I am not able to find in his article sufficient room for the consideration of the child's transitional object as a healthy early experience. Yet I do consider that transitional phenomena are healthy and universal. Moreover if we extend the use of the word fetish to cover normal phenomena we shall perhaps be losing some of the value of the term.

I would prefer to retain the word fetish to describe the object that is employed on account of a delusion of a maternal phallus. I would then go further and say that we must keep a place for the illusion of a maternal phallus, that is to say, an idea that is universal and not pathological. If we shift the accent now from the object on to the word illusion we get near to the infant's transitional object; the importance lies in the concept of illusion, a universal in the field of experience.

Following this, we can allow the transitional object to be potentially a maternal phallus but originally the breast, that is to say, the thing created by the infant and at the same time provided from the environment. In this way I think that a study of the infant's use of the transitional object and of transitional phenomena in general may throw light on the origin of the fetish object and of fetishism. There is something to be lost, however, in working backwards from the psycho-pathology of fetishism to the transitional phenomena which belong to the beginnings of experience and which are universal and inherent in healthy emotional development.

Summary

Attention is drawn to the rich field for observation provided by the earliest experiences of the healthy infant as expressed principally in the relationship to the first possession.

This first possession is related backwards in time to auto-erotic phenomena and fist and thumb sucking, and also forwards to the first soft animal or doll and to hard toys. It is related both to the external object (mother's breast) and to internal objects (magically introjected breast), but is distinct from each. The transitional objects and transitional phenomena belong to the realm of illusion which is at the basis of initiation of experience. This early stage in development is made possible by the mother's special capacity for making adaptation to the needs of her infant, thus allowing the infant the illusion that what the infant creates really exists.

This intermediate area of experience, unchallenged in respect of its belonging to inner or external (shared) reality, constitutes the greater part of the infant's experience and throughout life is retained in the intense experiencing that belongs to the arts and to religion and to imaginative living, and to creative scientific work.

A positive value of illusion can therefore be stated.

An infant's transitional object ordinarily becomes gradually decathected, especially as cultural interests develop.

In psychopathology:

addiction can be stated in terms of regression to the early stage at which the transitional phenomena are unchallenged;

fetish can be described in terms of a persistence of a specific object or type of object dating from infantile experience in the transitional field, linked with the delusion of a maternal phallus; pseudologia and thieving can be described in terms of an individual's unconscious urge to bridge a gap in continuity of experience in respect of a transitional object.

Notes

1. Based on a paper given at a Scientific Meeting of the British Psychoanalytical Society on 30 May, 1951. A shortened version was distributed to members beforehand, and Dr Winnicott confined his remarks to the section "Illusion-disillusionment".
2. It is necessary to stress that the word used here is "possession" and not "object". In the typed version distributed to members I did in fact use the word "object" (instead of "possession") in one place by mistake, and this led to confusion in the discussion. It was pointed out that the first not-me object is usually taken to be the breast.

    The reader's attention is drawn to the use of the word "transitional" in many places by Fairbairn in *Psychoanalytic Studies of the Personality* (Tavistock Publications, 1952), notably p. 35. (Also in this Journal, 22.)
3. Cf. Freud: "Case of Dora", *S.E.*, 3: 63–64; also Hoffer, Willi: *The Psychoanalytic Study of the Child*, Vol. III–IV, p. 51.
4. A recent example is the blanket-doll of the child in the film *A Child Goes to Hospital* by Robertson (Tavistock Clinic).
5. Here there could possibly be an explanation for the use of the term "wool-gathering", which means: inhabiting the transitional or inter-mediate area.
6. See W. C. M. Scott's recent paper on "Blathering".
7. See Illingworth, R. S., *B.M.J.*, 7 April, 1951, "Sleep disturbances in young children".
8. There are excellent examples in the one article I have found on this same

subject. Wulff (1946) ("Fetishism and object choice in early childhood", *Psychoanalytic Quarterly*, *15*, 450) is clearly studying this same phenomenon, but he calls the objects "fetish objects". It is not clear to me that this term is correct, and I discuss this below. I did not actually know of Wulff's paper until I had written my own, but it gave me great pleasure and support to find the subject had already been considered worthy of discussion by a colleague. See also Abraham: case description in "The first pregenital stage of the libido", *Selected Papers* p. 267, (London: Hogarth Press), and Lindner (1879) *Jahrbuch für Kinderheilkunde*, N.F., xiv.

9. The mother had "learned from her first child that it was a good idea to give one bottle feed while breast feeding", that is, to allow for the positive value of substitutes for herself, and by this means she achieved easier weaning than with X.

10. See also Freud: *Group Psychology and the Analysis of the Ego*, p. 65.

11. One effect, and the main effect, of failure of the mother in this respect at the start of an infant's life, is discussed clearly (in my view) by Marion Milner, in her paper appearing in the *Melanie Klein Birthday Volume*, Hogarth Press, 1952, also this Journal, 32 (1952), p. 181. She shows that because of the mother's failure there is brought about a premature ego-development, with precocious sorting out of a bad from a good object. The period of illusion (or my Transitional Phase) is disturbed. In analysis or in various activities in ordinary life an individual can be seen to be going on seeking the valuable resting-place of illusion. Illusion in this way has its positive value. See also Freud: *Aus den Anfängen der Psychoanalyse: Briefe an Wilhelm Fliess*. In 1895 Freud wrote (pp. 402 and 413) that only by outside help certain early functioning can proceed satisfactorily.

12. I include the whole technique of mothering. When it is said that the first object is the breast, the word "breast" is used, I believe, to stand for the technique of mothering as well as for the actual flesh. It is not impossible for a mother to be a good enough mother (in my way of putting it) with a bottle for the actual feeding.

    If this wide meaning of the word "breast" is kept in mind, and maternal technique is seen to be included in the total meaning of the term, then there is a bridge forming between the wording of Melanie Klein's statement of early history and that of Anna Freud. The only difference left is one of dates, which is in fact an unimportant difference which will automatically disappear in the course of time.

13. Cf. Riviere (1936). *International Journal of Psycho-Analysis*, *17*: p. 399.

Article citation

Winnicott, D. (1953). Transitional objects and transitional phenomena—a study of the first not-me possession. *International Journal of Psycho-Analysis, 34*: 89–97.

CHAPTER FOURTEEN

The nature of the child's tie to his mother[1]

John Bowlby

Psychoanalysts are at one in recognizing the child's first object relations as the foundation stone of his personality: yet there is no agreement on the nature and dynamics of this relationship. No doubt because of its very importance, differences are sharp and feelings often run high. In this paper I am taking it for granted that today we are all agreed on the empirical fact that within 12 months the infant has developed a strong libidinal tie to a mother-figure[2] and that our differences lie in how this has come about. What in fact are the dynamics which promote and underlie this tie?

My plan will be to begin by describing very briefly four alternative views which in greater or less degree of purity are to be found in the psychoanalytic and other psychological literature and to sketch a fifth which I believe may account more adequately for the data. I shall then attempt to assess what have been and are the views advanced in their writings by a number of leading analysts.

Before elaborating the view which I favour it will be necessary to discuss in rather summary fashion, first, some notions, including those of Piaget, regarding the development of perception and cognition and, secondly, some of the more recent theories of instinctual behaviour. Indeed, in writing it I have wondered whether this paper should not have been preceded by three others—one on cognitive development, a second on instinct, and a third on the comparative advantages and disadvantages on the one hand of direct observation of infants and on the other of reconstructions based on the psychoanalysis of older subjects. However, I have not taken this course, and instead am presenting a paper in which, I am acutely aware, despite its length a number of crucial matters are treated both controversially and cursorily.

The four theories regarding the positive aspects of the child's tie which are to be found in the literature can be described briefly. They are:

(i)   The child has a number of physiological needs which must be met, particularly for food and warmth, but no social needs. In so far as a baby becomes interested in and attached to a human figure, especially mother, this is the result of the mother meeting the baby's physiological needs and the baby in due course learning that she is the source of gratification. I propose to call this the theory of Secondary Drive, terminology which is derived from Learning Theory. It has also been called the cupboard-love theory of object relations.

(ii) There is in infants an in-built need to relate themselves to a human breast, to suck it and to possess it orally. In due course the infant learns that, attached to the breast, there is a mother and so relates to her also. I propose to call this the theory of Primary Object Sucking.

(iii) There is in infants an in-built need to be in touch with and to cling to a human being. In this sense there is a need for an object independent of food which is as primary as the need for food and warmth. I propose to call it Primary Object Clinging.

(iv) Infants resent their extrusion from the womb and seek to return there. This I shall call the theory of Primary Return-to-Womb Craving.

In this nomenclature, it should be noticed, the terms primary and secondary refer to whether the response is regarded as built-in and inherited or acquired through the process of learning; throughout the paper they will be used in this sense. The terms have no reference either to the period of life when the response appears or to the primary and secondary processes postulated by Freud.

THE NATURE OF THE CHILD'S TIE TO HIS MOTHER   225

The author is much indebted to Robert Hinde and Anthony Ambrose for discussions in which these ideas were clarified. The enquiry was undertaken as part of the work of the Tavistock Child Development Research Unit, which is at present supported by the National Health Service and by grants from the Josiah Macy Jr Foundation, the Foundations Fund for Research in Psychiatry and the Ford Foundation, to all of which our thanks are due. The review of literature was extensively revised whilst the author held a Fellowship at the Center for Advanced Study in the Behavioural Sciences.

The hypothesis which I am advancing incorporates the theories of Primary Object Sucking and Primary Object Clinging. It postulates that the attachment behaviour which we observe so readily in a baby of 12 months old is made up of a number of component instinctual responses which are at first relatively independent of each other. The instinctual responses mature at different times during the first year of life and develop at different rates; they serve the function of binding the child to mother and contribute to the reciprocal dynamic of binding mother to child. Those which I believe we can identify at present are sucking, clinging, and following, in all of which the baby is the principal active partner, and crying and smiling in which his behaviour serves to activate maternal behaviour. (By "following" I mean the tendency not to let mother out of sight or earshot, which is readily observed in human infants during the latter half of their first year and throughout their second and third years of life and in the young of other species sometimes almost from birth.) Whereas sucking is closely related to food-intake and crying may be so, the remaining three are non-oral in character and not directly related to food. In the normal course of development they become integrated and focused on a single mother figure: as such they form the basis of what I shall call "attachment behaviour".

In certain essential features I believe this theory to have much in common with the views advanced by Freud in his "Three essays on sexuality", in which he advanced the view that mature adult sexuality is to be conceived as built up of a number of individual component instincts which in infancy "are upon the whole disconnected and independent of one another", but which in adult life come to "form a firm organization directed towards a sexual aim attached to some extraneous sexual object" (*S.E. VII*, pp. 181, 197). Partly because of this similarity, but also because I believe it to be apt, I propose to call it the theory of Component Instinctual Responses.

The data which have influenced me in framing this hypothesis are culled less from the analysis of older subjects and more from the direct observation of babies and young children. I have also been deeply influenced by the accounts given me by mothers, both those whose children were prospering and those whose children were causing anxiety. The longer I contemplated the diverse clinical evidence the more dissatisfied I became with the views current in psychoanalytical and psychological literature and the more I found myself turning to the ethologists for help. The extent to which I have drawn on concepts of ethology will be apparent.

Although the hypothesis advanced incorporates the theories of Primary Object Sucking and Primary Object Clinging, it is essentially different from the theory of Secondary Drive. The theory of Primary Return-to-Womb craving is regarded as both redundant and biologically improbable.

It may be worth mentioning that this paper deals neither with ego nor superego. By confining itself to the instinctual roots of the child's tie, it is concerned only with an examination of certain parts of the id.

Review of literature

The hypotheses advanced during the past fifty years by psycho-analysts are numerous and diverse. As usual, we cannot understand Freud's evolving views without tracing them historically. In reading his works we are at once struck by the fact that it was not until comparatively late that he appreciated the reality of the infant's close tie to his mother, and that it was only in his last ten years that he gave it the significance we should all give it today. You will recall the passage in his paper of 1931 on "Female sexuality" in which he confesses how elusive everything connected with the first mother-attachment had seemed to him in his analytic work and how he had found it difficult to penetrate behind the strong father-transference which his women patients made to him. What then struck him as new, he tells us, was the "equally great attachment to the mother" which precedes the dependence on the father and the length of time this attachment lasts (C.P., V, pp. 254–255). Freud's failure to give due weight to this early tie until the last phase of his work has had (and I believe is still having) far-reaching effects on psychoanalytic theorizing. His first serious discussion of the matter was not until 1926 (Freud, 1938).

Realization of the tremendous importance of this first attachment seems to have been reached by Freud in a number of steps. Up to the early twenties he had held the view that, apart from a fleeting moment during which the oral component has the mother's breast as an object, all the components of libido start by being auto-erotic. This view, stemming from the "Three essays on sexuality", is succinctly expressed in his encyclopaedia article titled "Psycho-Analysis", written as late as 1922. "In the first instance the oral component instinct finds satisfaction by attaching itself to the sating of the desire for nourishment; and its object is the mother's breast. It then detaches itself, becomes independent and at the same time auto-erotic, that is, it finds an object in the child's own body. Others of the component instincts also start by being auto-erotic and are not until later directed on to an external object". Between the ages of two and five years "a convergence of sexual impulses occurs" the object of which is the parent of the opposite sex (S.E., XVIII, p. 245). In this account the phase we all now recognize when in both sexes there is a strong tie to the mother is conspicuous by its absence. Indeed, in the "Interpretation of dreams" there is a passage in which he expresses the view that "When people are absent, children do not miss them with any great intensity, [which] many mothers have learnt to their sorrow", a passage that, a little surprisingly, remains unamended and unqualified throughout later editions (S.E., IV, p. 255).

Nevertheless there are in various of Freud's earlier writings, statements suggesting that the infant is not so exclusively auto-erotic as his principal formulations assert. Thus in the "Three essays", after referring to the child sucking at his mother's breast as the prototype of later love relations, he writes, "But even after sexual activity has become detached from the taking of nourishment, an important part of this first and most significant of all sexual relations is left over ... All through the period of latency children learn to feel for other people who help them in their helplessness and satisfy their needs, a love which is on the model of, and a continuation of, their relation as sucklings to their nursing mother ... A child's intercourse with anyone responsible for his care affords him an unending source of sexual excitation and satisfaction from his erotogenic zones", and he proceeds to praise the mother who "by stroking, kissing and rocking him is fulfilling her task in teaching the child to love" (S.E., VII, pp. 222–223). We find a similar passage in his paper on "Narcissism" (1915) where he refers to the persons who have to do with the feeding, care and protection of the child becoming his earliest sexual objects. This type of object choice he terms the "anaclitic", because in this phase the sexual instincts find their satisfaction through "leaning up against" the self-preservative instincts (S.E., XIV, p. 87).

By 1920, we know, Freud had observed that an infant of 18 months dislikes being left alone ("Beyond the pleasure principle", S.E., XVIII, pp. 14–16), and six years later we find him discussing why the infant desires the presence of his mother and fears losing her ("Inhibitions, symptoms and anxiety", pp. 105–107). There remains, however, a disinclination to postulate any primary socially-oriented drive. Instead, he interprets the infant's anxiety that he may lose his mother as due to the danger that his body needs will not be gratified and that this will lead to "a growing tension due to need, against which it [the baby] is helpless". The real essence of the danger, he tells us, is the "economic disturbance caused by an accumulation of amounts of stimulation which require to be disposed of". That the infant fears the loss of his mother is, therefore, to be understood as a displacement: "When the child has found out by experience that an external, perceptible object can put an end to the dangerous situation which is reminiscent of birth, the nature of the danger it fears is displaced from the economic situation on to the condition which determined that situation, viz. the loss of the object" (pp. 106–108).

By 1931, as already remarked, the full significance of the phase during which the libidinal object is the mother has been grasped. However, in the paper on "Female sexuality" no account is attempted of how this relationship develops. In his final synthesis we find a pregnant but highly condensed paragraph ("An outline of psycho-analysis", 1938, p. 56). One notes at once the dramatic and colourful terms in which the relationship to the mother is described, terms which, so far as I know, are not found elsewhere in his writings on the subject. He describes it as "unique, without parallel, laid down unalterably for a whole lifetime, as the first and strongest love-object and as the prototype of all later love relations—for both sexes".

In delineating the dynamics of this newly evaluated relationship, Freud begins, as formerly, by telling us that "a child's first erotic object is the mother's breast which feeds him" and that "love in its beginning attaches itself to the satisfaction of the need for food". He proceeds to indicate that, because the child "makes no distinction between the breast and his own body", part of the "original narcissistic cathexis" is carried over on to the breast as an outside object. "This first object subsequently becomes completed into the whole person of the child's mother who not only feeds him but looks after him and thus arouses in him many other physical sensations pleasant and unpleasant. By her care of the child's body she becomes his first seducer. In these two relations lies the root of a mother's importance". This passage refers to the same dynamic that in his early writings he had attributed to the period of latency but which since the "twenties he had realized to be active in a much earlier phase of life".

Had he said no more we should have concluded with confidence that to the end of his life Freud espoused the theory of Secondary Drive; (although we should have been wise to note that he held it in a special form; in Freud's view the mother becomes important not only because she gratifies physiological needs but also because in so doing she stimulates the infant's erotogenic zones). These, however, are not his last words on the subject. Almost it might seem as an afterthought, at the end of this significant paragraph he expresses an opinion which differs radically from any previously expressed by him and which seems to contradict much of the earlier explanation. "The phylogenetic foundation", he writes, "has so much the upper hand in all this over accidental experience that it makes no difference whether a child has really sucked at the breast or has been brought up on the bottle and never enjoyed the tenderness of a mother's care. His development takes the same path in both cases". Our most conservative conclusion is that Freud was not wholly satisfied with his earlier accounts. A more radical one is that, towards the end of his life and imbued with a newly-found but vivid appreciation of the central importance of the child's tie to his mother, Freud was not only moving away from the theory of Secondary Drive but developing the notion that special drives built into the infant in the course of evolution underlie this first and unique love relationship.

I confess I would like to believe that this was so. My speculations are encouraged by a passage in his "Three essays" which, so far as I know, he never expanded. In discussing the activity of thumb-sucking and the independence of the sucking from the taking of nourishment Freud proceeds "In this connection a grasping-instinct may appear and may manifest itself as a simultaneous rhythmic tugging at the lobes of the ears or a catching hold of some part of another person (as a rule the ear) for the same purpose". (S.E., VII, pp. 179–180). Plainly here is a reference to a part-instinct even more independent than sucking of the taking of nourishment. It is a theme to which the Hungarian school has given particular attention and to which I shall be referring more fully when expounding my own views.

Whether or not we are right in thinking that in his later years Freud was in process of developing new ideas, it is evident that at most they were still no more than germinal when he died. That members of the Viennese school should have been little influenced by them is hardly surprising. In fact, as is well-known, Anna Freud and those who trained in Vienna before the war have continued to favour the theory of Secondary Drive. In a number of publications in the past ten years she has expressed the view with welcome clarity. "The relationship to the mother", she writes in a recent publication (1954), "is not the infant's first relationship to the environment. What precedes it is an earlier phase in which not the object world but the body needs and their satisfaction or frustration play the decisive part ... In the struggle for satisfaction of the vital needs and drives the object merely serves the purpose of wish fulfilment, its status being no more than that of a means to an end, a 'convenience'. The libidinal cathexis at this time is shown to be attached, not to the image of the object, but to the blissful experience of satisfaction and relief". In an earlier paper (1949) she describes how in the first year of life "the all-important step from primary narcissism to object-love should be taking place, a transition which happens in small stages". In accounting for this transition she follows Sigmund Freud in regarding the mother as a "seducer". "By means of the constantly repeated experience of satisfaction of the first body needs", she writes, "the libidinal interest of the child is lured away from exclusive concentration on the happenings in his own body and directed towards those persons in the outside world (the mother or mother substitute) who are responsible for providing satisfaction". In this same article, which is concerned with the origin of certain forms of social maladjustment, she describes how, when for any reason the mother fails to be a steady source of satisfaction, "the transformation of narcissistic libido into object-libido is carried out inadequately" and how as a result auto-erotism persists and the destructive urges remain isolated.

Although in her theoretical expositions Anna Freud seems unequivocal in her endorsement of the theory of Secondary Drive, there are passages in her clinical writings which hint at something different. The accounts which she and Dorothy Burlingham have given of the children in the Hampstead Nurseries include one of the few descriptions of the development of the child's tie which have been written by analysts on the basis of empirical observations (Burlingham & Freud, 1942). Two of their conclusions I wish to single out because I believe them to have been given too little weight in analytic theory. The first is their insistence that it is not until the second year of life that "the personal attachment of the child to his mother ... comes to its full development" (p. 50). The second is that "children will cling even to mothers who are continually cross and sometimes cruel to them. The attachment of the small child to his mother seems to a large degree independent of her personal qualities" (p. 47). Indeed, their observations make it plain that the potential for attachment is ever-present in the child and ready, when starved of an object, to fix on almost anyone. In the nursery setting, they tell us, "the emotions which [the child] would normally direct towards its parents ... remain undeveloped and unsatisfied, but ... are latent in [him] and ready to leap into action the moment the slightest opportunity for attachment is offered" (Burlingham & Freud, 1944, p. 43). The extent to which the attachment seems to be independent of what is received, which is very plain in these records (e.g. *ibid.*, p. 52) and which will be a main theme of this paper, emerges again in another report of the behaviour of young children for which Anna Freud is jointly responsible (Freud & Dann, 1951). This describes the behaviour of six children from a concentration camp, aged between three and four years, whose only persisting company in life had been each other. The authors emphasize that "the children's positive feelings were centered exclusively in their own group ... they cared greatly for each other and not at all for anybody or anything else". Was this, we may wonder, a result of one infant being instrumental in meeting the physiological needs of others? It is observations such as these that led Dorothy Burlingham and Anna Freud to describe the child's need "for early attachment to the mother" as an *"important instinctual need"* (Burlingham & Freud, 1944, p. 22, my italics)—a formulation which hardly seems compatible with the theory of Secondary Drive advanced elsewhere.

A discrepancy between formulations springing direct from empirical observations and those made in the course of abstract discussion seems almost to be the rule in the case of analysts with first-hand experience of infancy—for example Melanie Klein, Margaret Ribble, Therese Benedek, and Rene Spitz. In each case they have observed non-oral social interaction between mother and infant and, in describing it, have used terms suggesting a primary social bond. When they come to theorizing about it, however, each seems to feel a compulsion to give primacy to needs for food and warmth and to suppose that social interaction develops only secondarily and as a result of instrumental learning. Melanie Klein's basic theoretical concepts have their origin in ideas current before 1926. Although these basic concepts have persisted in her theorizing largely unmodified, first-hand observations of infants, made later, have resulted in a number of more empirically oriented concepts, often divergent in character, being juxtaposed.

In contrast to Anna Freud, Melanie Klein has for some years been an advocate of the view that there is more in the infant's relation to his mother than the satisfaction of physiological needs. Yet there is a very pronounced tendency for her theoretical formulations to be dominated by the interrelated themes of food, orality and the mother's breast. As regards food, she writes in the second of two chapters in which she discusses the matter (Klein *et al.*, 1952, Chapters 6 and 7): "The infant's relations to his first object, the mother, and towards food are bound up with each other from the beginning. Therefore the study of fundamental patterns of attitudes towards food seems the best approach to the understanding of young infants" (p. 238). She elaborates this in a number of passages where she relates particular attitudes toward food to particular forms taken later by psychic organization and development.

This concentration on orality and food, which has been such a conspicuous feature of Melanie Klein's theories since her early paper on "Infant analysis" (1926), seems in large measure to be due to the influence exerted on her thinking by Abraham's important papers on "The first pregenital stages" (1916) and "The development of the libido" (1924). In these works, as is well-known, Abraham gave special attention to orality. Nevertheless, his papers date from the period before the significance of the child's tie had been recognized and their basic concepts are little different from those of Freud's 1922 encyclopaedia article (see p. 245). Looking back at Melanie Klein's paper, it seems, the importance of the child's attachment is missed and only the oral component perceived. As a result, I believe, its influence has led to excessive emphasis being placed on orality and the first year of life and, as a consequence, to an underestimation of other aspects of the tie and events of the second and third years.

Turning again to the 1952 publication of Melanie Klein and her group, it is in keeping with her oral theory that we find her advancing the view that "the relation to the loved and hated—good and bad—breast is the infant's first object-relation" (p. 209) and that "the close bond between a young infant and his mother centres on the relation to her breast" (p. 243). Indeed, in an important note she postulates an inborn striving after the mother's breast: "the newborn infant unconsciously feels that an object of unique goodness exists, from which a maximal gratification could be obtained and that this object is the mother's breast" (p. 265). In discussing this notion she quotes approvingly Freud's statement regarding the significance of a phylogenetic foundation for early object relations which, it has already been observed, suggests that at the end of his life Freud was moving towards a formulation different from the theory of Secondary Drive which he had hitherto espoused.

Yet, despite this preoccupation in her theory with food, orality, and the mother's breast, Melanie Klein reports observations of infants from which she herself draws a different conclusion. Thus in one of the same chapters from which I have been quoting we find the following passage: "Some children who, although good feeders, are not markedly greedy, show unmistakable signs of love and of a developing interest in the mother at a very early stage—an attitude which contains some of the essential elements of an object-relation. I have seen babies as young as three weeks interrupt their sucking for a short time to play with the mother's breast or to look towards her face. I have also observed that young infants—even as early as in the second month—would in wakeful periods after feeding lie on the mother's lap, look up at her, listen to her voice and respond to it by their facial expression; it was like a loving conversation between mother and baby. Such behaviour implies that gratification is *as much related to the object which gives the food as to the food itself*" (p. 239, my italics).

Up to this point in Melanie Klein's writings (1952) the overall impression given is that, although she believes that the infant's first relation to the mother comprises more than one component instinct, she believes the oral component plays an overwhelmingly dominant part. As a result of this and her tendency to equate good breast and good mother, many of her formulations and those of her colleagues have given the impression of subscribing to the theory I have termed Primary Object Sucking. Nonetheless, perhaps the most accurate description is to say that she has oscillated between a foreground exposition of a theory of Primary Object Sucking and a variety of background references to a broader theory to which she had not then given systematic attention.[3]

In the opening pages of her most recent publication (Klein, 1957, pp. 3–5) we find the same oscillation. On the one hand is emphasis on the primacy of the breast and orality: there are references to "the primal good object, the mother's breast", to "the dominance of oral impulses", and to the feeling of security in relation to the mother being dependent "on the infant's capacity to cathect sufficiently the breast or its symbolic representative the bottle. ..." On the other hand the belief is expressed that there is from the first an awareness in the infant of something more: "there is in his mind", writes Melanie Klein, "already some indefinite connection between the breast and other parts and aspects of the mother. I would not assume that the breast is to him merely a physical object. The whole of his instinctual desires and his unconscious phantasies imbue the breast with qualities going far beyond the actual nourishment it affords".

Whereas, formerly, Melanie Klein had said little about the nature of this "something more", in her new publication she has ventured an hypothesis to explain it. She has in fact drawn upon the theory of Primary Return-to-Womb Craving. "This mental and physical closeness to the gratifying breast", she suggests, "in some measure restores, if things go well, the lost prenatal unity with the mother and the feeling of security which goes with it ... It may well be that his having formed part of the mother in the prenatal state contributes to the infant's innate feeling that there exists outside him something that will give him all he needs and desires". Later she refers to "the universal longing for the prenatal state" as though it were something self-evident. Thus Melanie Klein's most recent hypothesis regarding the dynamic underlying the child's tie seems to be that it combines a primary oral need to suck a breast with a primary craving to return to the prenatal state of unity with the mother.

In advancing the theory of Primary Return-to-Womb Craving to account for a tie which she believes to be more broadly founded than on orality alone, Melanie Klein has resuscitated a theory which has led an egregious existence in psychoanalysis for many years. So far as I know, it was advocated first in 1913 by Ferenczi in his "Stages in the development of the sense of reality". It is interesting to note, however, that Ferenczi did not advance the theory to account for the vigour with which the infant relates to his mother, but as an explanation of the fantasy of omnipotence.[4] When during its long history it was first borrowed by an analyst to account for the child's attachment to his mother I do not know, but we find it in Fairbairn (1943).[5] In any case, despite its place of origin, it does not seem to have played a major part in the thinking of the Hungarian school.

No doubt inspired by Ferenczi's interest in the mother–child relation, members of the Budapest Society gave much thought to our problem and during the 1930s published a number of papers about it. Hermann (1933, 1936) had noted that infant apes spend the early weeks of their lives clinging to their mother's bodies and also that there are many clasping and grasping movements to be seen in human babies, especially when they are sucking or feel threatened. As a result of these observations, and resuscitating the early and virtually discarded idea from Freud's *Three Essays*, he postulated as a primary component instinct in human beings an instinct to cling. It appears, however, that Hermann was reluctant to regard this as an object-relationship, so that it would probably be incorrect to say that he subscribed to the theory of Primary Object Clinging (see discussion in Appendix A).

Alice (1939) and Michael Balint (1937) express their indebtedness to Hermann, but go further than he does. Starting from Ferenczi's concept of passive object love, both reject the theory of primary narcissism and insist that from the first there is a primitive object relationship. Influenced, however, as they were by Hermann's work as well as by their own observations, they came to conceive of the infant as active in the relationship. Alice Balint in the appendix to her paper gives a vivid description of the development of their thought:

> ... The starting point of these ideas is Ferenczi's well-known concept of "passive object love". In my paper on this subject—printed in the Ferenczi memorial volume—I used only this term. Later, under the influence of M. Balint's ideas on the "new beginning" in which he emphasizes the active features in early infantile behaviour as well as partly under that of I. Hermann's work on the instinct to cling—I thought that the term passive was not a suitable description of a relation in which such markedly active tendencies as the instinct to cling play a paramount role. Since then I have used—as in the present paper—in place of "passive object love" mainly the terms "archaic" or "primary object relation" (object love). [A. Balint, 1939]

In describing this primitive but active object relationship, the Balints lay emphasis on two points. The first is the egoism of the relationship. After rejecting other notions Alice Balint concludes: "We come nearest to it with the conception of egoism. It is in fact an archaic, egotistic way of loving, originally directed exclusively at the mother", its main characteristic being a lack of any appreciation of the mother's own interests. The second point, though more controversial, is more germane to the present thesis. It is that the relationship is wholly independent of the erotogenic zones. "This form of object relation", writes M. Balint (1937), "is not linked to any of the erotogenic zones; it is not oral, oral-sucking, anal, genital, etc., love, but is something on its own. ...".

Reading these papers it seems clear that Primary Object Clinging is regarded as a major component in the Balints' conception of Primary Object Love but that, just as Melanie Klein's earlier views implied some dynamic beyond Primary Object Sucking, the views of the Balints go beyond Primary Object Clinging. Nevertheless in their work there is little discussion of the nature of other components.

It is curious, and to me disappointing, that in publications by British and American analysts during the past decade there has been so little interest shown in the ideas advanced in Budapest. One of the very few references to them is to be found in a footnote to a chapter by Paula Heiman (Klein *et al.*, 1952, p. 139). There, speaking in the name of the four authors of the book, she expresses agreement with Michael Balint's detailed critique of the theory of primary narcissism. She also records briefly that, with regard to the nature of the destructive impulses and the role of introjection and projection in early infancy, there is some disagreement. She fails, however, to note that, whilst the Hungarian group lays special emphasis on the non-oral components in the early object relation, the Kleinian group sees orality as dominating the relationship. The divergence plainly requires more attention than it has yet been given.

Furthermore, it must be emphasized, in so far as Melanie Klein has now dealt more fully with the non-oral component and has explained it as stemming from a primary craving to return to the womb, she is advocating a theory radically different from that of the Hungarians.

Winnicott's conception of the relationship seems always to have been far less dominated by food and orality than Melanie Klein's. Thus in a paper dated 1948 he lists a number of things about a mother which stand out as vitally important. His first two items refer to the fact that "she exists, continues to exist ... is there to be sensed in all possible ways" and that "she loves in a physical way, provides contact, a body temperature, movement and quiet according to the baby's needs". That she also provides food is placed fourth. In an important note to his paper on "Transitional objects" (1953) he discusses his usage of the term "mother's breast".

"I include the whole technique of mothering. When it is said that the first object is the breast, the word 'breast' is used, I believe, to stand for the technique of mothering as well as for the actual flesh. It is not impossible for a mother to be a good enough mother (in my way of putting it) with a bottle for the actual feeding". Food and mother's breast, therefore, are not in Winnicott's view central in the technique of mothering. Yet it is not clear how Winnicott conceptualizes the dynamic internal to the infant. In the note quoted above he hazards the view that "If this wide meaning of the word 'breast' is kept in mind, and maternal technique is seen to be included in the total meaning of the term, then there is a bridge forming between the wording of Melanie Klein's statement of early history and that of Anna Freud. The only difference left is one of dates". In this comment, it seems to me, Winnicott has failed to distinguish between a theory invoking primary instinctual responses and a theory of secondary drive.

Margaret Ribble (1944) also puts much emphasis on non-oral components, emphasizing that there is in infants an "innate need for contact with the mother", which she likens to that of hunger for food. This need, however, she relates very closely to the satisfactory functioning of physiological processes, such as breathing and circulation, and seems hardly to conceive as constituting a social bond in its own right. Indeed, in a separate section she discusses the development of the child's emotional attachment to his mother and appears to adopt a theory of Secondary Drive: "This attachment or, to use the psycho-analytic term, cathexis for the mother grows gradually out of the satisfactions it derives from her". Thus, like Klein and Winnicott, Ribble makes no reference either to a primary need to cling, or to a primary need to follow.

Like others who had their initial training in Budapest, Therese Benedek is also keenly alive to the emotional bond between mother and child, and has coined the term "emotional symbiosis" to describe it. She refers to "the need to be smiled at, picked up, talked to, etc." (1956, p. 403) and recognizes, further, that a crying fit may be caused, not "by a commanding physiologic need such as hunger or pain, but by the thwarting of an attempt at emotional (psychologic) communication and satisfaction" (p. 399). Nevertheless, as she herself admits, she finds this fact very difficult to understand. The upshot is that her theory is phrased in terms of what she describes as "the dominant tendency of childhood—the need to be fed" (p. 392)—an outcome which seems alien to her clinical descriptions. As a prisoner of orality theory she even postulates that the mother's bond to her child, about which she writes so insightfully, is also oral. Advancing the view (I believe rightly) that when a woman becomes a mother many of the same forces which bound her, as an infant, to her own mother are mobilized afresh to bind her, as a mother, to her infant, she cannot escape formulating the resulting relationship as reciprocally oral: "the post-partum symbiosis is oral, alimentary for both infant and mother" (p. 398).

Erikson, Sullivan and Spitz are similarly trapped—an expression intended to convey that I believe their clinical appreciation of the facts to be nearer the truth than their conventional theorizing. Erikson (1950), like Melanie Klein concerned to trace the origin of ambivalence in infancy, conceives it largely in terms of sucking and biting. Basic trust, on which he rightly places so much emphasis, has its origins, he believes, in orality: "The oral stages, then, form in the infant the springs of the basic sense of trust" (p. 75). Erikson, however, never formulates a Secondary Drive theory and seems at times to be assuming a theory of Primary Object Sucking.

Sullivan (1953), on the other hand, is very explicit about the primacy of physiological needs: "I regard the first needs that fall into the genus of the need for tenderness [from the mother] as needs arising in the necessary communal existence of the infant and the physico-chemical universe. [They] are direct derivatives of disequilibrium arising in the physico-chemical universe inside and outside the infant" (p. 40). Later, he thinks, infants may develop a primary need for contact and human relationships. The curious thing, however, is that he (or his editor) is so uncertain about it that discussion of this crucial issue is relegated to a footnote:

The only nonphysicochemically induced need that is probably somewhere near demonstrable during very early infancy and which certainly becomes very conspicuous not much later than this, is the need for contact ... The very young seem to have very genuine beginnings of purely human or interpersonal needs in the sense of requiring manipulations by and peripheral contact with the living, such as lying-against, and so on. But, when I talk as I do now of the first weeks and months of infancy, this can only be a speculation. .... [ibid., p. 40 note]

Spitz is also keenly alive to the need for contact and laments that "throughout the Western world skin contact between mother and child has been progressively and artificially reduced in an attempted denial of the importance of mother–child relations" (1957, p. 124). Nevertheless, in his theorizing he does not give it primacy and, instead, throughout adheres to Freud's formulation of primary narcissism and the theory of Secondary Drive. True object relations, he holds, stem from the need for food: "The anaclitic choice of object is determined by the original dependence of the infant on the person who feeds, protects and mothers him ... the drive unfolds anaclitically, that is by leaning onto a need for gratification essential for survival. The need which is gratified is the need for food" (1957, p. 83).

As we noted when describing Michael Balint's position, Freud's theory of primary narcissism has not gone unchallenged. Another who has given it much critical attention and who, also like Balint, centres his psycho-pathology on the child's relation to his mother is Fairbairn (1941, 1943). Fairbairn pictures infants partly in terms of a primary identification with the object ((an idea mooted by Freud in his Group Psychology (1921, S.E., XVIII, p. 105) but never developed by him)) and partly in terms of primary drives oriented towards social objects. In trying to explain the genesis of primary identification, Fairbairn invokes the theory of Primary Return-to-Womb Craving. In his concern with primary object seeking drives, on the other hand, he emphasizes the infant's real dependence on the mother and stresses orality. His belief that "infantile dependence is equivalent to oral dependence" (1952, p. 47) underlies much of his theorizing and leads him, like Melanie Klein, to infer that the crucial events in personality development take place in the first year of life. He admits, however, that this conclusion is not consistent with his clinical experience which is that schizoid and depressive psychopathology occur "when object-relationships continue to be unsatisfactory during the succeeding years of early childhood". To explain this he is forced to lean heavily on a theory of "regressive reactivation" (p. 55). In the most recent of his papers (1956), however, he appears to have changed his ground in some measure and to have moved nearer the position advanced in this paper: he protests against the "assumption that man is not by nature a social animal" and refers to ethology as demonstrating that object seeking behaviour is exhibited from birth.

It happens that one of the most systematic presentations of this last view was advanced in *The Origins of Love and Hate* (1935), the work of a British psychotherapist, Suttie, who, although much influenced by psychoanalysis, was not himself an analyst. Conceived and written at the same time as the work of the Hungarian school, Suttie and others of the pre-war Tavistock group postulated that "the child is born with a mind and instincts adapted to infancy", of which "a simple attachment-to-mother" is predominant. This need for mother is conceived as a primary "need for company" and a dislike of isolation, and is independent of the bodily needs which mother commonly satisfies. Had Suttie linked his ideas to those which Freud was advancing from 1926 onwards they might have been given attention in analytical circles and have led to a valuable development in theory. As it was, he couples them with a polemical attack on Freud which inevitably led to resentment of his book and neglect of his ideas.

In this paper I shall deal rather briefly with the views of others who are not psychoanalysts. First we may note that non-analysts are as divided in their views on this crucial issue as are analysts. On the one hand is the powerful school of Learning Theorists, adherents of which have long made the assumption that the only primary drives are those related to the physiological needs and that, in so far as an animal becomes interested in members of its own species, it is a result of a Secondary Drive. Although they claim legitimately that such assumptions fulfil the scientific demand for parsimony, it cannot be said that their explanations, in terms of instrumental response, social stimuli as conditioned or secondary reinforcers, and conditioned drives, are anything but complex and inelegant. One of them indeed (Gerwitz, 1956), admits that Learning Theory has been elaborated to account for phenomena which are relatively simpler and has, therefore, still to prove its relevance to our problem.

Holding an opposite view are the ethologists, who have never assumed that the only primary drives were those related to physiological needs. On the contrary, all their work has been based on the hypothesis that in animals there are many in-built responses which are comparatively independent of physiological needs and responses, the function of which is to promote social interaction between members of a species. In discussing the relation of young to parents in lower species, most if not all ethologists regard the theory of Secondary Drive as inadequate, and, though they are reluctant to commit themselves as regards a species they have not studied systematically, it is probably fair to say that no ethologist would expect the human infant's tie to his mother to be wholly explicable in terms of Learning Theory and Secondary Drive.

Empirical research workers such as Shirley (1933), Charlotte Bühler (1933), and Griffiths (1954), tend to side with this view. Each of them has been struck by the specificity of the responses babies show to human beings in the first weeks of life: they respond to the human face and voice in a way different to the way they respond to all other stimuli. Already in the first week, Shirley observed, some babies soberly watch an adult's face; by five weeks half of her sample of twenty odd babies were quietened by social interaction, such as being picked up, talked to, or caressed. It was similar observations which led Bühler to advance the view that there was something in the human face and voice which had a peculiar significance for the infant. Amongst her many published enquiries are those of her associates, Hetzer and Tudor-Hart (1927), who made a systematic study of the various responses which babies show to sounds of different kinds. As early as the third week of life the human voice was observed to evoke responses, for example sucking and expressions indicative of pleasure, which were unlike those evoked by any other sound. Griffiths has used some of these very early social responses in constructing her normative scale.

Plainly such observations do not rule out the possibility that the baby's early interest in human face and voice are the result of his learning that they are associated with the satisfaction of physiological needs: they cannot be taken to prove that there is an in-built interest. Nonetheless they support the contention of Melanie Klein and other analysts that even in the earliest weeks there is some special interest in human beings as such and at least raise the question whether learning accounts for all of it. A review of the many formulations which have been advanced shows them to fall into three main classes. On the one hand are those who commit themselves clearly to the Learning Theory standpoint. Next are the many who, whilst plainly dissatisfied with the theory of Secondary Drive, nonetheless find it difficult to put anything very explicit or plausible in its place. Finally, at the other end of the spectrum, are those, notably the Hungarian school of psychoanalysis and the ethologists, who postulate primary drives of clinging and/or following which are capable potentially of tying infant to mother. It is this third view which I believe will prove the right one.

Perceptual and cognitive aspects of the child's tie

Yet, even though there is good evidence that the human face and voice hold some special interest for the infant even in his earliest weeks, it is probably mistaken to suppose that at this age he entertains anything which remotely resembles the concept of "human being". This raises the question of the perceptual and cognitive aspects of the child's tie. Although this is as difficult and controversial a matter as is the dynamic aspect, I do not propose to deal with it in the same degree of detail. Whilst referring briefly to some of the current views, my main purpose in this section will be to describe my own views as a necessary preliminary to giving detailed attention to the problem of the dynamics of the relationship, which is the main theme of this paper.

All who have given thought to the subject seem agreed that it is only through a series of stages that the infant progresses to a state where he can order his cognitive world in terms of the concepts "human being" and "mother". There is wide agreement, too, that the earliest phase of all is probably one in which there is a total lack of differentiation between subject and object and that subsequently the infant passes through a phase during which he relates to part-objects, namely parts only of a complete human object. Beyond this, however, there is much difference of opinion.

Amongst analysts who have given special attention to these problems are Alice Balint, Melanie Klein, Winnicott, and Spitz.

A distinction to which several have drawn attention is between a phase of development when there is no concern for the object's own interests and a later one when there is. Thus Alice Balint (1939), Melanie Klein (1948), and Winnicott (1955), have all postulated a phase during which a primitive form of object relation is present without there being concern for the object. Alice Balint termed it a phase of "primary archaic object relation", for Melanie Klein it is the phase which precedes the attainment of the depressive position, and Winnicott characterizes it as one of "pre-ruth".

Spitz (1954) has introduced another distinction. On the one hand, there is a later phase when the infant enjoys a relationship with a libidinal object; in his opinion the essential qualities of such an object are that it is conceived as anticipating needs, protecting and satisfying, and continuing to do so despite its changing exterior attributes. On the other there is an earlier phase, revealed by Spitz's own experiments on the smiling response, in which it appears that what the infant is responding to is merely a gestalt signal, a superficial attribute of an object and not a conceptualized object at all. Here the distinction lies between the older infant who is responding to stimuli which he interprets as coming from a world of permanent objects existing in time and space and the younger infant who responds only to the stimulus presented in the here and now and without reference to any complex cognitive world. Referring to his work on the smiling response (Spitz & Wolf, 1946) Spitz writes: "This research led me to the conclusion that we are not justified in saying that perception of the human smile at three months is a real object relation. I have established that what the baby sees is not a partner, is not a person, is not an object but solely a signal". Nonetheless Spitz holds that, in so far as the gestalt signal belongs to and is derived from the face of the mother, it has a place in the "genealogy" of the libidinal object. For this reason he terms the response a pre-object relation (*une rélation pré-objectale*) and the signal a precursor of the object (Spitz, 1946, pp. 494–496). In thus qualifying his terminology for the earliest form of object relation, Spitz is following the lead given by Alice Balint who, in her term "primary archaic object relation", was plainly groping after a similar concept.

He is also on a track which Piaget has pioneered in his two important volumes on early cognitive development (1936, 1937). Basing his theories on the results of innumerable little experiments conducted on his own three children during their first 18 months of life, Piaget has developed a detailed account of how we may suppose the human infant gradually constructs his conceptual world. In particular he has given attention to how the infant progresses from a phase in which he appears to be influenced only by stimuli, familiar or unfamiliar, acting in the here and now, to a phase where he appears to conceptualize the world as one of permanent objects existing in time and space and interacting with each other, of which he is one. Like Freud and others, Piaget supposes that the initial phase is one in which there is no differentiation between subject and object. In the next phases, he suggests, although the infant is certainly responding to objects in the external world there is no reason to suppose that he is organizing his impressions of them in terms of permanently existing objects. Instead, he suggests, the infant is witness to a procession of images, visual, auditory, tactile, and kinaesthetic, each of which exists only in the here and now and belongs to nothing more permanent. As such it is a piecemeal world and responded to only by a series of *ad hoc* responses. This is a notion identical with that advanced by Spitz.

In my view the evidence that the infant in fact passes through such a phase is convincing. Further, pending other evidence, I am inclined to accept Piaget's conclusion that it is not much before the age of 9 months that the infant has finally constructed for himself a world of permanent objects, and that it is, therefore, not until after about this age that he is able to conceive of objects as endowed with certain of the attributes of human beings. This raises the question whether the infant can feel concern for his mother before he conceives of her as a human being existing in time and space. It may be that he can; but if he does so these feelings are likely to be at only a rudimentary level.

Nonetheless, even if Piaget proves right in putting the final construction as late as 9 months, it is evident that there is an important intermediate phase which starts at about 6 months. Prior to this the infant's differentiation, as measured by his responsiveness between familiar mother-figure and stranger is present but only evident on careful observation. After this phase has been reached, however, differential responses are very striking. In particular there is fear and avoidance of strangers and a pronounced turning to mother. This has been shown in a number of studies by Spitz (e.g. Spitz & Wolf, 1946) and confirmed recently by Schaffer (in press). Infants who lose their mothers after this point in development fret; those who lose them earlier do not.

This leads on to important and controversial issues regarding the age at which the child passes through the depressive position;

or, putting it into a wider theoretical context, the age during which the child passes through one of the critical phases in the development of his modes of regulating the conflict of ambivalence —for it seems likely that there is more than one. Since there is no space to discuss this issue at length I will remark only that, whilst I regard the stage in development when the infant first relates together his concepts of "good-mother-to-be-loved" and "bad-mother-to-be-hated" as a critical one for his future, I regard the dating of it suggested by Melanie Klein as debatable.

In constructing our picture of the infant's cognitive world I believe there are two fallacies into which it is easy to fall. The first is that because an infant responds in a typically "sociable" way he is aware of the human characteristics of the object to which he is responding; the second that because an infant recognizes a person (or a thing) he therefore perceives and thinks of him (or it) as something having a permanent existence in time and space. Let us consider them serially.

As already described, many observers have recorded how from the earliest weeks onward infants respond in special ways to the sight of a human face and the sound of a human voice; in particular we know that after about 6 weeks of age infants smile readily at the sight of a face. Is this not evidence, it may be thought, that they are aware of another human being? The answer is certainly in the negative. Both Spitz & Wolf (1946) and Ahrens (undated) have shown that they also smile at a mask painted with little more than a couple of eyes. Furthermore they do not smile at a real human face when it is in profile. These facts strongly support Spitz's view, described earlier, that in the second to fourth months the infant, on these occasions at least, is responding to the perception not of a human being but only of a visual gestalt signal.

The second fallacy is that of supposing that recognition of a person or thing requires the person or thing to be conceived as having existence in time and space. When we say that an infant recognizes a person as familiar we are basing our judgement on the fact that he responds differently to that person from the way he responds to others. In the same way we can say that ants recognize members of their own colony (by smell) when we observe that they respond to such members differentially. Yet, just as we should be rash to attribute to ants a capacity for perceiving the world in terms of many different ant colonies each with its own history and future, so should we be rash without further evidence to attribute to infants of 6 weeks[6] or even 6 months a capacity for perceiving the world in terms of a number of different human beings each with his or her own history and future. In this connexion, we should also remember, even machines can be constructed to recognize visual and auditory patterns. The fact, therefore, that in the second half of the first year infants are able readily to recognize familiar figures by sight and hearing cannot be taken by itself to indicate that the figures recognized are endowed by the infants with specific human characteristics. In my view it is quite possible that infants aged 6–9 months do not so endow them. This does not imply, however, that in this period there are no organized psychological processes relating them to the external world. On the contrary, I believe it is evident that throughout these early months psychic organization is developing apace and that much of it has the function of relating the infant to a mother-figure. It is now time to outline the view of the infant's perceptual and cognitive world which I favour and which I shall assume when I come to discuss the dynamics of the infant's tie to his mother. There appears to me good evidence for postulating a phase, which begins almost immediately after birth, when the infant responds in certain characteristic ways to certain inherently interesting stimulus patterns, by no means all of which are related to food. Thus, thanks to the human nature he inherits, the infant is predisposed to be interested, amongst other things, in the feel at his lips of something warm, moist, and nipple-like, or the sight of a pair of sparkling eyes, and is so made that he responds to them in certain characteristic ways, to the one by sucking and to the other by smiling. As the weeks and months pass he develops, first, an increasing capacity to recognize fragments of the perceptual world by one or another sense modality (probably starting with the kinaesthetic) and, secondly, a capacity to relate the fragments perceived and recognized by one sense modality to those perceived and recognized by another, so that ultimately all the fragments perceived in the here and now are attributed to one and the same source. There is reason to believe that this occurs at about five or six months. Only after this point has been reached is it possible for him to take the next steps, first to conceive of the source as existing outside himself, and secondly, for the familiar fragments to be attributed to a familiar object which has the rudiments of a past and a future. The age at which this finally occurs is uncertain; according to Piaget it may be as late as nine months.

These views I advance with much diffidence since I believe we still lack the data on which to base any which can be held with more confidence. My purpose in advancing them is to provide a sketch map of the perceptual and cognitive aspects of the child's ties as a background against which to consider its dynamic aspects, to which we will now return.

Theories of "instinct" and "instinctual response"

Since in constructing the hypothesis of Component Instinctual Responses I am leaning heavily on the work of the ethological school of animal behaviour studies, it is necessary to refer briefly to some of the ideas on instinct which have been developed in recent years. It must be recognized that these ideas differ in many significant respects from the theories of instinct which have for long been current in psychoanalysis. Yet it would be short-sighted were we not to avail ourselves of ideas stemming from other disciplines, particularly on this topic, about which Freud wrote forty years ago: "I am altogether doubtful whether any decisive pointers for the differentiation and classification of the instincts can be arrived at on the basis of working over the psychological material. This working-over seems rather itself to call for the application to the material of definite assumptions concerning instinctual life, and it would be a desirable thing if those assumptions could be taken from some other branch of knowledge and carried over to psychology" ("Instincts and their vicissitudes", S.E., XIV, p. 124). As is well known, Freud looked to biology for help in this matter. It seems best that, before attempting to relate these more recent theories of instinct to those advanced by Freud, a brief account is given of their basic principles.

Their most striking feature is a concentration of attention on certain limited and relatively precise behaviour patterns which are common to all members of a species and determined in large measure by heredity. They are conceived as the units out of which many of the more complex sequences are built. Once activated the animal of which they form a part seems to be acting with all the blind impulsion with which, as analysts, we are familiar.

Zoologists first became interested in these behaviour patterns because of the light they throw on taxonomy, namely the ordering of species with reference to their nearest relations alive and dead. For it has been found that, despite potential variability, the relative fixity of these patterns in the different species of fish and birds is such that they may be used for purposes of classification with a degree of reliability no less than that of anatomical structures. This interest goes back to Darwin (1875). In *The Origin of Species* he gives a chapter to "Instinct", in which he notes that each species is endowed with its own peculiar repertoire of behaviour patterns in the same way that it is endowed with its own peculiarities of anatomical structure. Emphasizing that "instincts are as important as corporeal structure for the welfare of each species", he advances the hypothesis that "all the most complex and wonderful instincts" have originated through the process of natural selection having preserved and continually accumulated variations which are biologically advantageous.

Since Darwin's time zoologists have been concerned to describe and catalogue those patterns of behaviour which are characteristic of each species and which, although in some degree variable and modifiable, are as much the hallmark of the species as the red breast of the robin or the stripes of the tiger. We cannot mistake the egg-laying activity of the female cuckoo for that of the female goose, the urination of the horse for that of the dog, the courtship of the grebes with that of the farmyard fowl. In each case the behaviour exhibited bears the stamp of the particular species and is, therefore, species-specific, to use a convenient if cumbersome term. Ethologists have specialized in the study of these species-specific behaviour patterns, or instincts as Darwin called them, the term deriving from the Greek "ethos" which signifies the nature of the thing.

It will be my thesis that the five responses which I have suggested go to make up attachment behaviour—sucking, clinging, following, crying, and smiling—are behaviour patterns of this kind and specific to Man. I propose to call them "instinctual responses" which I equate with the more cumbersome term "species-specific behaviour pattern".

My reason for preferring the term "instinctual response" to "instinct" or "part-instinct" will perhaps be clear. In psychoanalysis the term "instinct" (an unfortunate translation from the German *"Trieb"*) has been used to denote a motivating force. The term "instinctual response" used here describes something very different: it denotes an observable pattern of behaviour. Although this pattern results from the activation of a structure (which, since we know next to nothing of its neurological basis, is best conceived in purely psychic terms), the question of the nature and origin of the energy involved is deliberately left open.

This leads to a consideration of the dynamic of instinctual responses. Whereas Freud, with many earlier biologists, postulated instincts of sex and self-preservation to explain the motive force behind certain types of behaviour, ethologists point out that this is unnecessary—as unnecessary in fact as to postulate an instinct to see in order to explain the existence of the eye. Instead, just as the present efficiency of the eye as a seeing instrument can be explained as due to the process of natural selection having favoured the accumulation of variations leading to better vision, so the present efficiency of instinctual responses as the instruments of self-preservation and reproduction can be explained as due to similar processes having favoured the accumulation of favourable variations in these responses. In the same way that the eye can be said to have the function of sight, instinctual responses can be said to have the function, amongst other things, of safeguarding the individual and mediating reproduction.

It is contended, therefore, that it is redundant and misleading to invoke hypothetical instincts of sex and self-preservation as causal agents. Instead we may look to the conditions found necessary to activate a pattern as being in fact their causes.

In considering the conditions necessary to activate an instinctual response it is useful to distinguish between conditions internal to the organism and those external to it. Conditions internal to the organism which may be necessary before it will be exhibited include physiological conditions such as the hormonal state and stimuli of interoceptive origin. In Man they include also conditions such as thoughts and wishes, conscious and unconscious, which can be conceptualized only in psychological terms. All of these together put the organism into a responsive mood and sometimes lead to "seeking" behaviour well designed to lead to the next links in the chain of behaviour. It is on the nature of the conditions activating succeeding links that the ethologists have thrown a flood of light. What they have demonstrated is that, for most instinctual responses, activation only occurs in the presence of particular external conditions.

Heinroth was probably the first to point out that species-specific behaviour patterns may often be activated by the perception of fairly simple visual or auditory gestalts to which they are innately sensitive. Well-known examples of this, analysed by means of experiments using dummies of various shapes and colours, are the mating response of the male stickleback, which is elicited by the perception of a shape resembling a pregnant female, the gaping response of the young herring-gull, which is elicited by the perception of a red spot similar to that on the beak of an adult gull, and the attack response of the male robin which is elicited by the perception in his own territory of a bunch of red feathers, similar to those on the breast of a rival male. In all three cases the response seems to be elicited by the perception of a fairly simple gestalt, known as a "sign-stimulus".

A great deal of ethological work has been devoted to the identification of the sign-stimuli which elicit the various species-specific behaviour patterns in fish and birds. In so far as many of these behaviour patterns mediate social behaviour—courtship, mating, feeding of young by parents and following of parents by young—much light has been thrown on the nature of social interaction. In dozens of species it has been shown that behaviour subserving mating and parenthood is controlled by the perception of sign-stimuli presented by other members of the same species, such as the spread of a tail or the colour of a beak, or a song or a call, the essential characteristics of which are those of fairly simple gestalten. Such sign-stimuli are known as social releasers. They play an essential role in the activation of a response.

Oddly enough stimuli of a comparable kind often play an essential role also in the termination of a response. Psychoanalysis has for long thought of instinctive behaviour in terms of the flow of a hypothetical psychic energy. According to this view behaviour is activated when energy has accumulated within the organism and terminates when it has flowed away. So deeply is our thinking coloured by such concepts that it is by no means easy instead to conceive of an activity coming to an end because a set of stimuli, either internal or external to the organism, switch it off, much as the referee's whistle terminates a game of football. Yet this is a concept which has been elaborated during recent years and will, I believe, prove immensely fruitful.

Sometimes the stimuli which have a terminating effect, and which are conveniently termed consummatory stimuli, arise within the animal. Thus experiments using oesophagostomized dogs have demonstrated that the acts of feeding and drinking are terminated by proprioceptive and/or interoceptive stimuli which arise in the mouth, the oesophagus, and the stomach and which in the intact animal are the outcome of the performances themselves. Such cessation is due neither to fatigue nor to a satiation of the need for food or drink: instead the very act gives rise to the feed-back stimuli which terminate it. (For discussion see Deutsch, 1953; Hinde, 1954.)

In the case of other responses, it can be shown, termination results from stimuli arising in the organism's environment; for instance, Hinde has observed that in early spring the mere presence of a female chaffinch leads to a reduction of the male's courtship behaviour, such as singing and searching. When she is present he is quiet, when she is absent he becomes active. In this case, where a socially relevant behaviour pattern is terminated by consummatory stimuli emanating from another member of the same species, we might perhaps speak of a "social suppressor" as a term parallel to social releaser. I believe it to be a concept extremely valuable for helping us understand the problem before us. The basic model for instinctive behaviour which this work suggests is thus a unit comprising a species-specific behaviour pattern (or instinctual response) governed by two complex mechanisms, one controlling its activation and the other its termination. Although sometimes to be observed active in isolation, in real life it is usual for a number of these responses to be linked together so that adaptive behaviour sequences result. For instance sexual behaviour in birds can be understood as a sequence of a large number of discrete instinctual responses, in greater or less measure modified by learning, and so oriented to the environment, including other members of the species, and linked in time that reproduction of the species is commonly achieved. There are a large number of responses which, strung together in the right way, eventually lead to copulation; many others lead to nest-building, others again to brooding, and others again to care of young. It is interesting to note that, even in birds, those leading through courtship to copulation are far from few and fully confirm Freud's view that sexual activity is best understood in terms of the integration of a number of component "part-instincts". Plainly this integration occurs under the influence of forces operating at a high level and is proceeding in the perceptual as well as the motor field. Moreover it has a complex ontogeny. For instance it has been shown that, as in Man, during the development of members of lower species there are many hazards which must be avoided if co-ordinated and effective functioning is to be achieved in adult life. An example of failure is the case of the turkey cock, who, although he could copulate with turkey hens, could only court human males. Another is the case of the gander, all of whose sexual responses were fixated on a dog-kennel and who, moreover, behaved as though mourning when his dog-kennel was turned on its side.

In considering groups of instinctual responses patterned into behaviour sequences, concepts such as hierarchical structure and the availability of one and the same response for integration into more than one sequence are both of great interest; but their discussion would lead us too far afield on this occasion.

Two further points, however, need mention. First, to ensure survival of the individual and the species, it is necessary for the organism to be equipped with an appropriately balanced repertoire of instinctual responses at each stage of its ontogeny. No only must the adult be so equipped, but the young animal must itself have a balanced and efficient equipment of its own. This will certainly differ in many respects from that of the adult. Furthermore, not only do individuals of different sexes and at different stages of development require specialized repertoires, but in certain respects these need to be reciprocal. Male and female mating responses need to be reciprocal, and so also do those mediating on the one hand parental care and on the other parent-oriented activity in the young. It is my thesis that, as in the young of other species, there matures in the early months of life of the human infant a complex and nicely balanced equipment of instinctual responses, the function of which is to ensure that he obtains parental care sufficient for his survival. To this end the equipment includes responses which promote his close proximity to a parent and responses which evoke parental activity.

Not very much study has yet been given by ethologists to the process of transition from the infantile equipment to that of the adult (though there is one valuable paper by Meyer-Holzapfel, 1949). Let us hope this will be remedied, since it appears to me that it is precisely this transition in the human being which provides a main part of the subject matter of psychoanalysis.

My second point concerns how as human beings, we experience the activation in ourselves of an instinctual response system. When the system is active and free to reach termination, it seems, we experience an urge to action accompanied, as Lorenz (1950) has suggested, by an emotional state peculiar to each response. There is an emotional experience peculiar to smiling and laughing, another peculiar to weeping, yet another to sexual foreplay, another again to temper. When, however, the response is not free to reach termination, our experience may be very different: we experience tension, unease and anxiety. As observers when these responses are activated in another, we commonly think and speak of the individual as the subject of conscious and unconscious wishes and feelings.

All instinctual response systems which are not active are so potentially. As such they go to make up what has been described earlier as psychic structure. It is here, I believe, that concepts derived from ethology may link with those in regard to infantile phantasy which have been elaborated by Melanie Klein and her colleagues. Nevertheless, in making such linkages we need to walk warily, since there may well be processes in Man, such as imitation and identification, with their associated ego structures, which need for their understanding a different and complementary frame of reference. A full correlation of the two sets of concepts will be a long and difficult task.

In this brief account of ethological instinct theory I have concentrated on three main concepts: (a) the presence of species-specific behaviour patterns, or instinctual responses as I have called them; (b) the activation and termination of these responses by various conditions internal and external to the organism; and (c) their integration into more complex behaviour sequences. As such the approach starts with limited and observed behaviour and attempts to understand more complex behaviour as due to a synthesis, more or less elaborate, of these simpler units into greater wholes. In this respect it resembles Freud's earlier view of instinct as expressed in his "Three essays on sexuality" and "Instincts and their vicissitudes". It is the antithesis, however, of the approach he favoured later. In his essay "Beyond the pleasure principle" (1920) and later works, Freud starts with purely abstract concepts, such as those of psychic energy and Life and Death Instincts, and attempts to understand particular examples of behaviour as expressions of these hidden forces. Put briefly we might say that, whereas Freud's later theories conceive of the organism as starting with a quantum of unstructured psychic energy which during development becomes progressively more structured, ethology conceives of it as starting with a number of highly structured responses (some of which are active at birth and some of which mature later), which in the course of development become so elaborated, through processes of integration and learning, and in Man by imitation, identification and the use of symbols, that the resulting behaviour is of amazing variety and plasticity.[7] This picture of Man's behaviour may appear incredible to some, but before dismissing it we should be wise to recall that in other spheres we are used to the idea that from relatively few and simple components rich and varied structures may be created.

Indeed, in advocating the ethological approach, it is my hope that I am not underestimating the extraordinary complexities of behaviour characteristic of Man. By his skill in learning and his mastery of symbol he so conducts himself that the comparatively stereotyped behavioural units may well seem to have disappeared; and this may seem to be as true of the two-year-old as of the adult. Yet I believe this conclusion will prove false and that there will be found active beneath the symbolic transformations and other trappings of humanity, primeval dynamic structures which we share in common with lower species. Furthermore, I believe they will be found playing a dominant role in early infancy. As we go down the phylogenetic scale to simpler organisms we find instinctual responses increasingly in evidence; in the same way, I believe, as we trace Man back to his ontogenetic beginnings we shall find them responsible for an increasing proportion of his behaviour. I emphasize that at present this is no more than my belief and that whether or not ethology will prove a fruitful approach to psycho-analytic problems is yet to be shown. Speaking for myself, a main reason for preferring it to other approaches is the research which it suggests. With ethological concepts and methods it is possible to undertake a far-reaching programme of experimentation into the social responses of the preverbal period of infancy, and to this I attach much importance. Thus the repertoire of instinctual responses may be catalogued and the range of ages when each matures identified. Each response may be studied to discover the nature of the conditions which activate it and the nature of those which terminate it (often called consummatory stimuli), and why in some individuals responses come to be activated and terminated by unusual objects. The conditions which lead to certain responses being manifested at abnormal levels, either too low or too high an intensity, and the conditions which lead to a perpetuation of such a state may be explored. Other main interests will be the study of the conflicts arising when two or more incompatible responses are activated at once and the modes by which conflict is regulated. Finally, we may be interested to investigate the critical phases through which the modes of regulating conflict develop and the conditions which in an individual lead to one mode of regulation becoming dominant.

Even this brief sketch describes an extensive programme. Analysts will differ in their evaluation of it and in how they perceive its relatedness to the traditional research method of reconstructing early phases of development from the investigation of later ones. Since, however, we have yet to see the fruits of this new approach, it is perhaps premature to attempt to judge its likely value. For me it carries with it the hope that, by introducing experimental method to the investigation of early emotional development, we may be entering a phase when more reliable data will be available to us in our consideration of crucial theoretical issues.

The dynamic aspects of the child's tie—comparative studies

In presenting this brief and inadequate account of recent theories of instinctive behaviour I am keenly aware that they will be unfamiliar to many and controversial to all. I hope, in due course, time will be found when we can examine them in their own right and that meanwhile the account given will provide a background to my hypothesis.

Before proceeding I wish to emphasize again that I am discussing only the positive aspects of the child's tie and leaving an examination of its negative side to another occasion. My main thesis is that the positive dynamic is expressed through a number of instinctual responses, all of which are primary in the sense used in this paper and, in the first place, relatively independent of one another. Those which I am postulating are sucking, clinging, following, crying, and smiling, but there may well be many more.[8] In the course of the first year of life, it is suggested, these component instinctual responses become integrated into attachment behaviour. How this process of integration is related to the parallel process in the cognitive sphere is difficult to know. It seems not unlikely, however, that there are significant connexions between the two and that a disturbance in the one will create repercussions in the other.

The five responses postulated fall into two classes. Sucking, clinging, and following achieve their end, in the one case food and in the other close proximity to mother, with only a limited reciprocal response being necessary on the mother's part. Crying and smiling on the other hand depend for their results on their effect on maternal behaviour. It is my belief that both of them act as social releasers of instinctual responses in mothers. As regards crying, there is plentiful evidence from the animal world that this is so: probably in all cases the mother responds promptly and unfailingly to her infant's bleat, call, or cry. It seems to me clear that similar impulses are also evoked in the human mother and, furthermore, that the infant's smile has a comparable though more agreeable effect on her.

Since a main point of my thesis is that no one of these responses is more primary than another and that it is, therefore, a mistake to give pre-eminence to sucking and feeding, it may be useful to consider the evidence for such a view. Unfortunately, studies of human infants are inadequate for our purpose and the hypothesis, therefore, remains untested. In respect of other species, however, the data are unequivocal. In sub-human primates, as Hermann insisted twenty-five years ago, clinging is manifested independently of the oral response and food. The same is certainly true of following and "crying" in certain species of birds. Such observations are of great theoretical interest and merit detailed attention.

Clinging appears to be a universal characteristic of Primate infants and is found from the lemurs up to anthropoid apes and human babies. In every species save Man during the early weeks the infant clings to its mother's belly. Later the location varies, the mother's back being preferred in certain species. All accounts of infant–parent relations in sub-human Primates emphasize the extraordinary intensity of the clinging response and how in the early weeks it is maintained both day and night. Though in the higher species mothers play a role in holding their infants, those of lower species do little for them; in all it is plain that in the wild the infant's life depends, indeed literally hangs, on the efficiency of his clinging response.

In at least two different species, one of which is the chimpanzee, there is first-hand evidence that clinging occurs before sucking. As soon as it is born the infant either climbs up the ventral surface of the mother or is placed by her on her abdomen. Once there it "clings tenaciously with hands and feet to the hair or skin". Only later, sometimes after some hours, does it find the nipple and start to suck (carpenter, 1934; Yerkes & Tomlin, 1935). We may conclude, therefore, that in sub-human Primates clinging is a primary response, first exhibited independently of food.[9]

Similarly the response of following, which in nature is focused on a parent-figure, is known in certain species of birds to be independent of any other satisfactions and once again, therefore, primary. Although this response has the same function as clinging, namely to keep the infant animal in close proximity to its mother, it would be a mistake to regard the two as identical. Whereas clinging is virtually confined to Primates (and a few other mammals including bats and anteaters, see Burton, 1956), the following response is to be observed in a very great variety of species both of mammals, and birds. The species in which the following response is certainly primary include many ground-nesting birds, such as ducks, geese, and rails, the young of which are not fed by their parents but start foraging for themselves a day or so after birth. In systematic experiments Hinde et al. (1956) have shown that the mere experience of following an object reinforces the response; in other words the response increases in strength without any other reward being given.

The fact that clinging and following are undoubtedly primary responses in some species, it should therefore be noted, robs the theory of Secondary Drive of claim to special scientific status in regard to our problem; for it is shown not to fit the facts for certain species. It is particularly significant that these include Man's nearest relatives, the anthropoid apes.

Let us next consider crying. There is a widespread tendency to assume that crying is linked in a unique way to the needs for food and warmth. This, however, seems doubtful. In the species of birds already referred to in which the mother does no feeding of the young, the calls of the young serve the function of bringing mother to their side and thus prevent them from getting lost. Indeed, a common term for such calls is "lost piping". Evidence from chimpanzees is less conclusive but none the less suggestive. For instance, it is reported that infant chimpanzees are provoked to plaintive crying as much by being prevented from clinging to their mothers as by hunger (Tomlin & Yerkes, 1935). Further, perhaps it is not without interest that it is the same situation—being left alone or not being able to cling—which is by far the most frequent provoker of temper tantrums in the rather older infant chimpanzee (Kellogg & Kellogg, 1933).

The broad thesis which is being advanced is that each of the young animal's instinctual responses makes a distinctive contribution to the genesis of the infant–mother tie, and that the young of each species is equipped with its own peculiar repertoire of responses which mature at rates specific for the species. Thus, Ungulates have a fully active following response almost from birth but never demonstrate clinging; sub-human Primates have a fully developed clinging response at birth and develop a following response later. Both mammalian orders are equipped with a capacity to "cry" and thus to evoke maternal aid. What is the repertoire specific to Man?

The dynamic aspects of the child's tie—man

Perhaps largely as an adaptation required by his large head, in comparison to other Primates the human infant is born in a relatively immature state. Neither his clinging response nor his following response are yet effective. Indeed, apart from sucking, the only effective mother-related response available to the newborn human infant appears to be crying. This illustrates the extent to which in Man the survival of the young is dependent on the exertions of the mother.[10]

For reasons already given when considering the "crying" of chimpanzees, it is my thesis that in human infants the crying response is probably so designed that it is terminated not only by food but also by other stimuli connected with the mother's presence, initially probably kinaesthetic or tactile. As an example (but no proof) of this we may refer to the common experience that babies often cry when they are not hungry and that this crying may be quietened by touch or rocking, and later by voice. The mother thus provides the terminating (or consummatory) stimuli for crying, stimuli which may, rather aptly, be described as "social suppressors".

In addition to the baby's cry, maternal behaviour in the human mother is subjected to another social releaser: this is the baby's smile. As with other instinctual responses, maturation of smiling varies considerably from infant to infant; in most it is present by six weeks. At this time and for two or three months longer, smiling is sensitive to patterns much simpler than the whole human face: it is in fact activated at first by a sign stimulus comprising no more than a pair of dots (Ahrens, undated). Nevertheless, however activated, as a social releaser of maternal behaviour it is powerful. Can we doubt that the more and better an infant smiles the better is he loved and cared for? It is fortunate for their survival that babies are so designed by Nature that they beguile and enslave mothers.

Although in his early months the human infant is particularly dependent on his capacity to evoke maternal care, as he grows older and stronger responses mature such as clinging and following which require less reciprocal maternal action. By the third month he is following a person for a few seconds with his eyes (Griffiths, 1954) and as soon as he becomes mobile he will follow his mother by whatever means of locomotion he has available. Like the cock chaffinch referred to earlier, he is often restless and vocal when alone, content and quiet when in the presence of a mother-figure. For the following response as well as for crying, mother provides the consummatory stimuli.

Ordinary observation shows that the following response of human infants—the tendency to remain within sight or earshot of their mothers—varies both in the short term and over longer periods. In the short term it is particularly easily evoked if the child is tired, hungry, or in pain; it is also immediately activated if the child is afraid, a matter of great consequence for the theory of anxiety to which a later paper is devoted. In its sensitivity to these conditions it probably differs not a whit in principle from the comparable response in the young of all other species.

As regards the natural history of the response in the long term, so far as I know there has been no systematic study, but as in monkeys (Carpenter, 1934), there appears to be first a waxing and then a waning. No doubt its course varies from child to child, but in many a zenith seems to be reached in the period 18 to 30 months. This late dating may come as a surprise, especially to those who, equating psychological attachment with physiological dependence, presume that attachment must be at its maximum soon after birth. If we are right, however, in recognizing following as an instinctual response in its own right, there is no reason to expect it to be most active in the months following birth. On the contrary, it is to be expected that it would be at a maximum at a period of life after the child is capable of free and independent locomotion but before he is able to fend for himself in emergency. The chronology proposed is reasonably consistent with that advanced by Dorothy Burlingham and Anna Freud (1942), already quoted. Whether or not it is right, however, will have to be tested by research of a kind much more systematic than has yet been undertaken.

Although maturation no doubt plays a major role in determining this long-term waxing and waning, environmental conditions can greatly influence its course. Thus, any which result in strong unconscious hostility to the mother may also lead to high intensity following; and, whilst a limited degree of rejection and short separation may also lead to its exhibition at high intensity, massive rejection or the absence of a mother-figure may result either in its failure to mature or in maturation being overtaken later by repression. This, however, is not the occasion to concern ourselves in detail with the many conditions which influence its course: what I have attempted is to show that the following response is one which deserves systematic study in its own right.

The natural history of the clinging response appears to be rather similar though, unlike the following response, it is present in rudimentary form from the earliest days. It is well known that at birth human infants are able to support their weight by clinging with their hands. We know further that the response continues active in the early months, especially when the child is sucking, and that it is to be observed not only in the hands, as reported by Freud, but also the feet (Hermann, 1936). It seems to be rather chancy as to what the infant clings to, though Hermann holds that "the grasping instinct will show itself primarily in relation to another person". Whatever the facts, one has the impression that, in these early months, functionally, it is embryonic only.

Later it becomes more effective. Particularly when afraid, the infant will cling to his mother with great tenacity. Clinging is also especially apparent at bedtime or after a separation experience (see for example Burlingham and Freud, 1944, pp. 47–48). Sometimes it is directed towards mother or a part of mother, sometimes, as both Hermann and Winnicott (1953) have emphasized, towards a transitional object. Although this clinging is often thought to be an atavistic character related to an (imaginary) arboreal past, it seems far more reasonable to suppose that it is homologous with the infantile clinging of our Primate cousins. This view is strengthened by evidence that chimpanzee infants also cling tenaciously to transitional objects, objects moreover which, like "parent's" overalls, are plainly identified with the absent parent figure (Kellogg & Kellogg, 1933; Hayes, 1951).

When infants of other Primate species cling to their mothers they do so with arms and legs extended clutching their mothers' flanks. This extension of arms and legs may well explain the extension movements seen in human infants. In the presence of an adult, older babies and toddlers very frequently extend their arms in a way which is always interpreted by adults as a wish to be picked up; if we watch carefully, an extension of both arms and legs when an adult appears is to be seen also in infants as young as four months. If we are right in supposing that these movements are homologous with Primate clinging and that they activate the parental response to pick the baby up, we have a pretty example of an intention movement having become ritualized into a social releaser; this is an evolutionary process to which Daanje (1950) has called attention.

However that may be, there seems little doubt that, as in the case of following, clinging waxes, reaches a zenith, and then wanes, or that, again like following, the course of its development may be influenced by experience. In the short term, we know, anxiety and a period of separation both lead to its exhibition at high intensity.

In the account of the human infant's repertoire of positively directed mother-oriented instinctual responses, I have left sucking to the last. My reason is that psychoanalytical theory has tended to become fixated on orality and it is a main purpose of this paper to free it for broader development. Nevertheless sucking is plainly of great importance both in infancy and later and must be studied systematically. Furthermore, the phase during which sucking is one of the dominant responses continues for far longer than is sometimes supposed, a fact remarked upon by Anna Freud (1951). In my experience most infants through much of the second year of life need a great deal of sucking and thrive on milk from a bottle at bedtime. It is regrettable that, in Western culture, armchair doctrines regarding weaning at 9 months or earlier have led to a neglect of this obvious fact.

In this exposition I have emphasized the endogenous aspects of these instinctual responses. Their development in the individual, however, can never be free of change through processes of learning. In respect of smiling in infants aged 14–18 weeks, this has already been demonstrated experimentally by Brackbill (1956). What is of particular interest in her work is that the "reward" given was no more than a little social attention.

At this point I wish to emphasize that it is a main part of my thesis that each of the five instinctual responses which I am suggesting underlie the child's tie to his mother is present because of its survival value. Unless there are powerful in-built responses which ensure that the infant evokes maternal care and remains in close proximity to his mother throughout the years of childhood he will die—so runs the thesis. Hence in the course of our evolution the process of natural selection has resulted in crying and smiling, sucking, clinging and following becoming responses species-specific to Man. Their existence, it is claimed, is readily intelligible on biological grounds. In this respect they differ sharply from the hypothetical craving to return to the mother's womb. It is difficult to imagine what survival value such a desire might have and I am not aware that any has been suggested. Indeed, the hypothesis of Primary Return-to-Womb Craving has been advanced on quite other grounds and, so far as I know, lays no claim to biological status. I emphasize this to make clear my own position. The theory of Component Instinctual Responses, it is claimed, is rooted firmly in biological theory and requires no dynamic which is not plainly explicable in terms of the survival of the species. It is because the notion of a primary desire to return to the womb is not so rooted and because I believe the data are more readily explained in other ways that this theory is rejected.

In stressing the survival value of the five component instinctual responses we are put in mind of Freud's concepts of libido and Life instinct. Not only is there the same emphasis on survival, but the means of achieving it—a binding together—is the same: "Eros desires contact because it strives to make the ego and the loved object one, to abolish the barriers of distance between them" (Freud, 1926, p. 79). Despite the starting points of the two theories being so different, and their having different implications, the themes appear to be the same.

Although I have described these five responses as mother-oriented, it is evident that at first this is so only potentially. From what we know of other species it seems probable that each one of them has the potential to become focused on some other object. The clearest examples of this in real life are where sucking becomes directed towards a bottle and not to the mother's breast, and clinging is directed to a rag and not to the mother's body. In principle it seems likely that an infant could be so reared that each of his responses was directed towards a different object. In practice this is improbable, since all or most of the consummatory stimuli which terminate them habitually come from the mother-figure. No matter for what reason he is crying—cold, hunger, fear, or plain loneliness—his crying is usually terminated through the agency of the mother. Again, when he wants to cling or follow or to find a haven of safety when he is frightened, she is the figure who commonly provides the needed object. It is for this reason that the mother becomes so central a figure in the infant's life. For in healthy development it is towards her that each of the several responses becomes directed, much as each of the subjects of the realm comes to direct his loyalty towards the Queen; and it is in relation to the mother that the several responses become integrated into the complex behaviour which I have termed "attachment behaviour", much as it is in relation to the Sovereign that the components of our constitution become integrated into a working whole.

We may extend the analogy. It is in the nature of our constitution, as of all others, that sovereignty is vested in a single person. A hierarchy of substitutes is permissible but at the head stands a particular individual. The same is true of the infant. Quite early, by a process of learning, he comes to centre his instinctual responses not only on a human figure but on a particular human figure. Good mothering from any kind woman ceases to satisfy him—only his own mother will do.[11]

This focusing of instinctual responses on to a particular individual, which we find but too often ignored in human infancy, is found throughout the length and breadth of the animal kingdom. In very many species, mating responses are directed to a single member of the opposite sex, either for a season or for a lifetime, whilst it is the rule for parents to be solicitous of their own young and of no others and for young to be attached to their own parents and not to any adult. Naturally such a general statement needs amplification and qualification, but the tendency for instinctual responses to be directed towards a particular individual or group of individuals and not promiscuously towards many is one which I believe to be so important and so neglected that it deserves a special term. I propose to call it "monotropy", a term which, it should be noted, is descriptive only and carries with it no pretensions to causal explanation.[12]

In the case of human personality the integrating function of the unique mother-figure is one the importance of which I believe can hardly be exaggerated; in this I am at one with Winnicott who has constantly emphasized it (e.g. Winnicott, 1945). I see the ill-effects stemming from maternal deprivation and separation as due in large part to an interference with this function, either preventing its development or smashing it at a critical point. This is a view I have advanced in the past (Bowlby, 1951, p. 54) and to which I hope to give further attention.

In the final synthesis of these many responses into attachment behaviour directed towards a single mother-figure, it may well be that certain component responses play a more central part than others. Without much further research we cannot know which they may be. However, the ease with which sucking is transferred to objects other than the mother's breast leads me to think it will not prove the most important. Clinging and following seem more likely candidates for the role.

This view is strengthened by clinical observation. My impression in taking the histories of many disturbed children is that there is little if any relationship between form and degree of disturbance and whether or not the child has been breast-fed. The association which constantly impresses itself upon me is that between form and degree of disturbance and the extent to which the mother has permitted clinging and following, and all the behaviour associated with them, or has refused them. In my experience a mother's acceptance of clinging and following is consistent with favourable development even in the absence of breast feeding, whilst rejection of clinging and following is apt to lead to emotional disturbance even in the presence of breast feeding. Furthermore, it is my impression that fully as many psychological disturbances, including the most severe, can date from the second year of life when clinging and following are at their peak as from the early months when they are rudimentary. I am, of course, aware that these views contrast with those expressed by many other analysts and I make no special claim for their truth: like those of others, they rest only on a collection of not very systematic clinical impressions. In the long run this, like other scientific issues, will be decided on the quality of the empirical data presented.

This completes our review of the quintet of responses through which, it is suggested, the dynamic of the child's tie to his mother is expressed. It may be noted that all of them, even smiling, seem to reach a zenith and then to decline. As the years roll by first sucking, then crying, then clinging and following all diminish. Even the smiley two-year-old becomes a more solemn school-child. They are a quintet comprising a repertoire which is well adapted to human infancy but, having performed their function, are relegated to a back seat. Nevertheless none disappears. All remain in different states of activity or latency and are utilized in fresh combinations when the adult repertoire comes to mature. Furthermore, some of them, particularly crying and clinging, revert to an earlier state of activity in situations of danger, sickness, and incapacity. In these roles, they are performing a natural and healthy function and one which there is no need to regard as regressive.[13] Like old soldiers, infantile instinctual responses never die.

Conclusion

It will be noticed that in this account I have carefully avoided the term "dependence", although it is in common use. My reason is that to be dependent on someone and to be attached to them are not the same thing. The terms "dependence" and "dependency" are appropriate if we favour the theory of Secondary Drive, which has it that the child becomes oriented towards his mother because he is dependent on her as the source of physiological gratification. They are, however, inappropriate terms if we believe that dependence on physiological satisfactions and psychological attachment, although related to one another, are fundamentally different phenomena. On this view, we observe on the one hand that in the early weeks the infant is in fact dependent on its mother, whether or not there are forces in him which attach him to her, and on the other that he is attached to her by dynamic forces, whether or not, as in hospital, he is dependent on her physiologically. On this view, psychological attachment and detachment are to be regarded as functions in their own right apart altogether from the extent to which the child happens at any one moment to be dependent on the object for his physiological needs being met. It is interesting to note that, despite their adherence to the theory of Secondary Drive, both Sigmund Freud and Anna Freud nonetheless employ the term "attachment" (Freud, C.P., V, p. 252–253; (Burlingham & Freud, 1944).

Other terminological issues also arise. Thus we shall no longer regard it as satisfactory to equate breast and mother, to identify good feeding and good mothering, or even to speak of the earliest phase as oral and the first relationship as anaclitic. To some these may seem revolutionary consequences but, if the hypothesis advanced here is correct, terminological change is inescapable.

The hypothesis advanced, however, can be no more than tentative. Data are still scarce and it may well be many years before crucial evidence is available. Meanwhile I advance it as a working hypothesis, both as the best explanation of the facts as we now know them and above all as a stimulus to further research.

In most cases references to the works of Sigmund Freud are given in the text, wherever possible to the Standard Edition.

Notes

1. An abbreviated version of this paper was read before the British Psycho-Analytical Society on 19 June, 1957.

2. Although in this paper I shall usually refer to mothers and not mother-figures, it is to be understood that in every case I am concerned with the person who mothers the child and to whom he becomes attached rather than to the natural mother.

3. Following the discussion of this paper Mrs Klein drew my attention to the role which she attributes to anal and urethral impulses in the infant's relation to his mother. Although in her writings it is the hostile components of those impulses which seem to be most emphasized (an aspect of the relationship which lies outside the scope of this paper), it is evident that she also attaches importance to the pleasure in mastery and possession which are commonly attributed to anal erotism.

4. Ferenczi suggests that the foetus "must get from his existence the impression that he is in fact omnipotent" and that the child and the obsessional patient, when demanding that their wishes be at once fulfilled, are demanding no more than a return to those "good old days" when they occupied the womb.

5. Freud (1926) is struck by the functional similarity of mother's womb and mother's arms as modes of infant care (p. 109), which is a different matter. However, in postulating that the need for companionship in agoraphobia is due to "a temporal regression to infancy, or, in extreme cases, to prenatal days" (p. 89), he comes near to postulating a return-to-womb craving.

6. The age at which an infant differentiates reliably between individuals is uncertain. Griffiths (1954) states there is visual discrimination in the second month.

7. The many good theoretical reasons for being dissatisfied with Freud's notion of an unstructured id have been discussed by Fairbairn (1952) and Colby (1955). Moreover, Anna Freud (1951) in her empirical approach to child development has reached conclusions consistent with those advanced in the text. Discussing the theoretical implications of her Hampstead Nursery observations, she advances the view that "there exist in the child innate, preformed attitudes which are not originated, merely stimulated and developed by life experience".

8. It has been suggested to me that cooing and babbling may represent a sixth.

9. In 1957, Professor Harlow of the University of Wisconsin began a series of experiments on the attachment behaviour of young rhesus monkeys. Removed from their mothers at birth, they are provided with the choice

of two varieties of model to which to cling and from which to take food (from a bottle). Preliminary results (Harlow, in press) strongly suggest that the preferred model is the one which is most "comfy" to cling to rather than the one which provides food.

10. In lower Primates it is not so. Lemur mothers do little more than provide a moving milk tank with plenty of fur to which to grip. If the infant lemur does not fend for himself by clinging, locating a nipple, and sucking, he dies. In the higher Primates mothers play an increasingly active role (Zuckerman, 1933). Mother chimpanzees handle their infants gently and more or less skilfully, refuse to let them out of sight, and respond immediately to their cries (Yerkes & Tomlin, 1935). Fortunately for their offspring most human mothers do even better.

11. I am hesitant to name an age for this development. The studies of Spitz (1946) and Schaffer (in press) make it clear that it has already occurred by six or seven months.

12. Excellent examples of monotropy in young children are given in Infants without Families. For example "Bridget (2–2½ years) belonged to the family of Nurse Jean of whom she was extremely fond. When Jean had been ill for a few days and returned to the nursery, she constantly repeated: 'My Jean, my Jean.' Lillian (2–2½ years) once said 'my Jean' too, but Bridget objected and explained: 'It's my Jean, it's Lillian's Ruth and Keith's very own Ilsa'". (Burlingham & Freud, 1944, p. 44).

Robert Hinde has drawn my attention to the emphasis which William James gives to this process. In his chapter on "Instinct", James (1890) discusses two processes which lead to great variations in the manifestation of instinctual responses in different individuals. The first is the tendency for them to become focused on one object, and therefore to be inhibited in respect of other objects, which he terms "the law of inhibition of instincts by habits". The second refers to critical phases in the development of instinct. James' treatment of the whole problem is remarkably perspicacious.

13. In much theorizing (e.g. Benedek, 1956), all manifestations of attachment behaviour after infancy are conceived as "regressive". Since this term inevitably carries with it the connotation pathological or at least, undesirable, I regard it as misleading and failing to do justice to the facts.

References

Abraham, K. (1916). The first pregenital stage of the libido. In: *Selected Papers on Psychoanalysis*. London: Hogarth, 1927.

Abraham, K. (1924). A short study of the development of the libido, viewed in the light of mental disorders. In: *Selected Papers on Psychoanalysis*. London: Hogarth, 1927.

Ahrens, R. (Undated). Beitrag zur Entwicklung des Physiognomie- und Mimikerkennens. *Zeitschrift fur experimentelle und angewandte Psychologie II/3*: 412–454.

Balint, A. (1939). *Int. Z. f. Psa. u. Imago*, 24: 33–48. Trans. (1949). Love for the mother and mother-love. *International Journal of Psycho-Analysis*, 30: 251–259.

Balint, M. (1937). *Imago*, 23: 270–288. Trans. (abbreviated) (1949). Early developmental states of the ego. primary object love. *International Journal of Psycho-Analysis*, 30: 265–273.

Benedek, T. (1938). Adaptation to reality in early infancy. *Psychoanalytic Quarterly*, 7: 200–215.

Benedek, T. (1956). Toward the biology of the depressive constellation. *Journal of the American Psychoanalytic Association*, 4: 389–427.

Bowlby, J. (1951). *Maternal Care and Mental Health*. Geneva: W.H.O. Monograph No. 2.

Brackbill, Y. (1956). Smiling in infants: relative resistance to extinction as a function of reinforcement schedule. PhD Thesis, Stanford University.

Bühler, C. (1933). The social behaviour of children. In: *A Handbook of Child Psychology*. Worcester, Mass.: Clark Univ. Press.

Burlingham, D., & Freud, A. (1942). *Young Children in War-time*. London: Allen and Unwin.

Burlingham, D., & Freud, A. (1944). *Infants without Families*. London: Allen and Unwin.

Burton, M. (1956). *Infancy in Animals*. London: Hutchinson.

Carpenter, C. R. (1934). A field study of the behaviour and social relations of howling moneys (*Alouatta palliata*). *Comp. Psychol. Monograph*, 10: No. 48.

Colby, K. M. (1955). *Energy and Structure in Psycho-Analysis*. New York: Ronald Press.

Daanje, A. (1950). On locomotory movements in birds and the intention movements derived from them. *Behaviour*, 3: 48–98.

Darwin, C. (1875). *The Origin of Species Sixth Edition*. London: Murray.

Deutsch, J. A. (1953). A new type of behaviour theory. *Brit. J. Psychol.* (General Section), 44: 304–317.

Erikson, E. H. (1950). *Childhood and Society*. New York: W. W. Norton.

Fairbairn, W. R. D. (1941). A revised psychopathology of the psychoses and psychoneuroses. *International Journal of Psycho-Analysis*, 22 [Reprinted in *Psycho-Analytic Studies of the Personality*. London: Tavistock, 1952].

Fairbairn, W. R. D. (1943). The war neuroses—their nature and significance. *Psycho-Analytic Studies of the Personality*. London: Tavistock, 1952.

Ferenczi, S. (1916). Stages in the development of the sense of reality. In: *Contributions to Psycho-Analysis*. Boston: Badger.

Freud, A. (1949). Certain types and stages of social maladjustment. In: K. R. Eissler (Ed.), *Searchlights on Delinquency*. London: Imago Pub. Co.

Freud, A. (1951). Observations on child development. *Psychoanal. Study Child*, 6: 18–30.

Freud, A. (1954). Psychoanalysis and education. *Psychoanal. Study Child*, 9:

Freud, A., & Dann, S. (1951). An experiment in group upbringing. *Psychoanal. Study Child*, 6: 127–168.

Freud, S. (1926). (Trans. 1936). *Inhibitions, Symptoms and Anxiety*. London: Hogarth.

Freud, S. (1938). *An Outline of Psychoanalysis*. London: Hogarth.

Gerwitz, J. L. (1956). A program of research on the dimensions and antecedents of emotional dependence. *Child Development*, 27: 205–221.

Griffiths, R. (1954). *The Abilities of Babies*. London: Univ. of London Press.

Harlow, H. American Psychologist. (In press.)

Hayes, C. (1951). *The Ape in our House*. London: Gollancz.

Hermann, I. (1933). Zum Triebleben der Primaten. *Imago*, 19: 113, 325.

Hermann, I. (1936). Sich-Anklammern—AufSuche-Gehen. *Int. Z. Psa.*, 22: 349–370.

Hetzer, H., & Tudor-Hart, B. H. (1927). Die frühesten Reaktionen auf die menschliche Stimme. *Quellen und Studien zur Jugendkunde*, 5:

Hinde, R. A. (1954). Changes in responsiveness to a constant stimulus. *British Journal of Animal Behaviour*, 2: 41–45.

Hinde, R. A., Thorpe, W. N., & Vince, M. A. (1956). The following response of young coots and moorhens. *Behaviour*, 9: 214–242.

James, W. (1890). *Textbook of Psychology*. New York: Holt.

Kellogg, W. N., & Kellogg, L. A. (1933). *The Ape and the Child*. New York: Whittlesey House.

Klein, M. (1948). *Envy and Gratitude*. London: Tavistock.

Klein, M., Heimann, P., Isaacs, S., & Riviere, J. (1952). *Developments in Psychoanalysis*. London: Hogarth.

Lorenz, K. Z. (1950). The comparative method in studying innate behaviour patterns. In: *Physiological Mechanisms in Animal Behaviour No. IV of Symposia of the Society for Experimental Biology*, Cambridge University Press.

Meyer-Holzapfel, M. (1949). Die Beziehungen zwischen den Trieben Junger und Erwachsener Tiere. *Schweiz. Z. für Psychol. und ihre Anwendungen, 8*: 32–60.

Piaget, J. (1936). *La naissance de l'intelligence chez l'enfant*. Trans. (1953). *The Origin of Intelligence in the Child*. London: Routledge, 1953.

Piaget, J. (1937). *The Child's Construction of Reality*. London: Routledge, 1955 [trans.].

Ribble, M. A. (1944). Infantile experience in relation to personality development. In: Hunt (Ed.), *Personality and the Behaviour Disorders*, New York: Ronald Press.

Schaffer, H. R. (In press). Observations on personality development in early infancy. *British Journal of Medical Psychology*.

Shirley, M. M. (1933). *The First Two Years: Vols. II and III*. Minneapolis: University of Minnesota Press.

Spitz, R. A. (1946). Anaclitic depression. *Psychoanal. Study Child*, 2:

Spitz, R. A. (1954). Genèse des premièes relations objectales. *Revue française de psychanalyse, 18*: 479–575.

Spitz, R. A. (1957). *No and Yes*. New York: International Universities Press.

Spitz, R. A., & Wolf, K. M. (1946). The smiling response: a contribution to the onto-genesis of social relations. *Genetic Psychology Monographs, 34*: 57–125.

Sullivan, H. S. (1892–1949). *The Interpersonal Theory of Psychiatry*, Perry and Gawel (Eds.). New York: Norton, 1953.

Suttie, I. D. (1935). *Origins of Love and Hate*. London: Kegan Paul.

Tomilin, M. I., & Yerkes, R. M. (1935). Chimpanzee twins: Behavioural relations and development. *J. Genet. Psychol.*, 46: 239–263.

Winnicott, D. W. (1945). Primitive emotional development. *International Journal of Psycho-Analysis*, 26: 137–143.

Winnicott, D. W. (1948). Pediatrics and Psychiatry. *British Journal of Medical Psychology*, 21: 229–240.

Winnicott, D. W. (1953). Transitional objects and transitional phenomena. *International Journal of Psycho-Analysis*, 34: 1–9.

Winnicott, D. W. (1955). The depressive position in normal emotional development. *British Journal of Medical Psychology*, 28: 89–100.

Yerkes, R. M., & Tomilin, M. I. (1935). Mother-infant relations in chimpanzees. *J. Comp. Psychol.*, 20: 321–348.
Zuckerman, S. (1933). *Functional Affinities of Man, Monkeys and Apes*. London: Kegan Paul.

Article citation

Bowlby, J. (1958). The nature of the child's tie to his mother. *International Journal of Psycho-Analysis, 39*: 350–373.

CHAPTER FIFTEEN

Some remarks on the role of speech in psycho-analytic technique[1]

Rudolf M. Loewenstein

The discovery of the dynamic character of the unconscious, and the realization that most of the psychic processes usually observed in consciousness could be found also to exist preconsciously, led Freud to rely but little upon the presence or absence of conscious awareness in mental phenomena. Indeed, the factor of consciousness or its absence is elusive and deceptive, and the delimitation of the System Cs from the System Pcs cannot always be carried out unambiguously. Thus a conception of the psychic apparatus devised so as to include consciousness among its essential elements could not prove entirely satisfactory.

To these difficulties one might perhaps attribute the fact that Freud, as Ernest Jones reports in the second volume of his biography (1955), destroyed his manuscripts devoted to problems of consciousness. At any event, Freud cut through these complications by his fundamental change of the framework on which he proceeded to base the functioning of the mental apparatus. We know that the introduction of the structural approach to psychic phenomena became tremendously fruitful for the development of psychoanalysis. We also know that it permitted an understanding and a description of our technical procedure which before would have been impossible. The concept of the ego, in particular, had the advantage of encompassing conscious as well as preconscious and unconscious phenomena, and of uniting them within a common functional organization. However, it did not dispose of the existence of conscious as opposed to preconscious and unconscious processes, and of problems related to the functional differences between them.

Freud never thought that conscious mental processes should be considered mere epiphenomena of unconscious and preconscious ones (1900), and he never relinquished his interest in problems connected with them. In his posthumous *Outline of Psychoanalysis* (1939) he wrote: "Conscious processes on the (perceptual) periphery of the ego^2 and everything else in the ego unconscious—such would be the simplest state of affairs that we might picture. And such may in fact be the conditions prevailing in animals. But in man there is an added complication owing to which internal processes in the ego may also acquire the quality of consciousness. This complication is produced by the function of speech, which brings the material in the ego into a firm connexion with the memory-traces of visual and more particularly of auditory perceptions. Henceforth the perceptual periphery of the cortex of the ego can be stimulated to a much greater extent from inside as well; internal events such as consequences of ideas and intellective processes can become conscious; and a special apparatus becomes necessary in order to distinguish between the two possibilities—that is, what is known as reality-testing".[3]

Although less acute, the problem of the curative effect on neuroses being achieved by bringing unconscious phenomena to consciousness still remains. I shall try to contribute to its understanding by approaching it from a limited viewpoint; namely, that of the role of verbalization in the analytic procedure. But first I should like to make a few preliminary remarks about the term "bringing to consciousness".

Freud's original formulation of the aim of psychoanalytic therapy—to lift amnesias—was sufficient as long as only the undoing of the effects of repression was considered. But since psychoanalysis came to consider the results of other defensive mechanisms as well, the need has also arisen to encompass such processes as the re-establishment of connexions, for instance, and the correction of distortions produced by various mechanisms of defence. We refer here to the important role of the synthetic and organizing function in the therapeutic process. Under these circumstances we are justified, I believe, in supplementing the term "bringing to consciousness" by the more comprehensive one "gaining of insight" when we wish to designate the results of changes in the ego which make warded-off mental functions available to the conflictless sphere of the ego. This term comprises both the bringing to consciousness and the re-establishment of connexion (Bibring, 1937; Fenichel, 1937; Nunberg, 1937; Kris, 1950; Loewenstein, 1951).

It is true that the term "gaining insight" has been submitted to critical scrutiny, and the objection advanced that it is used also in other contexts and thus might lead to confusion or misunderstandings. We know how frequently patients nowadays use a so-called "insight" to form resistances by intellectualization (A. Freud, 1936; Kris, 1956). But we also know that a wallowing in emotions may likewise, and at least as frequently, be used as resistance; yet this fact does not lead us to deny the importance of affects in psychoanalytic therapy. Therefore I believe that for lack of a better expression we are entitled to continue our use of the term "analytic insight" to designate, not only the increase in awareness, but also the dynamic changes encompassed by it. For we know that such insight is gained only after certain dynamic changes have occurred, and that gaining of insight, in its turn, leads to other dynamic changes (Kris, 1950; Loewenstein, 1951).

This terminological digression will, I hope, prove useful for our discussion of verbalization. Psychoanalysis is both an investigative and a therapeutic procedure, a long-drawn-out experiment and process taking place entirely in the realm of speech. It is an exchange of particular communications between two people, a kind of dialogue, very different from all other dialogues. The analytic set-up, the fundamental rule and the role of the analyst make it unique. The patient is expected in fact to relinquish, to some extent, the exercise of an essential function of conscious phenomena: the aim-directed character of conscious thinking; the ability of the System Cs to select deliberately, from among all preconscious memories, only those which at the moment suit its aim. In exchange, this controlled regression of the ego (Kris, 1950) ultimately brings to the System Cs elements from the preconscious which otherwise would have remained outside the sphere of consciousness. These latter processes are facilitated, to a certain extent, by the protective role of the analyst and also by the fact that in the transference he happens to draw certain affects of the patient on to himself; but mainly by the role he plays in lending the help of his own ego functions to the weakened and restricted autonomous ego of the patient. He supplies the knowledge of mental phenomena, the understanding and objectivity which help the patient to face them.

In this peculiar dialogue the analyst is supposed to devote his entire attention to the mental phenomena of his patient, limiting his thoughts and words exclusively to the understanding of his interlocutor. One can say that in the person of the analyst the patient acquires an additional autonomous ego tending to enlarge the area of his System Cs over his unconscious.

Before going further into some details of the analytic procedure, let us dwell for a moment on the various functions of language.

Ferdinand de Saussure (1916) advanced the basic distinction between the two aspects which he designated, in French, by the terms *langue* and *parole*. Translated into English this is the differentiation between "language", defined as a system of distinctive signs corresponding to distinct ideas, on the one hand, and "speech", referring to utterances or spoken language, on the other. These two aspects of language are inseparable from one another, each being impossible without the other. Following de Saussure's formulations, the Viennese psychologist Karl Buehler (1934) devised a general classification of the various functions of speech. According to him, speech encompasses three functions between addressor and addressee: they may speak of objects and their relationships; or the addressor may express (i.e. communicate) what is in himself; or he may appeal to the addressee. The act of speech therefore comprises: (1) what Buehler called the *Darstellungsfunktion*, which could be translated as function of representation or, according to Roman Jakobson (Personal communication) as cognitive function, since it refers to the knowledge and description of things or objects and the connexions between them; (2) the function of expression, by which the speaker expresses something about himself; (3) the function of appeal, encompassing all those speech acts which appeal to the addressee to do something or to respond in some way; e.g. imploring, commanding, forbidding, seducing, etc.

In the analytic situation we might expect the patient's speech to be mainly confined to the expressive function and to that facet of the function of representation which deals mostly with the description of events. But experience shows that very soon the patient's thoughts lead him to exercise the third function, too, when his interest begins to centre on the analyst. The latter, in accordance with the rules of analytic technique, has two tasks. He refrains from responding to the appeal function which manifests itself as transference reactions. Furthermore, he aims at transforming the appeal function of the patient's speech into the expressive function by showing him, through interpretations, how he expresses or describes something about himself when he speaks of persons or things outside himself. In his own speech the analyst will exclude both the function of appeal and the expressive function, limiting himself specifically to the cognitive function in relation to facts concerning his present addressee: the patient. He will thus, in turn, promote the expressive function of the latter, since the interpretation will communicate to the patient knowledge about himself that will favour his recall and expression of hitherto unavailable facts about himself.

But at the same time the patient's knowledge about himself will enhance that aspect of the cognitive function to which we wish to ascribe a particular importance in the curative effect of analysis, the one on which working through is based and which leads to insight.

Indeed, there may exist a difference between the cognitive function in its application to the non-self and to the self. In the latter case, the cognitive and expressive functions might be intertwined in a very significant way.

These three main functions of speech, then, encompass its various secondary ones as they are known to analysts.

The concept of catharsis was based upon the idea that by recounting some hitherto uncommunicated events of one's past one, as it were, gets rid of them. The phrase "to let off steam" is a colloquial expression of the same idea. In this connexion, the various modalities in which a given patient utters or withholds information might be influenced by trends from the anal and urethral functions, leading to the retention or expulsion of words as though they were matter. A patient's way of talking may reveal that at times he uses speech for either seduction or aggression towards the analyst (Abraham, 1927; Fliess, 1949; Sharpe, 1950).

Nunberg (1955) has pointed at two important functions of speech in analysis. First, the magic one (which, by the way, to a certain extent enters into the cathartic function of speech). He stresses that, with words, human beings try to influence the fate of others: they bless or curse them; some try to cling to other persons by means of speech. "Thus," he states, "under the influence of libido, speech is used to perform positive as well as negative magic". We may say that there is actually no more powerful magic than that of words. This is perhaps the one realm where so-called magic is really operative. The communication of guilty acts or thoughts, confession, has a real psychological effect. It frequently makes an accomplice of the listener, thus determining his future behaviour in an important way.[4] From the consequences of so much knowledge about the hidden wishes and acts of others, from this role of an accomplice, perhaps only confessors and analysts can remain immune.

The second point emphasized by Nunberg is that speech is a substitute for action. Indeed, speaking involves motor discharge by means of the vocal organs and in this respect plays a role in the therapeutic action of psychoanalysis. Even if one stresses the discharge value of affects in analysis, they have this property only while the memory-contents are remembered, and this only inasmuch as they are being told to the analyst.

Superego, id and ego do not equally partake of the action of speech. As far as the superego is concerned, the confession of guilty acts or intentions may lead to actual change in the person. The sharing of experience and feelings, which is achieved through communication, might be in the service of the id. Although speech is but a poor substitute for sexual gratification, it plays an important role in the expression of love and in the conquest of a love object. It is most powerful, however, in the service of aggression. Here, words are not merely a substitute for action. Insults and expressions of irony or contempt are often more adequate than deeds, and sometimes hurt more than physical blows. But it is in its function for the ego, which mainly concerns us here, that speech seems to play the most interesting and significant role.

In psychoanalytic practice, we often encounter considerable resistances in our patients to verbalizing certain thoughts and emotions of which they have always been perfectly aware. Some of them, we find, delay for a long time before telling the analyst about some conscious thought or memory, and at times will experience highly painful physical sensations when they finally do so. We all know that this resistance against reporting things which are entirely conscious reappears, time and again, throughout the analytic treatment. Thus we must conclude that a barrier exists not only between the unconscious and preconscious and between the latter and the conscious, but also between conscious thoughts or emotions and their verbalization.

Every analyst knows that this resistance to verbalizing conscious phenomena manifests itself in all kinds of areas. Some patients are reluctant to reveal specific facts of their lives; others, to divulge certain details of their past or present sex life; still others are ashamed of their emotions.[5] For most of them the telling of their daydreams is a particularly difficult task, and we all know how strong is the resistance in patients to expressing their conscious feelings and thoughts about the analyst. Undoubtedly one reason for the existence of this barrier between conscious experiences and their verbalization is the fear of letting another know one's most intimate secrets, the fear of loss of love and esteem from the analyst, fear of punishment in its various forms.[6]

Indeed, the analyst is a kind of superego to the patient. But he is also a witness. He is like an additional memory acting to remind the patient of certain facts when he may want, in periods of increased resistance, to forger or disregard what he had revealed before. At such moments a reluctant patient can sometimes be heard to say: "I know I told it to you, so it must be true". This role of a witness and a memory is, in fact, a part of the analyst's functions which we defined as being the patient's additional autonomous ego. But this very fact leads us to consider the resistance against verbalization from yet another point of view. It is not uncommon in analysis that, after reluctantly talking about certain consciously remembered events of his life, the patient will add that now, since he has told them, these events have become more real.

I should like to add here that often the mere fact of communicating such conscious thoughts or memories to the analyst makes hitherto hidden material (or important missing details of other material) easily available to the analysand, so that the latter either reaches some additional insight by himself or becomes ripe to grasp an interpretation.

What makes a memory more real when it is recounted than while it was kept secret? We might think of several explanations. That speech is a substitute for action has already been mentioned; this substitute action may render an experience more real, when it is verbalized, than one that is merely remembered. Another explanation is that the inner experience may, while being told, acquire an additional reality value through its auditive perception.

Furthermore, spoken words are products of the speech act. The function of objectivation, which Cassirer (1944, 1946) stressed in language, plays an important part in the analytic process itself, in the assimilation by the ego of hitherto warded-off elements, as pointed out by Bibring (1937) and Hartmann (1951). But this is not all. It is true that "unspoken words are our slaves, and spoken ones enslave us". The mere conscious awareness of psychological realities still keeps them in the realm of privacy; communicated, they become an objective and social reality.

A particular problem in analytic therapy centres around the verbalization of emotions and affects in the transference situation. Warded-off affects may emerge spontaneously in the transference or as a result of previous interpretation. But the mere experiencing of affects in analysis must be followed by their verbal expression. Moreover, although in the analytic process such verbal expression may be a necessary step, this process is not completed until the connexions of the affects with specific contents have been re-established. Only thus can the affects be re-integrated as a part of defences as well as of instinctual drives; in other words, in their place within the structural framework of id, ego, and superego. The establishment of these connexions is likewise achieved with the help of verbalization. (The difficulty of dealing analytically with the impact of experiences stemming from preverbal stages in the patient's life is well known.)[7]

Affects expressed in words are henceforth external as well as internal realities. The words denoting these affects are now being perceived by both patient and analyst; they have become realities of the outside world in a factual and in a social sense.

Moreover, by analysing the patient's transference phenomena or acting out, we endeavour to transform his repetitive behaviour in the transference into thinking, into the achievement of insight into his intentions and motivations through their verbalization. This may lead the patient ultimately to remember the conflicts, situations, and traumatic events of his past, which thus far he had been unconsciously repeating.

Resistance against the analysis of the transference situation may manifest itself at each of the points just mentioned. Moreover, resistance against the verbalization of affect can be traced to two types of motivation. One is based on the fear of being carried away too far by such expression of emotions, a fear that the affect might thus reach too much intensity and also have an effect on the analyst. The other motive seems to be of an opposite kind; some patients can indulge in their emotional states as long as they do not talk about them, but to put these emotions into words interrupts their silent gratification; it "breaks the spell", one might say. To the discharge function through verbalization we must therefore add another, equally important one: the binding, as it were, of affects by speech. To a purely expressive function a reflective, cognitive function is added which may have an inhibiting influence on the discharge of affects. Both the discharge function and the binding function[8] of verbalization underlie the curative effect of insight in psychoanalysis. In turn both may at times be used by the forces of resistance for defensive purposes.

Summarizing our remarks about resistance to verbalization, we can say that at the point of verbal expression a last struggle is put up by the ego's defences against bringing the unconscious to consciousness. We must conclude that in the formation of analytic insight, verbalization is an essential step.

Man has the ability, either by concealment or lies or by communicating the truth, to influence or to create social realities through the spoken word. Language plays a decisive role in the formation and the development of thought processes (Sapir, 1921, 1949). The thought processes that particularly interest us here are those which deal with understanding or knowing oneself. Every analyst has had occasion to observe that a patient may express some idea or affect and then suddenly realize that such thought or feeling was hitherto completely unknown to him. The fact of having expressed it in words makes him recognize its existence. Let me give a recent example of such an incident. One of my patients, a man in his forties, conspicuously presented the consequences of the mechanisms of isolation and repression of affect. It was not until the beginning of his analysis, for instance, that he became aware of ever in his life having been jealous. He was equally unaware that he might ever have wanted to be loved by his mother. All his life he lived, to use his own words, in the illusion of being the preferred child of his parents. When once, in a situation where he imagined that I might take sides with an adversary of his, he brought up the "illusion of communion" with the analyst and hesitantly spoke of feelings of jealousy, I remarked that his sentence was not complete. Reluctantly, and with a disbelieving chuckle, he finished the sentence which expressed that he wanted to be loved by his analyst. This wish had never occurred to him before uttering these words. (Needless to add that when the patient was reminded of this incident a week later, it had been forgotten by him.) Here, one might say, words carried to the surface of conscious awareness a thought and an affect which had been unconscious before. In these instances, language performs the function of a kind of scaffolding that permits conscious thought to be built inside.

Another category of the phenomena based on verbalization, with which we are familiar in psychoanalysis, consists in interpretations given by the analyst. These, too, might to some extent be compared to a kind of scaffolding which the patient's thought can gradually fill. They then play the role stressed by Kris (1950), when he spoke of recognition as an important step in the recall of repressed memories.

Not infrequently the interpretations are misused by the patient in the service of resistance. Thus intellectualization may use mere words, instead of insights; the empty scaffolding alone, without a building. This kind of resistance can sometimes be avoided by a judicious attention to tact, timing, and wording of interpretations. When the analyst believes, on the basis of preparatory work, that the time has come, that the patient is ready for it, he lends him the words, so to speak, which will meet the patient's thoughts and emotions half-way. In the peculiar dialogue going on between patient and analyst, their mutual understanding is based on the general property of human speech to create states of mind in the interlocutor akin to those expressed by the spoken words. The function of representation in speech elicits images and representations in the addressee which are similar to those used by the addressor. The expressive function tends to arouse emotions or states similar to those expressed. The function of appeal potentially creates the reactions corresponding to the appeal. As far as the analyst is concerned, we expect that the patient's speech shall elicit in him only those potential responses which may act as signals[9] for his understanding of the patient, and which ultimately may be used by him in interpreting the latter's utterances.

Freud advised listening to the patient's words while trying, at the same time, also to understand a second, a kind of coded message conveyed by them. The fundamental rule, since it requires the patient to relinquish the aim-directed character of his thought to some extent, brings this "coded message" closer into the foreground. This is another way of saying that we observe that the patient's utterances become more obviously influenced by the primary process. We know that in the psychic phenomena which are under the sway of the primary process, the relationship between word representation and object representation—or, to use Ferdinand de Saussure's terms, between the signifying and the signified—is altered as compared to thoughts within the framework of the secondary process. To put it still differently: one might say that next to the usual vocabulary of any human language—i.e. to a definite set of meaningful relations between signs and ideas, "signifying" and "signified"—there exists another which is limited in scope, less definite, usually unconscious, and unintelligible, and which gains a partial hold upon the human mind on certain conditions; e.g. in dreams, in neurotic and psychotic thought processes. However, the use of the same kind of vocabulary in wit, jokes, and in actual love life often is conscious, intentional, and perfectly understandable to others.[10]

I do not intend to go into a detailed discussion of the various types of altered relations between "signifying" and "signified". Let me give just two examples, out of a countless number common in analytic experience. An aeroplane phobia results from emotional reactions to the fact that, to a given patient, an aeroplane means not only a flying machine, but also a symbolic representation of a penis. In a case of compulsive neurosis, the anxiety created by sitting down in a taxicab was based upon the unconscious meaning of the act for this patient, which centred around the French colloquial connotation of "sitting on somebody": an expression of contemptuous indifference.

In respect to the primary and secondary processes, the analytic process has a twofold effect. On the one hand, analysis elicits expressions of the unconscious vocabulary. On the other hand, it causes these thoughts to be translated into words of the ordinary language. Being confronted with them, as it were, by means of the speech act, the patient during the analysis is led to a gradual gaining of insight into phenomena that are under the sway of the primary process. By putting them into words, he subjects them to the influence of the secondary process.

In the passage quoted above, Freud (1939) ascribed to the function of speech the very fact that "processes in the ego may ... acquire the quality of consciousness", since it "brings the material in the ego into a firm connexion with the memory-traces of visual and more particularly of auditory perceptions"; adding that, as a consequence, "a special apparatus becomes necessary in order to distinguish between ..." (stimulations from inside and from outside) "—that is, what is known as reality-testing".

The analytic set-up "creates for the patient a situation where attention and reality-testing are withdrawn from the outside world (the analyst) and shifted on to the inner experience of the patient" (Lowenstein, 1951).[11] Insight which a patient may gain during analysis widens his capacity for reality-testing in the area of his mental processes and permits a far more differentiated use of it. He may learn to distinguish the role of his own unconscious drives or thoughts in the evaluation of situations involving other people; he may learn to discern the complexity of his motivations where only rationalization was used before; he may learn to understand the mental states of other persons; and he may acquire the ability to differentiate between the past and present of his own experience as well as of outside reality. The latter point is crucial in the therapeutic effects of psychoanalysis. All these acquisitions of reality-testing in the area of the patient's mental processes are acquisitions of the System Cs, and are gained with the help of and by means of speech as it is used in the analytic procedure. Indeed, the use of language permits human beings to give actuality even to events that are remote in time and space, and yet to distinguish them from those which exist here and now.

Why is it that certain psychic phenomena may have a pathogenic effect so long as they remain unconscious, but become harmless after having been brought to consciousness?

Freud attempted to account for this peculiar state of affairs when he used the comparison with archaeology to explain the effect of analytic therapy. He compared it with the perennialness of the remnants of antiquity buried in Pompeii, and their speedy disintegration when brought out into the light (Freud, 1933). Their apparent timelessness was due to their being removed from the effects of the outside world; and their disintegration, once brought to the surface, was caused by various physical and chemical factors, by the influences of air and humidity from which they had so long been removed. What is it, then, that corresponds to these physical and chemical influences upon the unearthed Roman relics? What causes our psychic antiquities to disintegrate when they become conscious? In their unconscious state they have a pathogenic effect because, unlike the buried Roman remains, they continue to exert an action in the present: namely, on the personality of the patient. Brought to consciousness, they become harmless because insight and verbalization subject them to reality-testing and thus unravel the effects of the pathogenic intertwinement between past and present.

We know the therapeutic effect of analysis to be a lasting one, even though the insights and recollections achieved during treatment may apparently be forgotten once more. By undergoing conscious experience they have acquired a resistivity to repression, whether or not they remain available to conscious awareness. This resistivity of hitherto pathogenic memories to repression is ascribed by Kris (1950) to the fact that, as a result of analytic insight, they have become part of a context. Freud (1915) advanced a hypothesis according to which there are two types of memory traces: those deposited by unconscious and those deposited by conscious–preconscious processes. One might then presume that the latter contain elements of having been part of a context, of having undergone insight and reality-testing, which may account for an increased resistivity to both repression and regression.

Before concluding, I should like to discuss certain limitations and qualifications that must be attached to my presentation.

We know that various modes of communication and understanding, other than verbal ones, exist between human beings.

Certainly we do not underestimate the importance of the immediate understanding of the unconscious between two people, of the intuitive grasping of non-verbal forms of emotional expressions; and these important ways of communication might lie quite outside the realm of verbalization. They even may play a part in the analyst's understanding of his patient. However, the essential factor in the investigative and therapeutic function of psychoanalysis is based upon the use of speech between patient and analyst. To be sure, not all relevant processes during an analysis occur on the level of consciousness; nor are all of them ever verbalized. And yet, without verbalization on the part of the patient, without interpretations, without gaining of insight, there would be no analysis and thus no such processes.

Communication may have a considerable and enriching influence on the development of the human personality (Rapaport, 1951). However, the importance of verbalization in the therapeutic procedure of analysis should not lead us to assume that communication *per se* has a title to therapeutic efficiency. First of all, communication is not the whole of either language or speech (Sapir, 1921, 1949; Piaget, 1948). Moreover, people do not change just because they communicate with others. What counts in analysis is, not communication by itself, but what is being communicated on the part of both patient and analyst, what leads to communication, and what psychic processes and changes occur as a result of this communication as such and of its contents.

A most pertinent consideration arises, however, with regard to the therapeutic effects of self-analysis. Most psychoanalysts, I presume, experience its effectiveness only in the form of a continuation of a previous analysis with an actual analyst. As far as I know, it is then usually a solitary continuation of dialogue with the latter or with an imaginary analyst. In this respect it might be viewed as an imaginary dialogue in which the subject is able to play both parts, that of a patient and that of an analyst, and thus to some extent involving inner speech.

Nevertheless, the possibility of a therapeutic self-analysis serves to confirm what we would suspect in any case: that if verbalization and speech play an essential role in the therapeutic effects of the gaining of insight, they are not the only factors to do so.

Notes

1. Based on a paper presented at a meeting of the New York Psychoanalytic Society on 11 March, 1952, and at the Annual Meeting of the American Psychoanalytic Association in Atlantic City on 11 May, 1952. An abbreviated version of the present text was read in the Symposium on "The theory of technique" held at the Centenary Scientific Meetings of the British Psycho-Analytical Society in London on 5 May, 1956.
2. Poetzl's work and the recent experimental studies by Charles Fisher (1954, 1956) indicate the existence of perception without consciousness.
3. Freud had discussed these problems previously in *The interpretation of dreams* (1900), "The unconscious" (1915) and *Moses and Monotheism* (1937).
4. This is one of the most striking examples showing that it is human language, the communicability of human experience and its psychological consequences for the speaker and the listener, which makes it even more difficult to create a scientific psychology based exclusively on concepts used by the learning theory which describes man in terms of drive–stimulus–response.
5. In some emotionally charged states, such as grief, awe, or communion with a love object, talking is experienced as a desecration. The same may be true of the reluctance to reveal highly valued beliefs or ideals: a refusal "to cast pearls before swine".
6. The role of warded-off exhibitionistic tendencies in these resistances is obvious.
7. Human beings learn to speak from their mothers. In the transference, the analytic situation with all its emotional over- and undertones might well at times reawaken this remote period of a patient's life.
8. This binding of the affect by words may be a factor in the neutralization of drive energies to which Kris (1956) ascribes the therapeutic function of insight.
9. A similar idea was expressed by Kris (1956).
10. Benveniste (1956) attempts to describe these phenomena in terms of well-known figures of style.
11. Hartmann recently expressed similar ideas in a "Discussion on defence mechanisms" at the Midwinter Meeting of the American Psychoanalytic Association in 1953.

References

Abraham, K. (1927). The influence of oral erotism on character formation. *Selected Papers* (pp. 393–406). London: Hogarth.

290 INFLUENTIAL PAPERS FROM THE 1950s

Benveniste, É. (1956). Remarques sur la fonction du langage dans la découverte Freudienne. In: J. Lacan (Ed.), *Sur la Parole et le Langage. La Psychanalyse, 1*: 3–16.

Bibring, E. (1937). On the theory of the therapeutic results of psychoanalysis. *International Journal of Psycho-Analysis, 18*: 170–189.

Buehler, K. (1934). *Sprachtheorie. Die Darstellungsfunktion der Sprache.* Jena: Fischer.

Cassirer, E. (1944). *An Essay on Man.* New Haven: Yale University Press.

Cassirer, E. (1944). *Language and Myth.* New York: Harper.

Fenichel, O. (1937). On the theory of the therapeutic results of psychoanalysis. *International Journal of Psycho-Analysis, 18*: 133–138.

Fisher, C. (1954). Dreams and perception: the role of preconscious and primary modes of perception in dream formation. *Journal of the American Psychoanalytic Association, 2*: 389–445.

Fisher, C. (1956). Dreams, images, and perception: a study of unconscious–preconscious relationships. *Journal of the American Psychoanalytic Association, 4*: 5–48.

Fliess, R. 91949). Silence and verbalization: a supplement to the theory of the "Analytic Rule". *International Journal of Psycho-Analysis, 30*: 21–30.

Freud, A. (1936). *The Ego and the Mechanisms of Defence.* London: Hogarth.

Freud, S. (1900). The interpretation of dreams. *S.E.,* 4 and 5. London: Hogarth, 1953.

Freud, S. (1915). The unconscious. *Coll. Papers* 4: 98–136. London: Hogarth, 1925.

Freud, S. (1933). *New Introductory Lectures on Psychoanalysis.* New York: Norton.

Freud, S. (1937). *Moses and Monotheism.* New York: Knopf, 1949.

Freud, S. (1939). *An Outline of Psychoanalysis.* New York: Norton, 1949.

Hartmann, H. (1951). Technical implications of ego psychology. *Psychoanalytic Quarterly, 20*: 31–43.

Jakobson, R. Personal communication.

Jones, E. (1955). *The Life and Work of Sigmund Freud, 2: Years of Maturity.* New York: Basic Books.

Kris, E. (1950). On preconscious mental processes. *Psychoanalytic Quarterly, 19*: 540–560.

Kris, E. (1951). Ego psychology and interpretation in psychoanalytic therapy. *Psychoanalytic Quarterly, 20*: 15–30.

Kris, E. (1956). On some vicissitudes of insight. Contribution to the Symposium on "The Theory of Technique" held at the Centenary Scientific Meeting of the British Psycho-Analytical Society, London, 5 May, 1956.

Loewenstein, R. M. (1951) The problem of interpretation. *Psychoanalytic Quarterly, 20*: 1–14.

Nunberg, H. (1932). *Principles of Psychoanalysis. Their Application to the Neuroses*. New York: International Universities Press, 1955.

Nunberg, H. (1937). On the theory of the therapeutic results of psycho-analysis. *International Journal of Psycho-Analysis, 18*: 161–169.

Piaget, J. (1948). *Le Langage et la Pensée chez l'enfant*. Neuchâtel and Paris: Delachaux et Niestlé.

Rapaport, D. (1951). *Organization and Pathology of Thought*. New York: Columbia University Press.

Sapir, E. (1921). *Language. An Introduction to the Study of Speech*. New York: Harcourt, Brace.

Sapir, E. (1949). *Selected Writings*, D. G. Mandelbaum (Ed.). Berkeley and Los Angeles: University of California Press.

Saussure, F. de (1916) Cours de Linguistique Générale, C. Bally & A. Sechehaye (Eds.). Lausanne and Paris: Payot.

Sharpe, E. F. (1950). Psycho-physical problems revealed in language: an examination of metaphor. *Collected Papers on Psycho-Analysis* (pp. 155–169). London: Hogarth.

Article citation

Loewenstein, R. (1956). Some remarks on the role of speech in psycho-analytic technique. *International Journal of Psycho-Analysis, 37*: 460–468.

CHAPTER SIXTEEN

Some reflections on the ego[1]

Jacques Lacan

The development of Freud's views on the ego led him to two apparently contradictory formulations. The ego takes sides against the object in the theory of narcissism: the concept of libidinal economy. The bestowal of the libidinal cathexis on one's own body leads to the pain of hypochondriasis, while the loss of the object leads to a depressive tension which may even culminate in suicide.

On the other hand, the ego takes sides with the object in the topographic theory of the functioning of the perception–consciousness system and resists the id, i.e. the combination of drives governed solely by the pleasure-principle.

If there be a contradiction here, it disappears when we free ourselves from a naive conception of the reality-principle and take note of the fact—though Freud may have been clear on this point, his statements sometimes were not—that while reality precedes thought, it takes different forms according to the way the subject deals with it.

Analytic experience gives this truth a special force for us and shows it as being free from all trace of idealism, for we can specify concretely the oral, anal, and genital relationships which the subject establishes with the outer world at the libidinal level.

I refer here to a formulation in language by the subject, which has nothing to do with romantically intuitive or vitalistic moods of contact with reality, of his interactions with his environment as they are determined by each of the orifices of his body. The whole psychoanalytic theory of instinctual drives stands or falls by this.

What relation does the "libidinal subject" whose relationships to reality are in the form of an opposition between an *Innenwelt* and an *Umwelt* have to the ego? To discover this, we must start from the fact—all too neglected—that verbal communication is the instrument of psychoanalysis. Freud did not forget this when he insisted that repressed material such as memories and ideas which, by definition, can return from repression, must, at the time when the events in question took place, have existed in a form in which there was at least the possibility of its being verbalized. By dint of recognizing a little more clearly the supra-individual function of language, we can distinguish in reality the new developments which are actualized by language. Language has, if you care to put it like that, a sort of retrospective effect in determining what is ultimately decided to be real. Once this is understood, some of the criticisms which have been brought against the legitimacy of Melanie Klein's encroachments into the preverbal areas of the unconscious will be seen to fall to the ground.

Now the structure of language gives us a clue to the function of the ego. The ego can either be the subject of the verb or qualify it. There are two kinds of language: in one of them one says "I am beating the dog" and in another "There is a beating of the dog by me". But, be it noted, the person who speaks, whether he appears in the sentence as the subject of the verb or as qualifying it, in either case asserts himself as an object involved in a relationship of some sort, whether one of feeling or of doing. Does what is expressed in such statements of the ego give us a picture of the relationship of the subject to reality?

Here, as in other examples, psychoanalytical experience substantiates in the most striking way the speculations of philosophers, in so far as they have defined the existential relationship expressed in language as being one of negation.

What we have been able to observe is the privileged way in which a person expresses himself as the ego; it is precisely this—*Verneinung*, or denial.

We have learned to be quite sure that when someone says "It is not so" it is because it is so; that when he says "I do not mean" he does mean; we know how to recognize the underlying hostility in most "altruistic" statements, the undercurrent of homosexual feeling in jealousy, the tension of desire hidden in the professed horror of incest; we have noted that manifest indifference may mask intense latent interest. Although in treatment we do not meet head-on the furious hostility which such interpretations provoke, we are nevertheless convinced that our researches justify the epigram of the philosopher who said that speech was given to man to hide his thoughts; our view is that the essential function of the ego is very nearly that systematic refusal to acknowledge reality (*méconnaissance systématique de la réalité*) which French analysts refer to in talking about the psychoses.

Undoubtedly every manifestation of the ego is compounded equally of good intentions and bad faith and the usual idealistic protest against the chaos of the world only betrays, inversely, the very way in which he who has a part to play in it manages to survive. This is just the illusion which Hegel denounced as the Law of the Heart, the truth of which no doubt clarifies the problem of the revolutionary of today who does not recognize his ideals in the results of his acts. This truth is also obvious to the man who, having reached his prime and seen so many professions of faith belied, begins to think that he has been present at a general rehearsal for the Last Judgement.

I have shown in my earlier works that paranoia can only be understood in some such terms; I have demonstrated in a monograph that the persecutors were identical with the images of the ego-ideal in the case studied.

But, conversely, in studying "paranoiac knowledge", I was led to consider the mechanism of paranoiac alienation of the ego as one of the preconditions of human knowledge.

It is, in fact, the earliest jealousy that sets the stage on which the triangular relationship between the ego, the object and "someone else" comes into being. There is a contrast here between the object of the animal's needs which is imprisoned in the field of force of its desire, and the object of man's knowledge.

The object of man's desire, and we are not the first to say this, is essentially an object desired by someone else. One object can become equivalent to another, owing to the effect produced by this intermediary, in making it possible for objects to be exchanged and compared. This process tends to diminish the special significance of any one particular object, but at the same time it brings into view the existence of objects without number.

It is by this process that we are led to see our objects as identifiable egos, having unity, permanence, and substantiality; this implies an element of inertia, so that the recognition of objects and of the ego itself must be subjected to constant revision in an endless dialectical process.

Just such a process was involved in the *Socratic Dialogue*: whether it dealt with science, politics, or love, Socrates taught the masters of Athens to become what they must by developing their awareness of the world and themselves through "forms" which were constantly redefined. The only obstacle he encountered was the attraction of pleasure.

For us, whose concern is with present-day man, that is, man with a troubled conscience, it is in the ego that we meet this inertia: we know it as the resistance to the dialectic process of analysis. The patient is held spellbound by his ego, to the exact degree that it causes his distress, and reveals its nonsensical function. It is this very fact that has led us to evolve a technique which substitutes the strange detours of free association for the sequence of the *Dialogue*.

But what, then, is the function of this resistance which compels us to adopt so many technical precautions?

What is the meaning of the aggressiveness which is always ready to be discharged the moment the stability of the paranoiac delusional system is threatened?

Are we not really dealing here with one and the same question?

In trying to reply by going into the theory a little more deeply, we were guided by the consideration that if we were to gain a clearer understanding of our therapeutic activity, we might also be able to carry it out more effectively—just as in placing our role as analyst in a definite context in the history of mankind, we might be able to delimit more precisely the scope of the laws we might discover.

The theory we have in mind is a genetic theory of the ego. Such a theory can be considered psychoanalytic in so far as it treats the relation of the subject to his own body in terms of his identification with an imago, which is the psychic relationship *par excellence*; in fact, the concept we have formed of this relationship from our analytic work is the starting point for all genuine and scientific psychology.

It is with the body-image that we propose to deal now. If the hysterical symptom is a symbolic way of expressing a conflict between different forces, what strikes us is the extraordinary effect that this "symbolic expression" has when it produces segmental anaesthesia or muscular paralysis unaccountable for by any known grouping of sensory nerves or muscles. To call these symptoms functional is but to confess our ignorance, for they follow the pattern of a certain imaginary Anatomy which has typical forms of its own. In other words, the astonishing somatic compliance which is the outward sign of this imaginary anatomy is only shown within certain definite limits. I would emphasize that the imaginary anatomy referred to here varies with the ideas (clear or confused) about bodily functions which are prevalent in a given culture. It all happens as if the body-image had an autonomous existence of its own, and by autonomous I mean here independent of objective structure. All the phenomena we are discussing seem to exhibit the laws of gestalt; the fact that the penis is dominant in the shaping of the body-image is evidence of this. Though this may shock the sworn champions of the autonomy of female sexuality, such dominance is a fact and one moreover which cannot be put down to cultural influences alone.

Furthermore, this image is selectively vulnerable along its lines of cleavage. The fantasies which reveal this cleavage to us seem to deserve to be grouped together under some such term as the "image of the body in bits and pieces" (*imago du corps morcelé*) which is in current use among French analysts. Such typical images appear in dreams, as well as in fantasies. They may show, for example, the body of the mother as having a mosaic structure like that of a stained-glass window. More often, the resemblance is to a jig-saw puzzle, with the separate parts of the body of a man or an animal in disorderly array. Even more significant for our purpose are the incongruous images in which disjointed limbs are rearranged as strange trophies; trunks cut up in slices and stuffed with the most unlikely fillings, strange appendages in eccentric positions, reduplications of the penis, images of the cloaca represented as a surgical excision, often accompanied in male patients by fantasies of pregnancy. This kind of image seems to have a special affinity with congenital abnormalities of all sorts. An illustration of this was provided by the dream of one of my patients, whose ego development had been impaired by an obstetrical brachial plexus palsy of the left arm, in which the rectum appeared in the thorax, taking the place of the left sub-clavicular vessels. (His analysis had decided him to undertake the study of medicine.)

What struck me in the first place was the phase of the analysis in which these images came to light: they were always bound up with the elucidation of the earliest problems of the patient's ego and with the revelation of latent hypochondriacal preoccupations. These are often completely covered over by the neurotic formations which have compensated for them in the course of development. Their appearance heralds a particular and very archaic phase of the transference, and the value we attributed to them in identifying this phase has always been confirmed by the accompanying marked decrease in the patient's deepest resistances.

We have laid some stress on this phenomenological detail, but we are not unaware of the importance of Schilder's work on the function of the body-image, and the remarkable accounts he gives of the extent to which it determines the perception of space.

The meaning of the phenomenon called "phantom limb" is still far from being exhausted. The aspect which seems to me especially worthy of notice is that such experiences are essentially related to the continuation of a pain which can no longer be explained by local irritation; it is as if one caught a glimpse here of the existential relation of a man with his body-image in this relationship with such a narcissistic object as the lack of a limb.

The effects of frontal leucotomy on the hitherto intractable pain of some forms of cancer, the strange fact of the persistence of the pain with the removal of the subjective element of distress in such conditions, leads us to suspect that the cerebral cortex functions like a mirror, and that it is the site where the images are integrated in the libidinal relationship which is hinted at in the theory of narcissism.

So far so good. We have, however, left untouched the question of the nature of the imago itself. The facts do, however, involve the positing of a certain formative power in the organism. We psychoanalysts are here reintroducing an idea discarded by experimental science, i.e. Aristotle's idea of Morphe. In the sphere of relationships in so far as it concerns the history of the individual we only apprehend the exteriorized images, and now it is the Platonic problem of recognizing their meaning that demands a solution.

In due course, biologists will have to follow us into this domain, and the concept of identification which we have worked out empirically is the only key to the meaning of the facts they have so far encountered.

It is amusing, in this connexion, to note their difficulty when asked to explain such data as those collected by Harrison in the *Proceedings of the Royal Society*, 1939. These data showed that the sexual maturation of the female pigeon depends entirely on its seeing a member of its own species, male or female, to such an extent that while the maturation of the bird can be indefinitely postponed by the lack of such perception, conversely the mere sight of its own reflection in a mirror is enough to cause it to mature almost as quickly as if it had seen a real pigeon.

We have likewise emphasized the significance of the facts described in 1941 by Chauvin in the *Bulletin de la Société entomologique de France* about the migratory locust, *Schistocerca*, commonly known as a grasshopper. Two types of development are open to the grasshopper, whose behaviour and subsequent history are entirely different. There are solitary and gregarious types, the latter tending to congregate in what is called the "cloud". The question as to whether it will develop into one of these types or the other is left open until the second or third so-called larval periods (the intervals between sloughs). The one necessary and sufficient condition is that it perceives something whose shape and movements are sufficiently like one of its own species, since the mere sight of a member of the closely similar Locusta species (itself non-gregarious) is sufficient, whereas even association with a *Gryllus* (cricket) is of no avail. (This, of course, could not be established without a series of control experiments, both positive and negative, to exclude the influence of the insect's auditory and olfactory apparatus, etc., including, of course, the mysterious organ discovered in the hind legs by Brunner von Wattenwyll.)

The development of two types utterly different as regards size, colour and shape, in phenotype, that is to say, and differing even in such instinctual characteristics as voraciousness is thus completely determined by this phenomenon of Recognition. M. Chauvin, who is obliged to admit its authenticity, nevertheless does so with great reluctance and shows the sort of intellectual timidity which among experimentalists is regarded as a guarantee of objectivity.

This timidity is exemplified in medicine by the prevalence of the belief that a fact, a bare fact, is worth more than any theory, and is strengthened by the inferiority feelings doctors have when they compare their own methods with those of the more exact sciences.

In our view, however, it is novel theories which prepare the ground for new discoveries in science, since such theories not only enable one to understand the facts better, but even make it possible for them to be observed in the first place. The facts are then less likely to be made to fit, in a more or less arbitrary way, into accepted doctrine and there pigeon-holed.

Numerous facts of this kind have now come to the attention of biologists, but the intellectual revolution necessary for their full understanding is still to come. These biological data were still unknown when in 1936 at the Marienbad Congress I introduced the concept of the "Mirror Stage" as one of the stages in the development of the child.

I returned to the subject two years ago at the Zürich Congress. Only an abstract (in English translation) of my paper was published in the *Proceedings of the Congress*. The complete text appeared in the *Revue française de Psychanalyse*.

The theory I there advanced, which I submitted long ago to French psychologists for discussion, deals with a phenomenon to which I assign a twofold value. In the first place, it has historical value as it marks a decisive turning-point in the mental development of the child. In the second place, it typifies an essential libidinal relationship with the body-image. For these two reasons the phenomenon demonstrates clearly the passing of the individual to a stage where the earliest formation of the ego can be observed.

The observation consists simply in the jubilant interest shown by the infant over eight months at the sight of his own image in a mirror. This interest is shown in games in which the child seems to be in endless ecstasy when it sees that movements in the mirror correspond to its own movements. The game is rounded off by attempts to explore the things seen in the mirror and the nearby objects they reflect.

The purely imaginal play evidenced in such deliberate play with an illusion is fraught with significance for the philosopher, and all the more so because the child's attitude is just the reverse of that of animals. The chimpanzee, in particular, is certainly quite capable at the same age of detecting the illusion, for one finds him testing its reality by devious methods which shows an intelligence on the performance level at least equal to, if not better than, that of the child at the same age. But when he has been disappointed several times in trying to get hold of something that is not there, the animal loses all interest in it. It would, of course, be paradoxical to draw the conclusion that the animal is the better adjusted to reality of the two!

We note that the image in the mirror is reversed, and we may see in this at least a metaphorical representation of the structural reversal we have demonstrated in the ego as the individual's psychical reality. But, metaphor apart, actual mirror reversals have often been pointed out in *Phantom Doubles*. (The importance of this phenomenon in suicide was shown by Otto Rank.) Furthermore, we always find the same sort of reversal, if we are on the look-out for it, in those dream images which represent the patient's ego in its characteristic role; that is, as dominated by the narcissistic conflict. So much is this so that we may regard this mirror-reversal as a prerequisite for such an interpretation.

But other characteristics will give us a deeper understanding of the connexion between this image and the formation of the ego. To grasp them we must place the reversed image in the context of the evolution of the successive forms of the body image itself on the one hand, and on the other we must try to correlate with the development of the organism and the establishment of its relations with the Socius those images whose dialectical connexions are brought home to us in our experience in treatment.

The heart of the matter is this. The behaviour of the child before the mirror seems to us to be more immediately comprehensible than are his reactions in games in which he seems to wean himself from the object, whose meaning Freud, in a flash of intuitive genius, described for us in "Beyond the pleasure principle". Now the child's behaviour before the mirror is so striking that it is quite unforgettable, even by the least enlightened observer, and one is all the more impressed when one realizes that this behaviour occurs either in a babe in arms or in a child who is holding himself upright by one of those contrivances to help one to learn to walk without serious falls. His joy is due to his imaginary triumph in anticipating a degree of muscular co-ordination which he has not yet actually achieved.

We cannot fail to appreciate the affective value which the gestalt of the vision of the whole body-image may assume when we consider the fact that it appears against a background of organic disturbance and discord, in which all the indications are that we should seek the origins of the image of the "body in bits and pieces" (*corps morcelé*).

Here physiology gives us a clue. The human animal can be regarded as one which is prematurely born. The fact that the pyramidal tracts are not myelinated at birth is proof enough of this for the histologist, while a number of postural reactions and reflexes satisfy the neurologist. The embryologist too sees in the "foetalization", to use Bolk's term, of the human nervous system, the mechanism responsible for Man's superiority to other animals—*viz.* the cephalic flexures and the expansion of the fore-brain.

His lack of sensory and motor co-ordination does not prevent the newborn baby from being fascinated by the human face, almost as soon as he opens his eyes to the light of day, nor from showing in the clearest possible way that from all the people around him he singles out his mother. It is the stability of the standing posture, the prestige of stature, the impressiveness of statues, which set the style for the identification in which the ego finds its starting-point and leave their imprint in it for ever.

Miss Anna Freud has enumerated, analysed and defined once and for all the mechanisms in which the functions of the ego take form in the psyche. It is noteworthy that it is these same mechanisms which determine the economy of obsessional symptoms. They have in common an element of isolation and an emphasis on achievement; in consequence of this one often comes across dreams in which the dreamer's ego is represented as a stadium or other enclosed space given over to competition for prestige.

Here we see the ego, in its essential resistance to the elusive process of Becoming, to the variations of Desire. This illusion of unity, in which a human being is always looking forward to self-mastery, entails a constant danger of sliding back again into the chaos from which he started; it hangs over the abyss of a dizzy Assent in which one can perhaps see the very essence of Anxiety.

Nor is this all. It is the gap separating man from nature that determines his lack of relationship to nature, and begets his narcissistic shield, with its nacreous covering on which is painted the world from which he is for ever cut off, but this same structure is also the sight where his own milieu is grafted on to him, i.e. the society of his fellow men.

In the excellent accounts of children provided by the Chicago observers we can assess the role of the body-image in the various ways children identify with the Socius. We find them assuming attitudes, such as that of master and slave, or actor and audience. A development of this normal phenomenon merits being described by some such term as that used by French psychiatrists in the discussion of paranoia, *viz.* "transivitism". This transivitism binds together in an absolute equivalent attack and counter-attack; the subject here is in that state of ambiguity which precedes truth, in so far as his ego is actually alienated from itself in the other person.

It should be added that for such formative games to have their full effect, the interval between the ages of the children concerned should be below a certain threshold, and psychoanalysis alone can determine the optimum such age interval. The interval which seems to make identification easiest may, of course, in critical phases of instinctual integration, produce the worst possible results.

It has perhaps not been sufficiently emphasized that the genesis of homosexuality in a body can sometimes be referred to the imago of an older sister; it is as if the boy were drawn into the wake of his sister's superior development; the effect will be proportionate to the length of time during which this interval strikes just the right balance.

Normally, these situations are resolved through a sort of paranoiac conflict, in the course of which, as I have already shown, the ego is built up by opposition.

The libido, however, entering into narcissistic identification, here reveals its meaning. Its characteristic dimension is aggressiveness.

We must certainly not allow ourselves to be misled by verbal similarities into thinking, as so often happens, that the word "aggressiveness" conveys no more than capacity for aggression.

When we go back to the concrete functions denoted by these words, we see that "aggressiveness" and "aggression" are much more complementary than mutually inclusive terms, and, like "adaptability" and "adaptation", they may represent two contraries.

The aggressiveness involved in the ego's fundamental relationship to other people is certainly not based on the simple relationship implied in the formula "big fish eat little fish", but upon the intrapsychic tension we sense in the warning of the ascetic that "a blow at your enemy is a blow at yourself".

This is true in all the forms of that process of negation whose hidden mechanism Freud analysed with such brilliance. In "he loves me. I hate him. He is not the one I love", the homosexual nature of the underlying "I love him" is revealed. The libidinal tension that shackles the subject to the constant pursuit of an illusory unity which is always luring him away from himself, is surely related to that agony of dereliction which is Man's particular and tragic destiny. Here we see how Freud was led to his deviant concept of a death instinct.

The signs of the lasting damage this negative libido causes can be read in the face of a small child torn by the pangs of jealousy, where St Augustine recognized original evil. "Myself have seen and known even a baby envious; it could not speak, yet it turned pale and looked bitterly on its foster-brother" (... *nondum loquebatur, et intuebatur pallidus amaro aspectu conlactaneum suum*).

Moreover, the whole development of consciousness leads only to the rediscovery of the antinomy by Hegel as the starting-point of the ego. As Hegel's well-known doctrine puts it, the conflict arising from the coexistence of two consciousnesses can only be resolved by the destruction of one of them.

But, after all, it is by our experience of the suffering we relieve in analysis that we are led into the domain of metaphysics.

These reflections on the functions of the ego ought, above all else, to encourage us to re-examine certain notions that are sometimes accepted uncritically, such as the notion that it is psychologically advantageous to have a strong ego.

In actual fact, the classical neuroses always seem to be by-products of a strong ego, and the great ordeals of the war showed us that, of all men, the real neurotics have the best defences. Neuroses involving failure, character difficulties, and self-punishment are obviously increasing in extent, and they take their place among the tremendous inroads the ego makes on the personality as a whole.

Indeed, a natural process of self-adjustment will not alone decide the eventual outcome of this drama. The concept of self-sacrifice, which the French school has described as *oblativité*, as the normal outlet for the psyche liberated by analysis seems to us to be a childish over-simplification.

For every day in our practice we are confronted with the disastrous results of marriages based on such a self-sacrifice, of commitments undertaken in the spirit of narcissistic illusion which corrupts every attempt to assume responsibility for other people.

Here we must touch on the problem of our own historical evolution, which may be responsible both for the psychological impasse of the ego of contemporary man, and for the progressive deterioration in the relationships between men and women in our society.

We do not want to complicate the issues by straying too far from our main topic, and so shall confine ourselves to mentioning what comparative anthropology has taught us about the functions in other cultures of the so-called "bodily techniques" of which the sociologist Mauss has advocated a closer study. These bodily techniques are to be found everywhere; we can see them maintaining the trance-states of the individual, as well as the ceremonies of the group, they are at work in ritual mummeries and ordeals of initiation. Such rites seem a mystery to us now; we are astonished that manifestations which among us would be regarded as pathological, should in other cultures, have a social function in the promotion of mental stability. We deduce from this that these techniques help the individual to come through critical phases of development that prove a stumbling-block to our patients.

It may well be that the Oedipus complex, the corner-stone of analysis, which plays so essential a part in normal psycho-sexual development, represents in our culture the vestigial relics of the relationships by means of which earlier communities were able for centuries to ensure the psychological mutual interdependence essential to the happiness of their members.

The formative influence which we have learned to detect in the first attempts to subject the orifices of the body to any form of control allows us to apply this criterion to the study of primitive societies; but the fact that in these societies we find almost none of the disorders that drew our attention to the importance of early training, should make us chary of accepting without question such concepts as that of the "basic personality structure" of Kardiner.

Both the illnesses we try to relieve and the functions that we are increasingly called upon, as therapists, to assume in society, seem to us to imply the emergence of a new type of man: *Homo psychologicus*, the product of our industrial age. The relations between this *Homo psychologicus* and the machines he uses are very striking, and this is especially so in the case of the motor-car. We get the impression that his relationship to this machine is so very intimate that it is almost as if the two were actually conjoined—its mechanical defects and breakdowns often parallel his neurotic symptoms. Its emotional significance for him comes from the fact that it exteriorizes the protective shell of his ego, as well as the failure of his virility.

This relationship between man and machine will come to be regulated by both psychological and psychotechnical means; the necessity for this will become increasingly urgent in the organization of society.

If, in contrast to these psychotechnical procedures, the psychoanalytical dialogue enables us to re-establish a more human relationship, is not the form of this dialogue determined by an impasse, that is to say by the resistance of the ego?

Indeed, is not this dialogue one in which the one who knows admits by his technique that he can free his patient from the shackles of his ignorance only by leaving all the talking to him?

Note

1. Read to the British Psycho-Analytical Society on 2 May, 1951.

Article citation

Lacan, J. (1953). Some reflections on the ego. *International Journal of Psycho-Analysis*, 34: 11–17.